Network Forensics with Wireshark

Build Practical Expertise in Network Monitoring, Threat Detection, and Cyber Forensics with Wireshark

Bhavik Shah

www.orangeava.com

First Published: November 2025

Published By: Orange Education Pvt Ltd, AVA®

Address: 9, Daryaganj, Delhi, 110002, India

275 New North Road Islington Suite 1314 London,
N1 7AA, United Kingdom

ISBN (PBK): 978-93-49888-45-6
ISBN (E-BOOK): 978-93-49888-67-8

Dedicated To

My Wife, Sujata and My Daughter, Dityaa
And

My Parents and Late Sister, Smt Sharmilly Shah.

About the Author

Bhavik Shah has over 17 years of experience in Cyber Security, with deep expertise in designing and architecting networks where security is a primary focus. He has been a speaker at several universities, delivering talks on Network Forensics, and also at Cybersecurity Communities like Null. He has also spoken at Cisco Live on topics related to AI security and its various components. Through his first book, ***Network Forensics with Wireshark***, Bhavik aims to highlight the significance of Wireshark, and how it can help in analyzing Network Traces efficiently.

About the Technical Reviewer

Om Karrahe is an Implementation Engineer with over three years of experience in the telecom and networking domain, specializing in protocol testing and packet-level analysis. He has worked extensively with tools such as Wireshark and the Seagull simulator to validate and troubleshoot signaling flows across 4G and 5G networks. His expertise spans key telecom components including CHF, PCRF, PCF, OCS, NRF, and OCSDRA, with practical knowledge of interfaces like Gy, Gx, Sy, and Ro.

Om's strong foundation in Linux, SQL, and application configuration complements his deep interest in network protocols such as SIP, TCP, UDP, and Diameter. He has hands-on experience in analyzing PCAP traces, identifying anomalies, and ensuring system performance under load. His ability to connect theoretical protocol concepts with real-world packet behavior makes him an enthusiastic contributor to knowledge resources in the networking field.

As a Technical Reviewer with AVA™ – An Orange Education Label, Om brings his practical insights into packet flows and system testing to support authors in producing high-quality educational content. His work on this book reflects his passion for demystifying complex packet-level interactions and helping learners build confidence in analyzing networks through Wireshark.

Passionate about continuous learning and growth, Om is dedicated to contributing to the telecom and networking community by bridging the gap between theory, real-world testing, and evolving automation practices.

Acknowledgments

Network Forensics with Wireshark has become an indispensable part of my life. It took me a couple of years to create this book by working extensively on the content, and also making sure it is unique than the books currently available on Wireshark. I have made sure to keep the content practical, and also add some novelty which would not only help in understanding the Network better but also how to use Wireshark in troubleshooting Critical Issues. I have tried to include all the practical scenarios which I observed while working on Large Networks, and tried to bring the approach in solving issues at the basic level.

This is the first edition of the book, and I would like to thank Jatin Sachdeva, Vinay Saini, Akshay Dubey and Prof Vinod P for reviewing this book technically, and making suggestions which were highly beneficial in bringing the best version of the book. I would also like to thank my colleagues, Akshay Dubey and Prapanch Ramamoorthy for contributing to the Malware section. Any errors, omissions and inconsistencies that remain are, alas, my responsibility.

I thank my wife, Sujata and my daughter, Dityaa for being patient with me, while I was engrossed in writing this book. I also thank my parents, and my late sister for giving their blessings, without which it would have been impossible to complete this book.

Finally, my heartfelt gratitude to the Editorial team at Orange Education Pvt. Ltd. for being so patient and supportive, and also giving me several valuable suggestions in making this book better. I hope every author gets a publisher who is cooperative, knowledgeable and supportive as Orange Education Pvt. Ltd.

Preface

In the first edition, the seven chapters of this book are structured to enable readers to learn both Networking and Wireshark skills efficiently, completing the material in seven one-hour sessions. This approach allows readers to build foundational knowledge in Networking and apply it to practical troubleshooting using Wireshark. Feedback from readers is highly encouraged to enhance the quality of future editions.

The book begins with an introduction to the TCP/IP model, the fundamental framework of networking on which various application stacks are built. It then progresses to explain how enterprise networks function in real-world scenarios and how network activities can be observed using Wireshark. Subsequent chapters introduce tools for analyzing Wireshark traces, along with methods to automate this analysis. The book concludes with an exploration of malware behavior within networks and techniques to identify and verify malware activity through Wireshark traces.

Get a Free eBook

We hope you are enjoying your recently purchased book! Your feedback is incredibly valuable to us, and to all other readers looking for great books.

If you found this book helpful or enjoyable, we would truly appreciate it, if you could take a moment to leave a short review with a 5 star rating on Amazon. It helps us grow, and lets other readers discover our books.

As a thank you, we would love to send you a free digital copy of this book, and a **30%** discount code on your next cart value on our official websites:

www.orangeava.com

www.orangeava.in (For Indian Subcontinent)

☑ **Here's how:**

Leave a review for the book on Amazon.

Take a screenshot of your review, and send an email to **info@orangeava.com** (it can be just the confirmation screen).

Once, we receive your screenshot, we will send you the digital file, within 24 hours.

Thank you so much for your support – it means a lot to us!

Downloading the code bundles and colored images

Please follow the links or scan the QR codes to download the
Code Bundles and Images of the book:

https://github.com/ava-orange-education/Network-Forensics-with-Wireshark

The code bundles and images of the book are also hosted on
https://rebrand.ly/e1e938

In case there's an update to the code, it will be updated on the existing GitHub repository.

Errata

We take immense pride in our work at **Orange Education Pvt Ltd,** and follow best practices to ensure the accuracy of our content to provide an indulging reading experience to our subscribers. Our readers are our mirrors, and we use their inputs to reflect and improve upon human errors, if any, that may have occurred during the publishing processes involved. To let us maintain the quality and help us reach out to any readers who might be having difficulties due to any unforeseen errors, please write to us at :

errata@orangeava.com

Your support, suggestions, and feedback are highly appreciated.

DID YOU KNOW

Did you know that Orange Education Pvt Ltd offers eBook versions of every book published, with PDF and ePub files available? You can upgrade to the eBook version at **www.orangeava.com** and as a print book customer, you are entitled to a discount on the eBook copy. Get in touch with us at: **info@orangeava.com** for more details.

At **www.orangeava.com**, you can also read a collection of free technical articles, sign up for a range of free newsletters, and receive exclusive discounts and offers on Print Books and eBooks.

PIRACY

If you come across any illegal copies of our works in any form on the internet, we would be grateful if you would provide us with the location address or website name. Please contact us at **info@orangeava.com** with a link to the material.

ARE YOU INTERESTED IN AUTHORING WITH US?

If there is a topic that you have expertise in, and you are interested in either writing or contributing to a book, please write to us at **business@orangeava.com**. We are on a journey to help developers and tech professionals to gain insights on the present technological advancements and innovations happening across the globe and build a community that believes Knowledge is best acquired by sharing and learning with others. Please reach out to us to learn what our audience demands and how you can be part of this educational reform. We also welcome ideas from tech experts and help them build learning and development content for their domains.

REVIEWS

Please leave a review. Once you have read and used this book, why not leave a review on the site that you purchased it from? Potential readers can then see and use your unbiased opinion to make purchase decisions. We at Orange Education would love to know what you think about our products, and our authors can learn from your feedback. Thank you!

For more information about Orange Education, please visit **www.orangeava.com**.

Table of Contents

CHAPTER 1

Overview of TCP/IP Model

Introduction

This chapter will focus on understanding the TCP/IP model on which different applications are built. Each application has a TCP/IP stack, which helps in the communication between the client and server. Before we understand tracing packets in Wireshark, it is important to build the foundation and understand the OSI model in detail. Have you ever realized that different things we use in our day-to-day life work on a model where our actions are linked to each other? For example, when we drive a next-gen automobile, what are the main components of its Infotainment System?

Structure

In this chapter, we will cover the following topics:

- Main Components of Infotainment Systems
- Understanding the OSI Model

Main Components of Infotainment Systems

- **Integrated Head Unit:** Touch-screen-based tablet-like device with a user-friendly HMI that acts as a control center for the infotainment system.
- **Heads-up Display:** Automotive heads-up display is an integral part of high-end infotainment systems, which displays vehicle real-time information on the transparent screen integrated with the vehicle windshield.
- **Operating Systems:** Infotainment systems require operating systems that are capable of supporting connectivity, convenience functions, and downloadable applications to integrate new functions in the system.

- **CAN and Other Network Protocol Support:** The hardware components in infotainment systems are interconnected with certain standard communication protocols, such as Controller Area Network (CAN), which allows microcontrollers and devices to communicate with each other.
- **Connectivity Modules:** Infotainment systems encompass GPS, Wi-Fi, and Bluetooth modules to provide internet connectivity.
- **Digital Cluster:** Infotainment systems have transformed cockpit designs from static displays of in-vehicle instruments to digital clusters. Digital instrument clusters fetch information from the vehicle ECU unit via OBD port-II and display it in the display screen of the infotainment system.

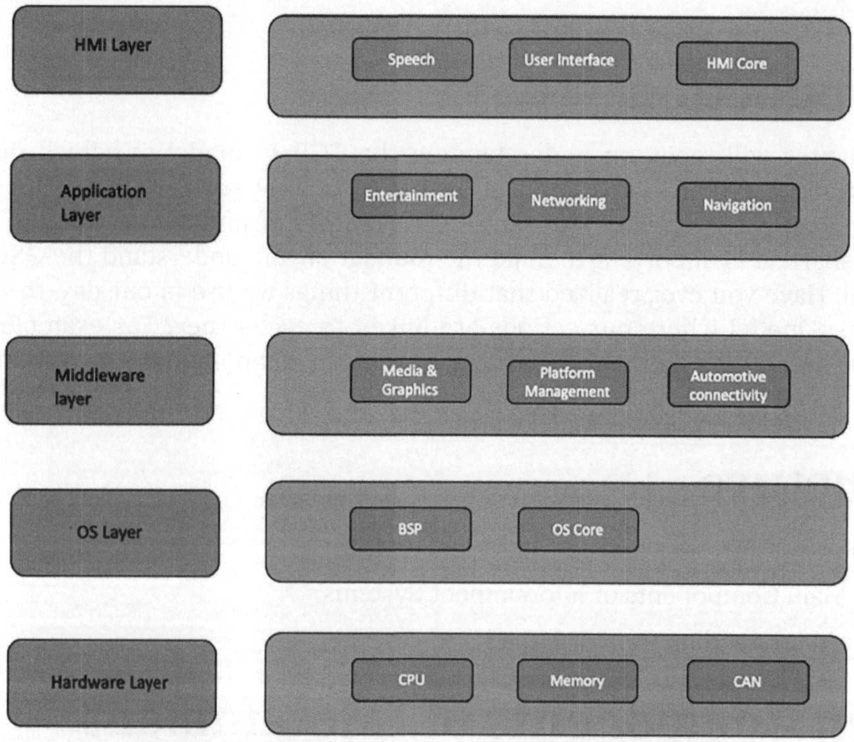

Figure 1.1: *Understanding the Infotainment Components*

The idea is not to explain how CAN works in Infotainment for Automobiles, but to demonstrate the correlation between CAN and the OSI model.

Need for CAN

CAN protocol is a method of communication between electronic devices embedded in a vehicle, such as central locking, air conditioning, and airbags. A vehicle contains a network of electronic devices that share data and information with one another. A spark-ignition engine, for instance, requires a spark to initiate the combustion chamber. To ensure this occurs accurately, it communicates with the vehicle engine control unit, which chooses the ideal time for the ignition to provide the power and fuel efficiency.

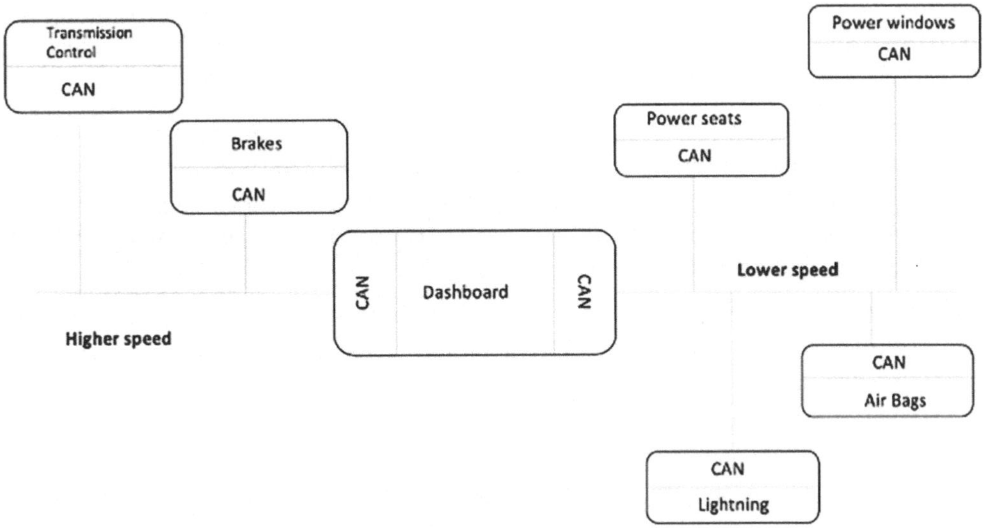

Figure 1.2: *Interconnection between Different Components*

CAN identifies each electronic device as a node that is connected via a common serial bus.

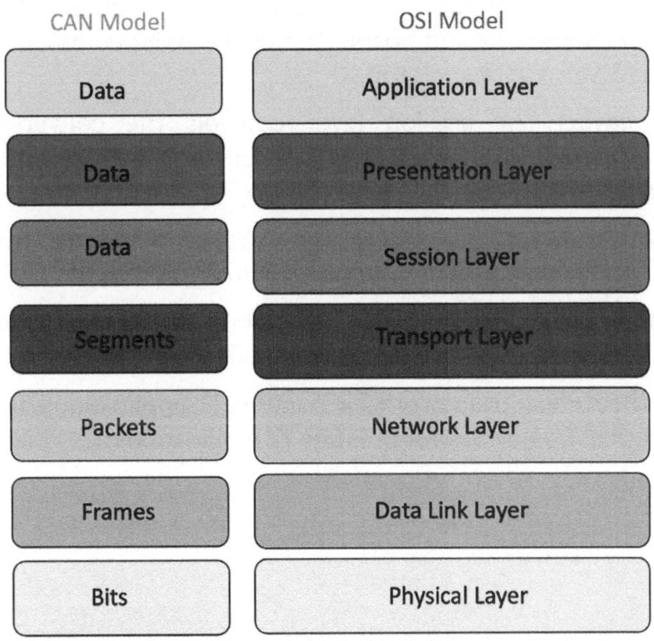

Figure 1.3: *Correlation between CAN and OSI Models*

Understanding the OSI Model

The Open Systems Interconnection Model is a conceptual framework used to describe the functions of networking systems. It has fundamental concepts to understand how the entire IT systems work, and most importantly, how different applications are built.

- **Physical Layer:** The lowest layer of the OSI model is concerned with transmitting raw, unstructured data bits across the network from the physical layer of the sending device to the physical layer of the receiving device. At the physical layer, one might find physical resources such as network switches, routers, and network modems at home.
- **Data Link Layer:** At the data link layer, directly connected nodes are used to perform node-to-node data transfer, where data gets packaged in frames. The data link layer also corrects errors that may have occurred at the physical layer. Media Access Control (MAC) provides flow control and multiplexing for device transmissions over the network.
- **Network Layer:** The network layer is responsible for receiving frames from the data link layer and delivering them to the destinations based on the address contained inside the frame. The network layer finds the destination by using logical addresses such as Internet Protocol (IP).
- **Transport Layer:** The transport layer manages the error checking and delivery of data packets. It regulates size, sequencing, and ultimately, the transfer of data between systems and hosts. One of the most common examples of the Transport layer is TCP and UDP.
- **Session Layer:** The session layer controls the conversations between different computers. Session layer services also include authentication and reconnections.
- **Presentation Layer:** The Presentation layer translates the data for the application layer based on the syntax or semantics that the application accepts.
- **Application Layer:** At this layer, the user directly communicates with the applications. For example, SaaS based applications such as O365 and Gmail.

OSI layer is the theoretical framework for building IT applications, while the TCP/IP model is the practical framework for building IT applications.

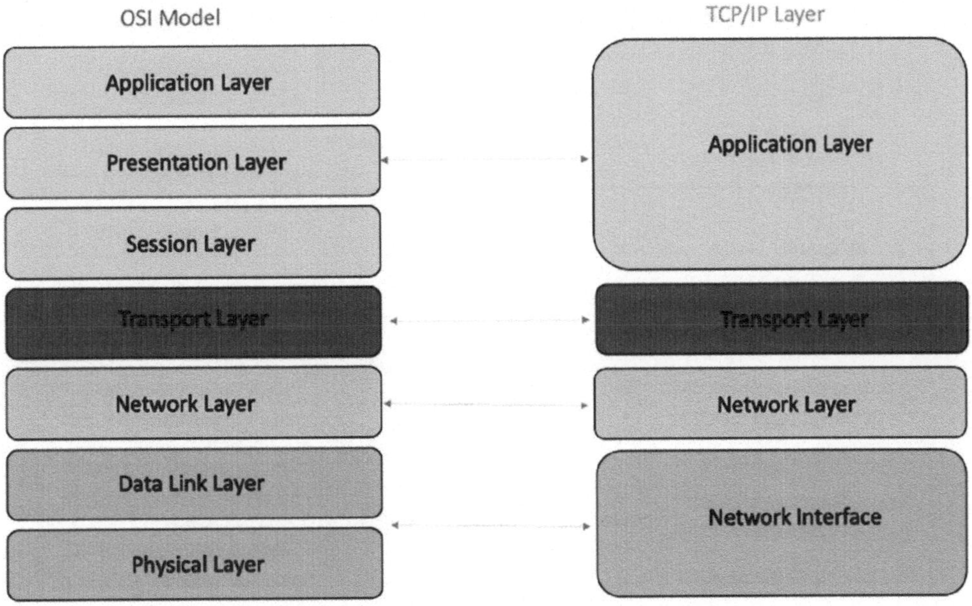

Figure 1.4: *Correlation between OSI and TCP/IP Model*

The OSI Model is being developed by the International Organization for Standardization (ISO). TCP/IP is being developed by Advanced Research Projects Agency Network (ARPANET). Though there are subtle differences between them, both are equally important in building the Network Architecture over which applications can communicate over the Internet.

TCP provides the bridge over which different applications can communicate with each other. For example, when you dial a number, the call gets routed through the service provider network and then gets routed to the calling party. The service provider provides the Network Infrastructure and also the path for the call to reach the destination calling party. Once the call gets connected, the communication happens over TCP or UDP, which is the transport layer over which the session is being established.

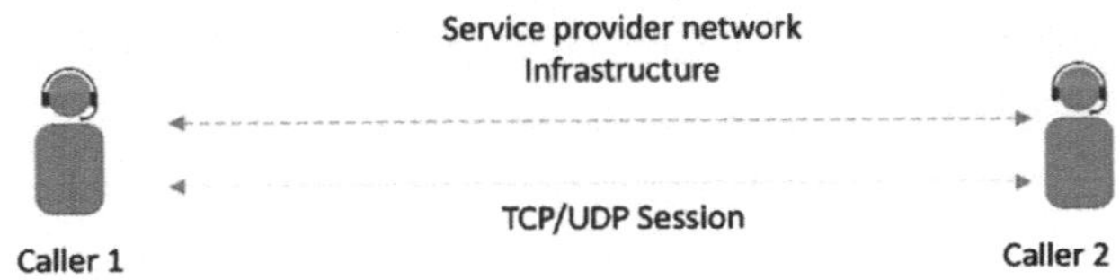

Figure 1.5: *Establishing a TCP Session*

TCP is a connection-oriented protocol, the details of which we will examine later.

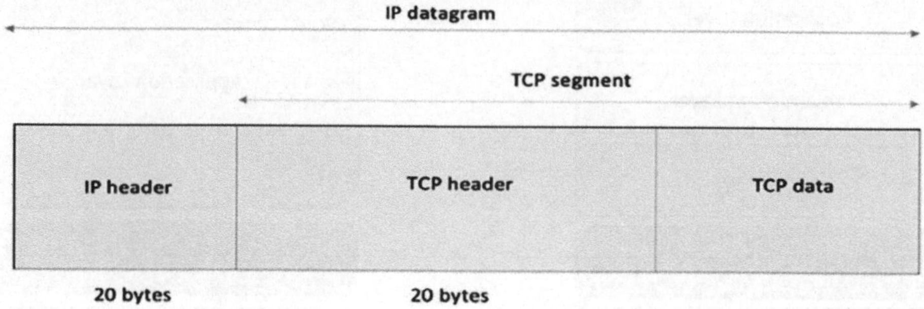

Figure 1.6: *Encapsulation of TCP Data in an IP Datagram*

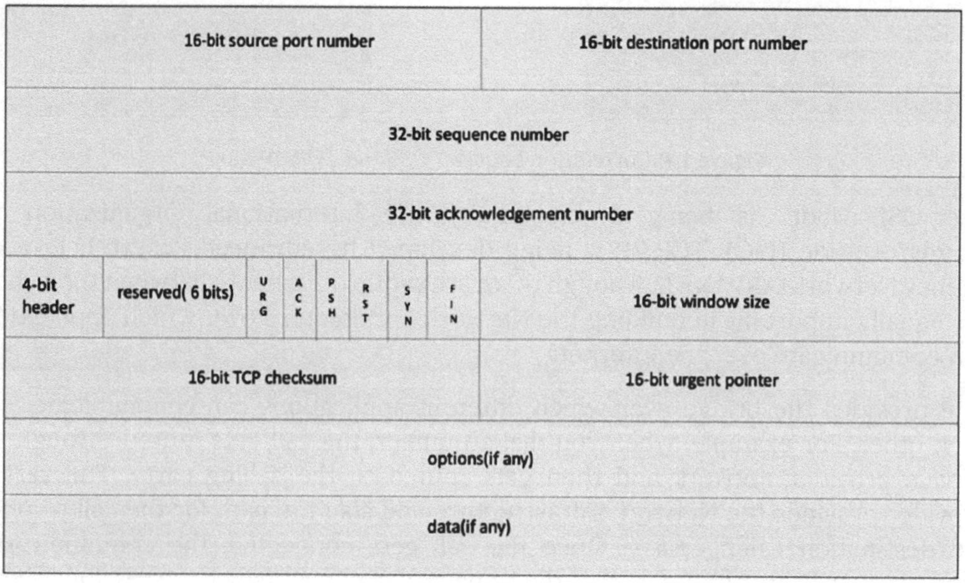

Figure 1.7: *TCP Header*

Each TCP segment contains source and destination port numbers to identify sending and receiving applications. These two values, along with the source and destination IP address in the IP header, identify a connection.

The combination of IP address and port number is called a socket. The socket pair is a 5-tuple, which consists of the client IP address, client port number, server IP address, server port number, and transport protocol TCP/UDP.

The sequence number identifies the stream of bytes flowing between two applications. The acknowledgment number contains the next sequence number that the sender of the acknowledgment expects to receive. TCP provides full-duplex service to the application layer. This means that data can flow in each direction, which means each end of the connection must maintain a sequence number for the data flowing in each direction.

The header length gives the length of the header in 32-bit words. This is required because the length of the options field is variable. Without options, the normal size is 20 bytes.

There are six flags in the TCP header such as:

- **URG:** This is for the sender to transmit emergency data to the receiver.
- **ACK:** The acknowledgement number is valid.
- **PSH:** The receiver should pass data to the application as soon as possible.
- **SYN:** Synchronize sequence numbers to initiate connection.
- **FIN:** The sender is finished sending data.
- **TCP:** This flow control is provided by each end advertising a window size. This is the number of bytes that the receiver is willing to accept.

The checksum covers the entire TCP segment, including both the TCP header and the TCP data. This is calculated and stored by the sender, which is then verified by the receiver. The urgent pointer is valid if the URG flag is set.

The most common option field is the maximum segment size, called MSS. Each end of a connection specifies an option on the first segment exchanged. It specifies the maximum-sized segment that the sender wants to receive.

Following is a sample TCP conversation captured in Wireshark:

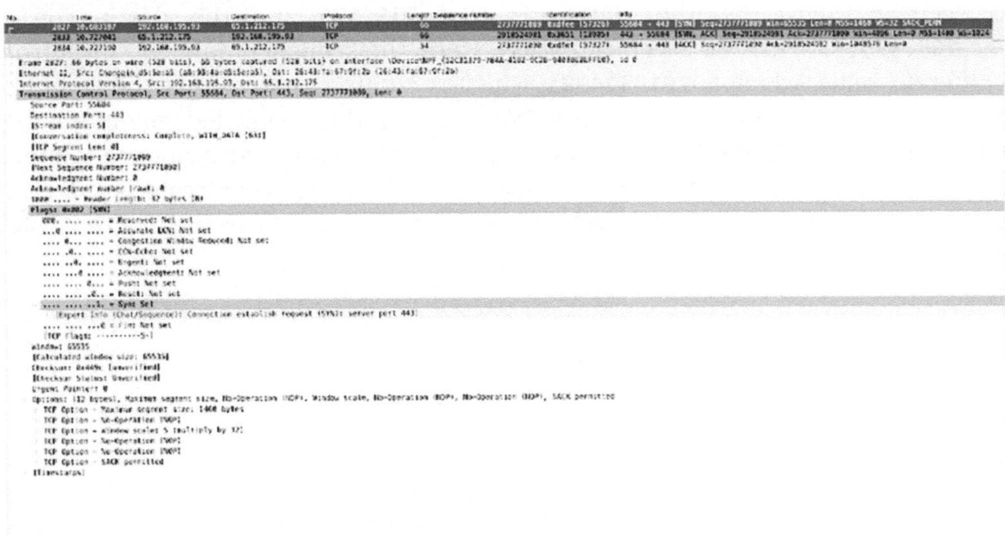

Figure 1.8: *TCP Parameters in Wireshark*

As seen in *Figure* 1.8, each TCP communication happens with a successful 3-way handshake starting with a **SYN**, **SYN-ACK**, and **ACK** packet.

As we look at the diagram, we see the source port and the destination port in the TCP header with source port as **55684** and destination port as **443**. The sequence number starts with **2737771089** from the source as **192.168.195.93** and the destination as **65.1.212.175**. As you can see, the next sequence number is always **SYN + 1**. The ack number would be 0, as it always starts from 0. The window size is of length **65535**, and the max TCP port range is from 0-65535. The MSS size is **1460** bytes.

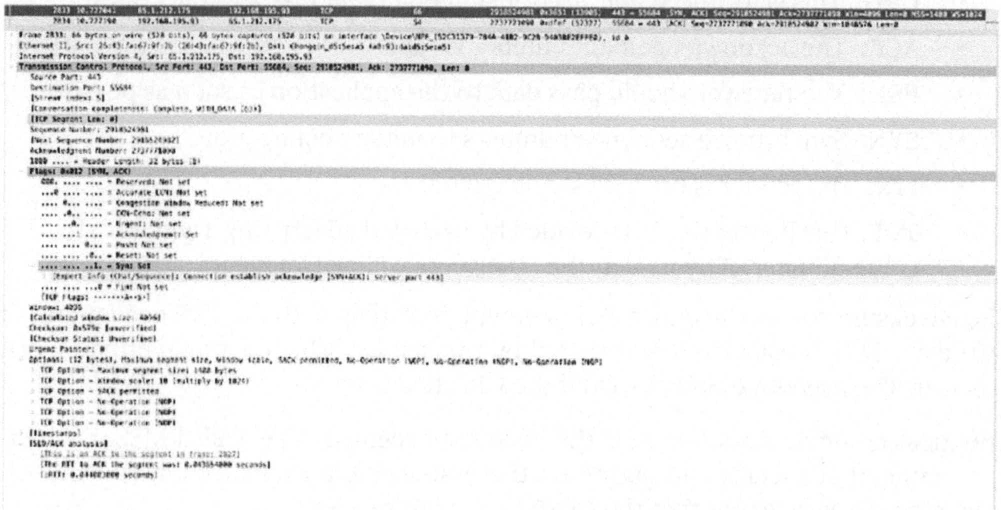

***Figure* 1.9:** *TCP MSS and Window Size*

As seen in *Figure* 1.9, the source is **65.1.212.175** and the destination is **192.168.195.93**. This is a **SYN ACK** packet. Here, the sequence number starts from a different value, which is **2918524981**, which is a different stream as the source is different. The next sequence number is **SYN + 1**. Now the acknowledgement number is not 0 but **2737771090**, which is SYN + 1(2737771089 + 1)== next sequence number. The acknowledgement is equal to the SYN+1(2737771089) as the stream is the reply to the **SYN** initiated from source **192.168.195.93**. The MSS advertised here is **1400** bytes.

Figure 1.10: *Sequence Number in TCP Header*

As seen in *Figure* 1.10, the source is again **192.168.195.93**, and as seen, it is an acknowledgement to the **SYN ACK** packet. The sequence number is **2737771090**, which is the next sequence number of the first packet, which was **SYN** with source as **192.168.195.93**. As can be seen, the sequence number is equal to the next sequence number of the source **192.168.195.93** of the first packet. The Acknowledgement number is **2918524982**, which is == to the next sequence number of the **SYN-ACK** packet whose source is **65.1.212.175**.

What have we learnt so far?

Each TCP transaction starts with a 3-way handshake. Each stream would have its own TCP sequence number. The next sequence number would always be SYN + 1. The acknowledgement number would always be equal to the next sequence number of the previous packet, as TCP works in sequence and keeps a track of all transactions; as a result, it is being mentioned as a reliable protocol.

How is the next sequence number calculated?

The next sequence number for a **SYN** or **SYN ACK** packet = sequence number + 1 – if the TCP data payload is 0.

The next sequence number for a TCP packet is = sequence number + TCP data payload.

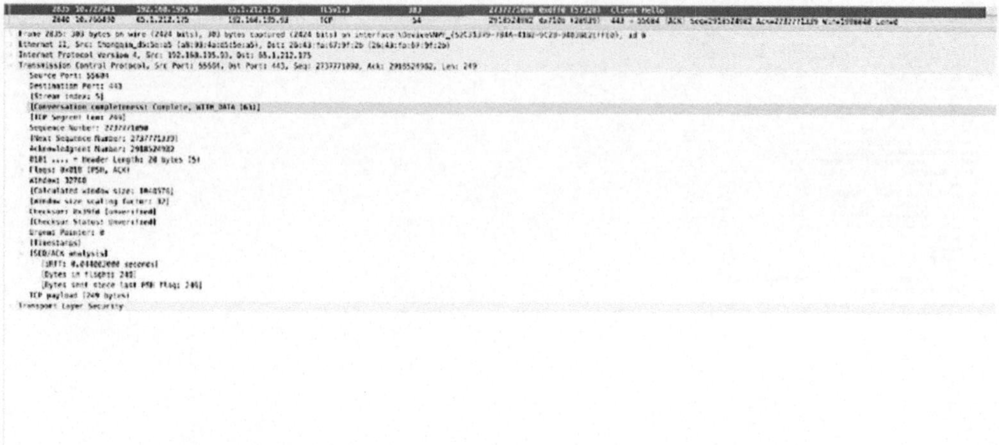

Figure 1.11: *Validating Next Sequence Number in TCP Header*

As seen in *Figure* 1.11, the TCP packet is a Client Hello, which is sent after the initial `SYN` from the source **`192.168.195.93`**. As seen, the next sequence number = Seq number(2737771090) + TCP payload(249) = **`2737771339`**.

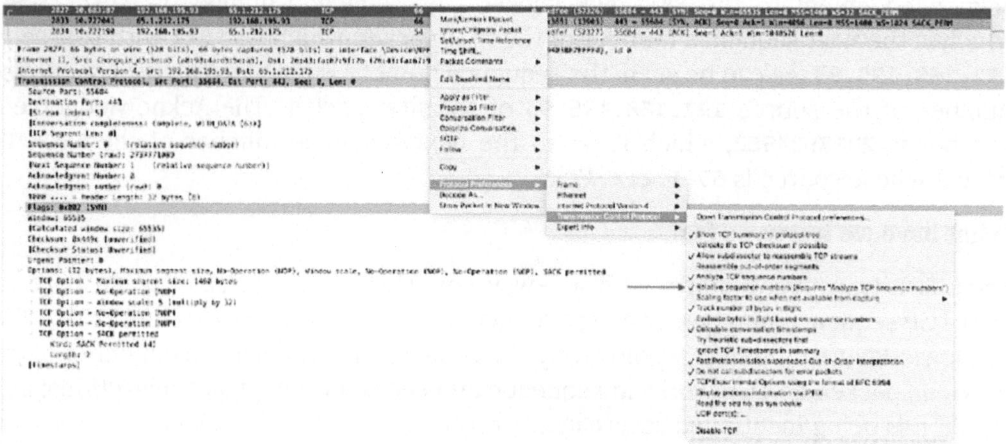

Figure 1.12: *Enabling Relative Sequence Number*

We can always enable the Relative sequence number while working on TCP sequence number analysis. As seen in *Figure* 1.12, right click any **`TCP packet`** > **`Protocol preferences`** > **`TCP`** > **`Relative sequence number`**.

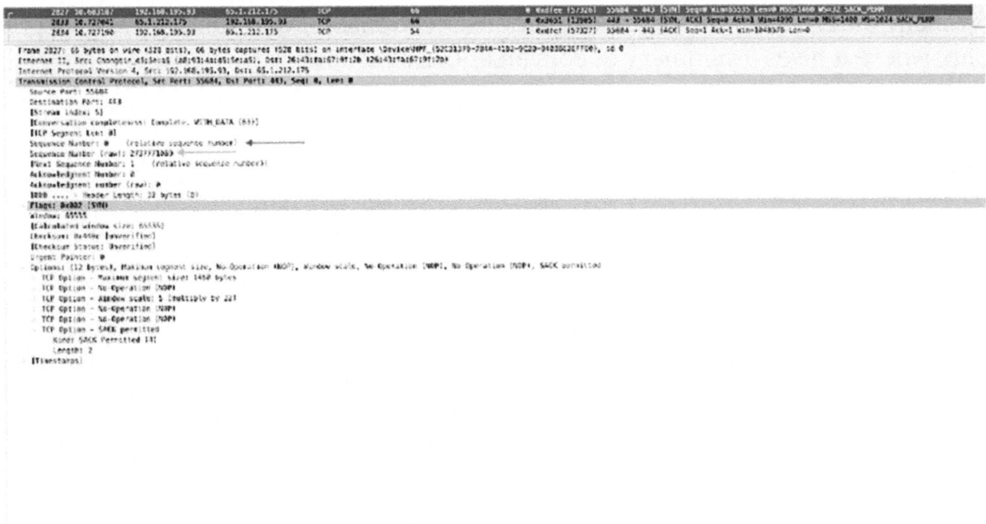

Figure 1.13: *Validating Relative Sequence Number*

As seen in *Figure* 1.13, the term relative means that it starts from 0. One can always see the raw sequence number and also the relative sequence number. The relative sequence number helps in troubleshooting TCP stream issues with a lower offset number, rather than the actual sequence number, which is a large number.

Figure 1.14: *Client Hello with Relative Sequence Number*

As seen in *Figure* 1.14, the client hello packet is shown with a relative sequence number enabled. The next sequence number is 250, as it is sequence number + TCP payload length = 1 + 249.

With a larger pcap file, it is important to understand how many different streams are available and what are the different transport protocols TCP/UDP available, and how many different sources and destinations are available. Wireshark gives us a great utility where it gives a summary of conversations as follows.

Open `Wireshark` > `Statistics` > `Conversations`

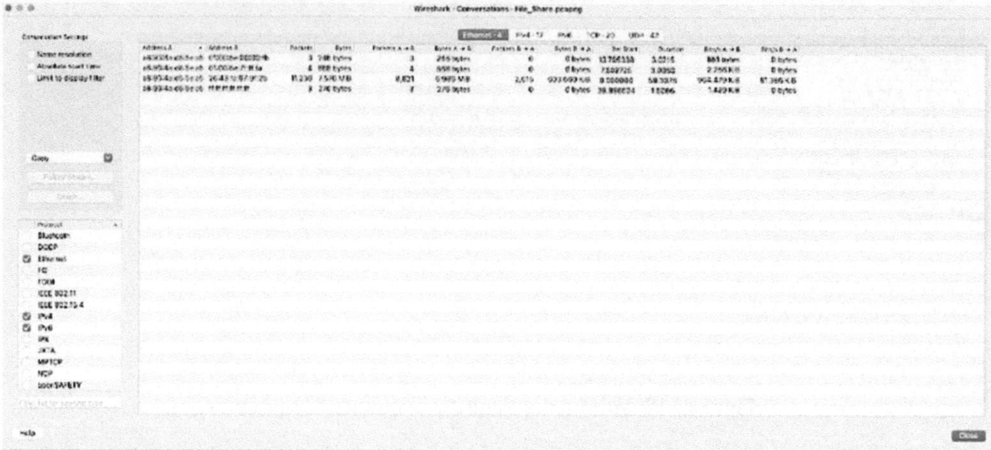

***Figure 1.15:** Conversation Summary in Wireshark*

As seen in *Figure* 1.15, there are 5 columns:

1. **Ethernet:** Layer 2 mac address
2. **IPV4**: IPv4 address for different conversations
3. **IPV6**: IPV6 address for different conversations
4. **TCP:** The 4-tuple information of TCP transaction
5. **UDP**: The 4-tuple information of UDP transaction

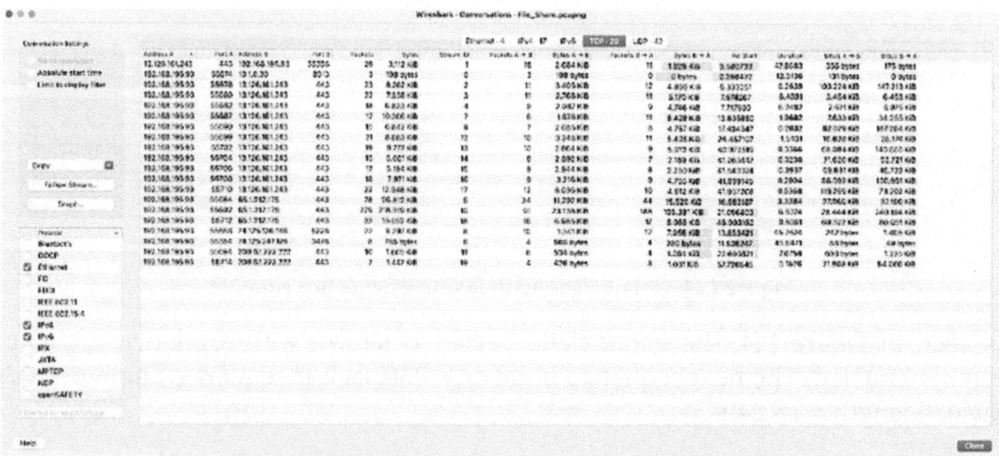

***Figure 1.16:** Conversation Summary with TCP Sessions*

As seen in *Figure* 1.16, the information under the TCP column gives the source and destination IP address and also the source and destination port, which are labeled as Port A and Port B. It also gives the information about the bytes transferred for each connection. One of the important columns is the stream id, which is the Wireshark way of filtering specific transactions.

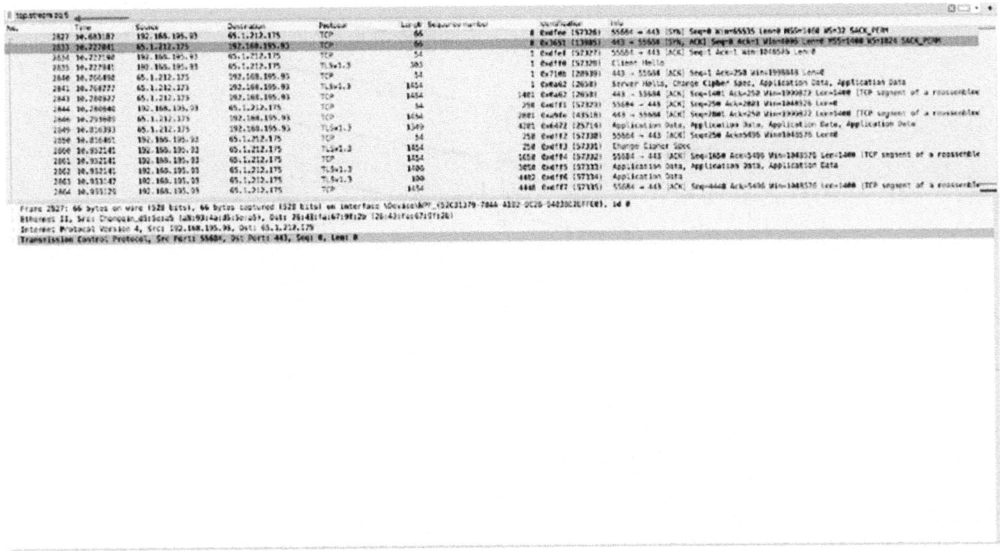

Figure 1.17: *Filtering Wireshark with TCP Stream Id*

With this filter, one can look at all the conversations happening for a specific stream index.

Let us look at how the TCP acknowledgement works for different segments, and then we will look into the selective acknowledgement functioning.

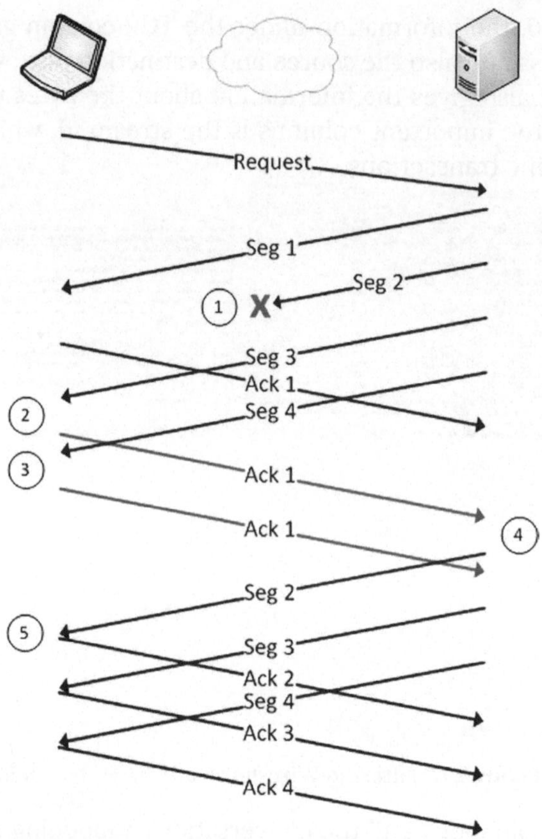

Figure 1.18: *Reliable Communication in TCP with Acknowledgement for Missing Segments*

The preceding diagram shows the client sending a request to the server and the server formulates the response into 4 TCP segments (packets). As seen in the diagram, segment 2 is lost, and the Server keeps on sending other segments, where the client keeps on sending an acknowledgement of the first packet, post which the server sends segment 2 again, after which the Client sends an acknowledgement for other segments. As seen, the client always acknowledges the packet which it has received till now, and by sending the acknowledgement of the first packet server understands that segment 2 was lost in between it retransmits all packets from segment 2,3,4.... One of the disadvantages is that it results in the server retransmitting the packets, which can result in loss of bandwidth and is considered as not efficient.

Selective Acknowledgement

Selective Acknowledgement was introduced in TCP flow to manage the loss of segments. In order to better manage the bandwidth of the link a range was defined to identify the start and the end of the Segments which were lost so that the receiver knows from where the retransmission of the Segments to start selectively.

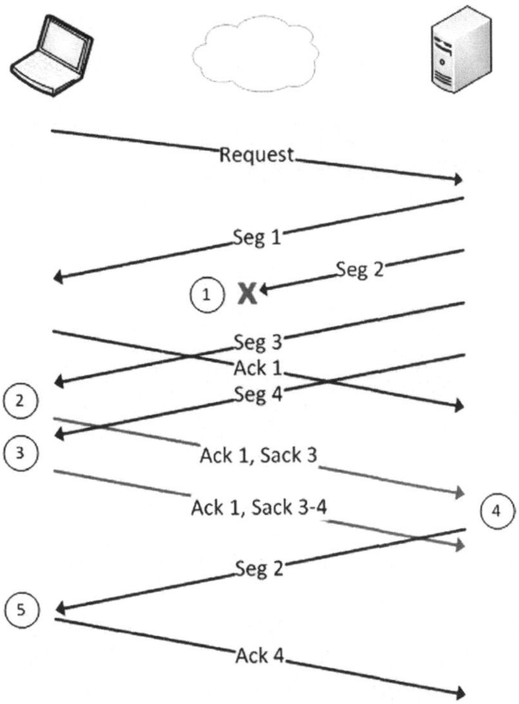

Figure 1.19: *Selective Acknowledgement*

The preceding diagram shows the server sending segments requested by the client. As seen, segment 2 is not received by the client. The client, along with sending an acknowledgement of segment 1, also sends an acknowledgement with the Sack field that segments 3 and 4 are also received. Thus, the server sends only segment 2 and does not retransmit the other.

As seen in *Figure 1.20*, the packet #30 sent by the server is not received by the client.

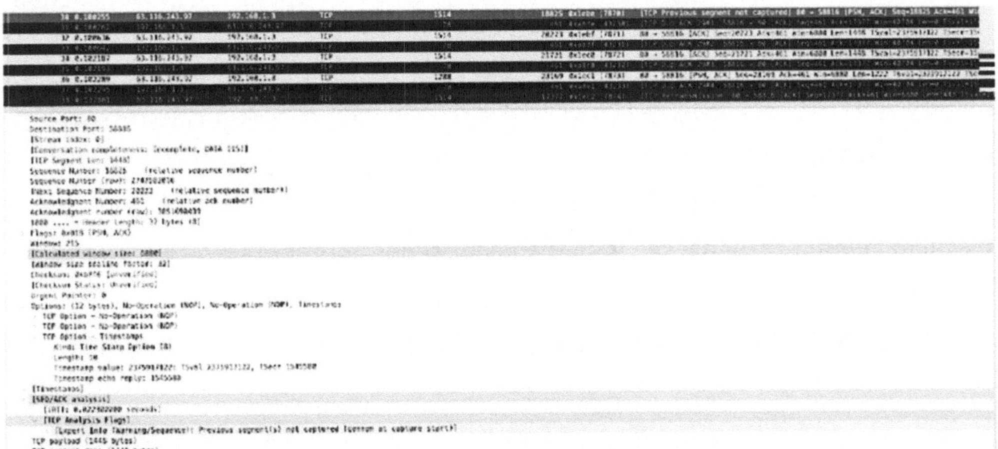

Figure 1.20: *Selective Acknowledgement Field in Wireshark*

As seen in *Figure* 1.21, the client in packet #31 sends an acknowledgement by mentioning the segments in the Sack field which are not received by the client.

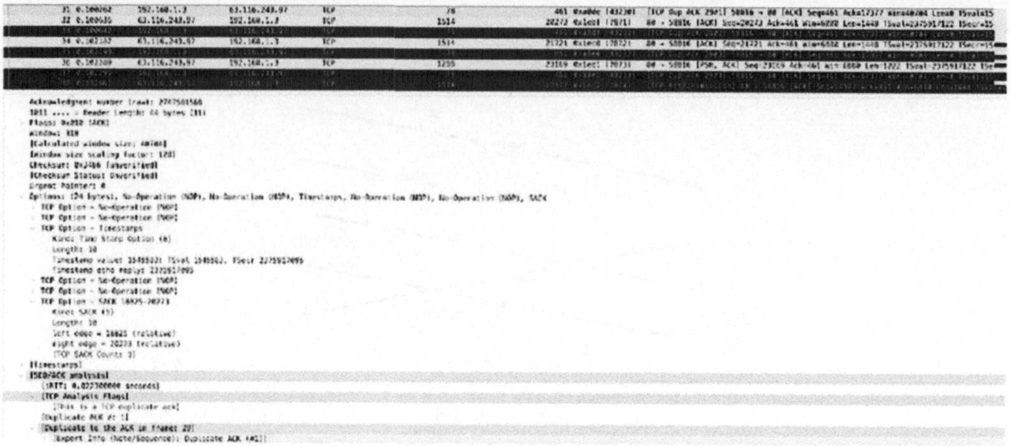

Figure 1.21: *Receiver acknowledging the Segments Not received*

Client sends another packet #33, where it sends an acknowledgement by mentioning the segments in the Sack field which are not received by the client. The client also sends the non-contiguous segments that the server has been sending. As seen, the right edge keeps on increasing, which is now **21721**.

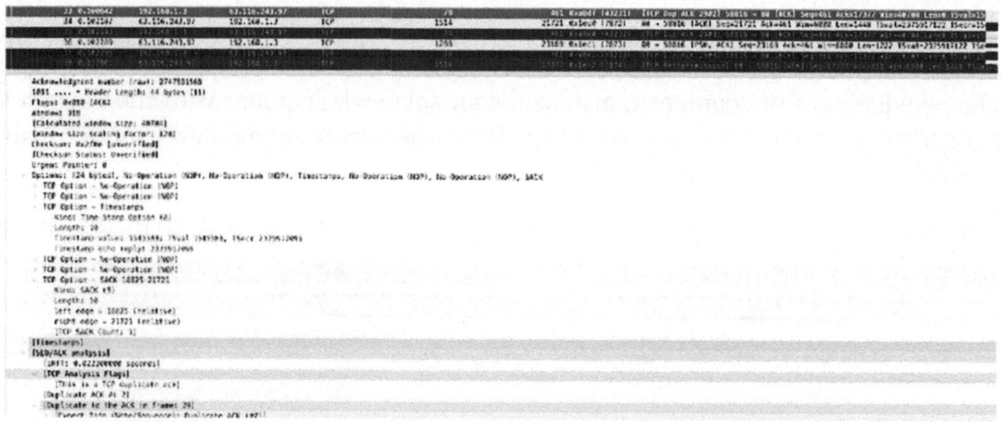

Figure 1.22: *Client sending the Segments requested by the Receiver*

As seen in *Figure* 1.22, in packet #35, the client sends another **Dup Ack** with the right edge of Sack as **23169**.

As seen in packet #38, the server retransmits the packet with the seq no **18825**.

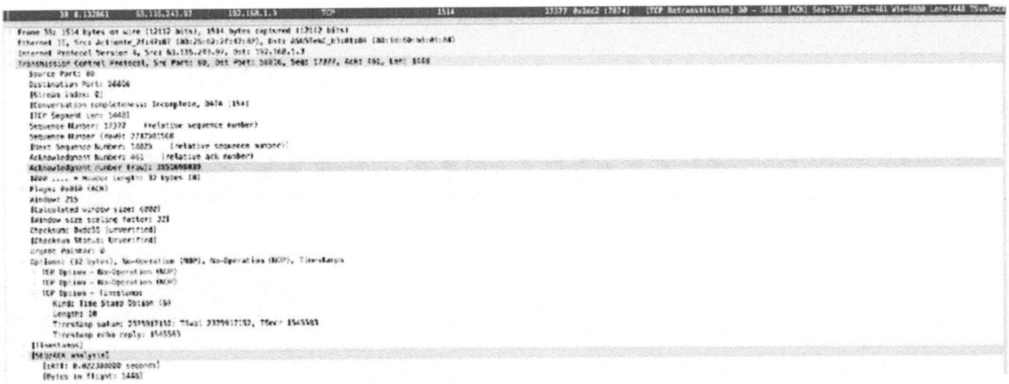

Figure 1.23: *Server retransmitting the Packet*

Conclusion

We started by looking at the building blocks of Infotainment Systems. We then understood the basics of the OSI model and also looked at the actual packet captures to understand the different packet handshakes in the TCP protocol. We also looked at how the TCP protocol is a reliable protocol and also how the TCP 3-way handshake works. The next chapter will explain how the Internet traffic works when you are working from home.

CHAPTER 2
Flow of Internet Traffic

Introduction

This chapter will focus on how the Internet traffic works when you are working from home. This chapter will give insights into how different components of the OSI layer model work while the traffic is initiated to the Internet. It would highlight the DNS resolution and how the connection is made to different websites. We would set up a private Web Server and perform decryption in Wireshark using the server's private key and TLS pre-master secret. We will conclude by taking a remote capture on the Apache server using Wireshark.

Structure

In this chapter, we will cover the following topics:

- Basic Home Internet Connectivity
- Analyzing Practical SSL Decryption
- Applying Remote Capture Using Wireshark

Basic Home Internet Connectivity

Let us start with a basic setup, where the machine is connected to the Home Wifi. The Home Wifi provides Internet connectivity.

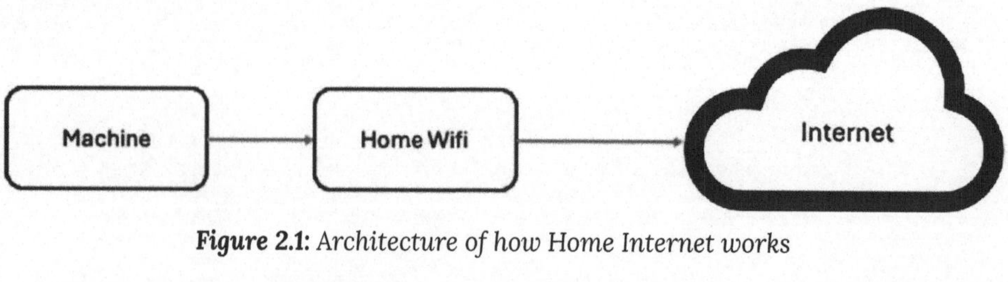

Figure 2.1: *Architecture of how Home Internet works*

In order to access the Internet, the Network needs to have a public IP, which would allow Internet communication. If the Network only has a private IP, then the Internet traffic access would not work. The list of private IP addresses is mentioned in https://datatracker.ietf.org/doc/html/rfc1918.

I log in to my Home Wifi router. By default, the IP address of the Wifi router is 192.168.1.1. The Wifi router can be accessed on http://192.168.1.1 . The default login username and password would generally be admin/admin, depending on the Wifi router model.

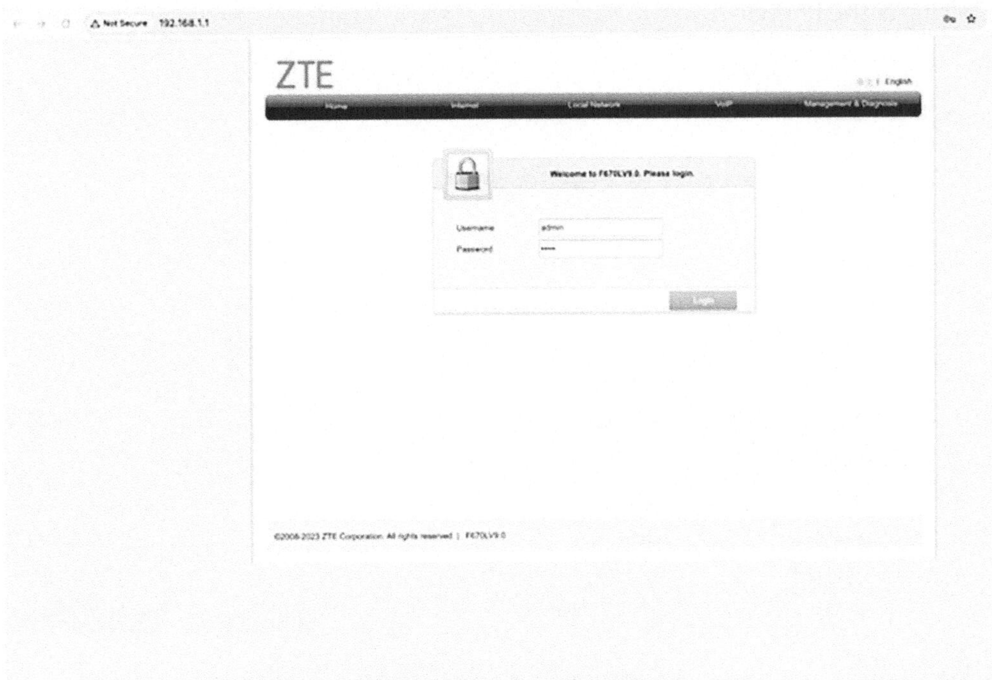

Figure 2.2: *Wifi Router Login Page*

Figure 2.3: *The Machines connected to the WiFi Server*

Here, it shows the machines that are connected to the Wifi router. As we can see, the private IP address is being displayed as **`192.168.1.3`**. Verifying on the machine CLI, we can see the same IP address being configured.

```
en0: flags=8863<UP,BROADCAST,SMART,RUNNING,SIMPLEX,MULTICAST> mtu
1500
        options=6460<TSO4,TSO6,CHANNEL_IO,PARTIAL_CSUM,ZEROINVERT_
        CSUM>
        ether e2:a9:5b:86:e6:84
```

```
inet6 fe80::840:493e:edd9:c2ef%en0 prefixlen 64 secured
scopeid 0xe
inet 192.168.1.3 netmask 0xffffff00 broadcast 192.168.1.255
nd6 options=201<PERFORMNUD,DAD>
media: autoselect
status: active
```

The question comes from where the IP address pool is being configured and how the IP address is assigned to the machine. Under **Lan Settings> DHCP Server**, the following is the IP pool:

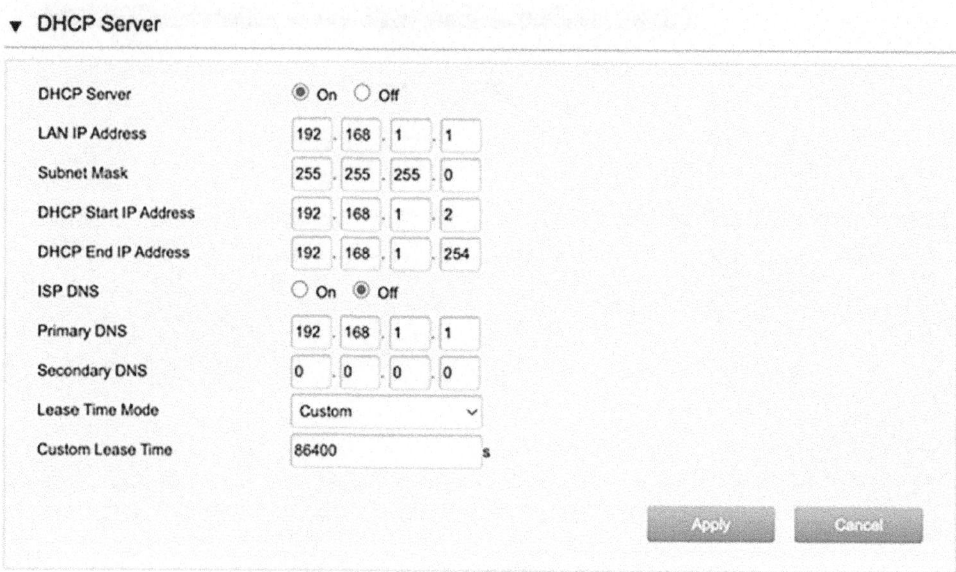

Figure 2.4: *DHCP Server Settings on the Wi-Fi Router*

There is a DHCP server configured on the Wifi router, which allocates IP to the machines that get connected. We can also see that the DNS server is configured at **192.168.1.1**. Why is the DNS server important? Let us say a user initiates the traffic to the Internet at google.com. The first step that happens is the user's machine forwards the DNS resolution to the DNS server configured, which is provided by the Home Wifi Provider.

The user sends the DNS request to the DNS server, which is **192.168.1.1**. As we learnt initially, for the network to access the Internet, it needs to have a public IP, and similarly, the DNS server should also have a public DNS server for resolving public domains. The public DNS server is configured as follows on the Wifi router:

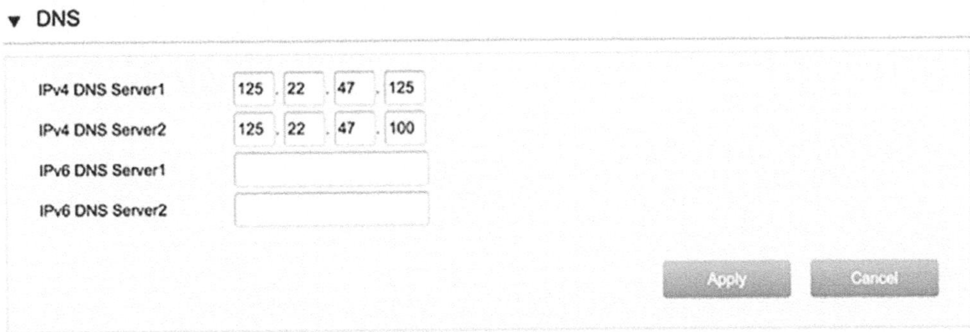

Figure 2.5: *DNS Server Setting on the Wi-fi Router*

The Wifi provider is Airtel, and they use the following DNS server range. https://www.dnsknowledge.com/name-servers/india/airtel-dns-server-address/

Let us check this DNS communication on Wireshark. The user has initiated traffic to 3 public websites: news18.com, youtube.com, and google.com

In order to filter all the traffic, we would use the filter **dns** in Wireshark.

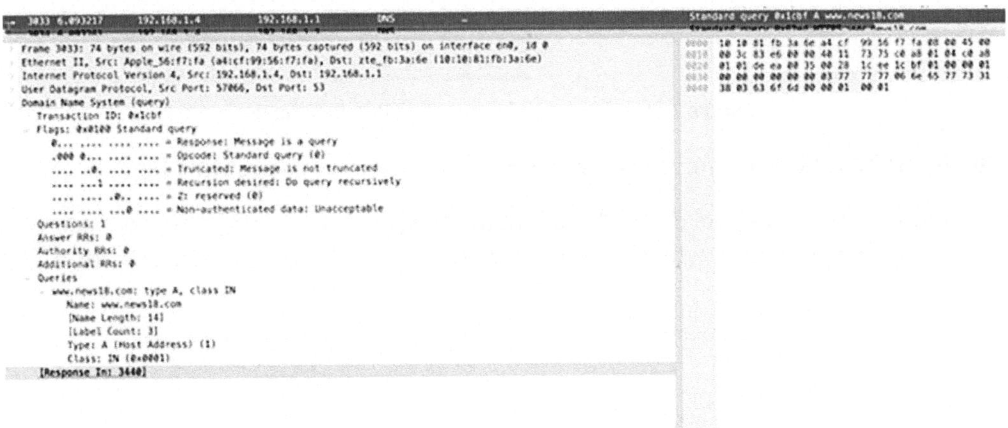

Figure 2.6: *Verifying DNS Request on Wireshark*

Let us first try to view the first dns query made for the first request made by the user to news18.com.

As we see packet no `3033`, the source IP of the DNS query is `192.168.1.4`, and the destination IP is `192.168.1.1`, which is the DNS server. The DNS server `192.168.1.1` redirects to the public DNS server, which would not be seen on the capture. As can be seen, the DNS response for the DNS query made on packet no 3033 is on packet no `3440`. Once we view the packet no 3440, we see the response coming from the DNS server to the endpoint machine.

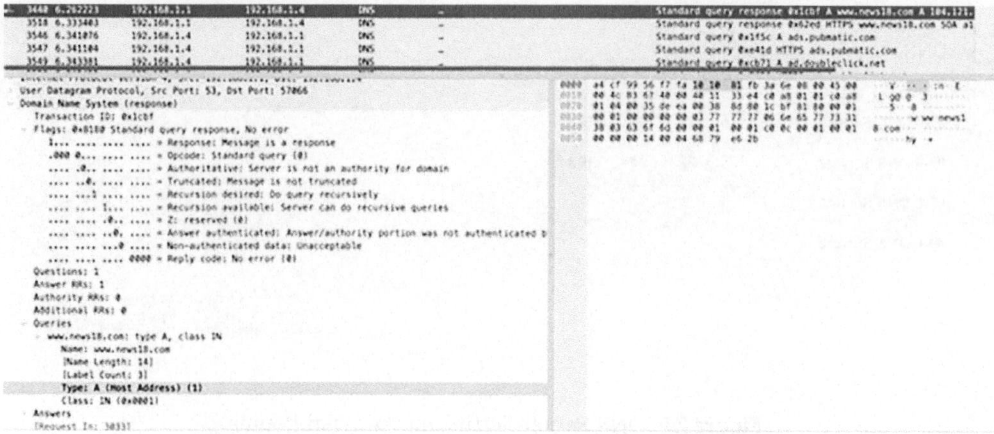

Figure 2.7: *DNS Response to the Query initiated by the User*

As seen in Wireshark, the Information field mentions that it is a DNS response. When we look at the DNS Flags in the packet, it specifies a Response message. We do not see any IP address information in the DNS packet header. We only see Type A as the Host address with no IPv4 information in it. When we look at the Info field, the IP address information is visible.

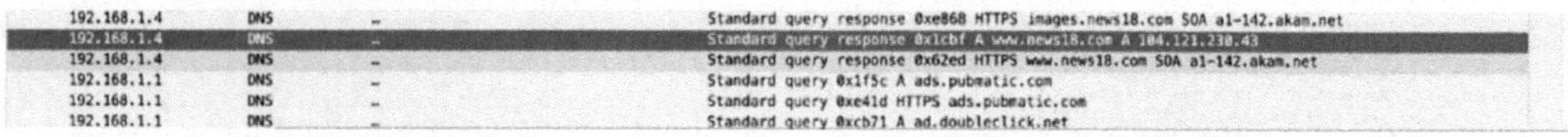

Figure 2.8: *IP Information for the DNS Response*

Why is the IP address information not visible in the DNS packet header?

Let us look at the DNS packet header again in the Queries section. When we select to Query the domain name, which is news18.com, we also look at the Information field in Pane 3.

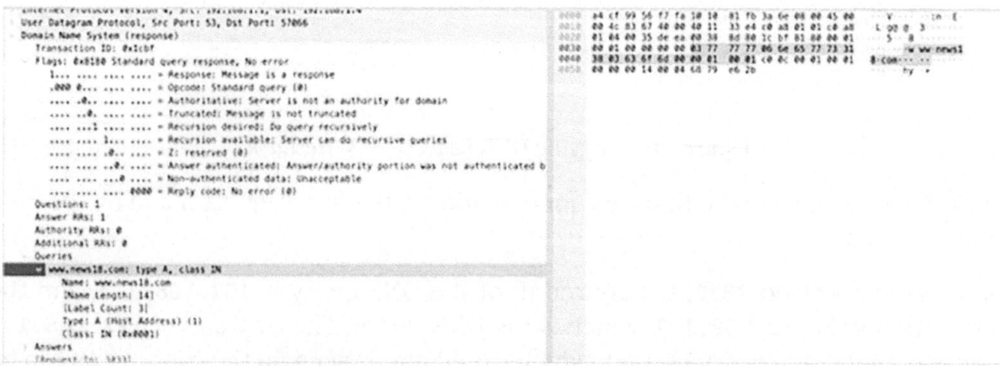

Figure 2.9: *Dissecting the DNS Query Packet*

We can see that the highlighted portion in pane 3 stops at 01. If we look at Pane 3, there are some Integers in place. Let us try to dissect what those Integers represent.

The first part of the domain is www. If you use https://www.rapidtables.com/convert/number/ascii-to-hex.html and try to convert the ascii character www to hexadecimal, we get **77 77 77**. The next part of the domain is news18, which gives hexadecimal output of **6E 65 77 73 31 38**. The last part of the domain is com, which gives hexadecimal output of **63 6F 6D**.

Similarly, we check the DNS query packets for other domains such as youtube.com. Here we are using the filter **dns.qry.name** to only list out the packets which has youtube.com as the dns query.

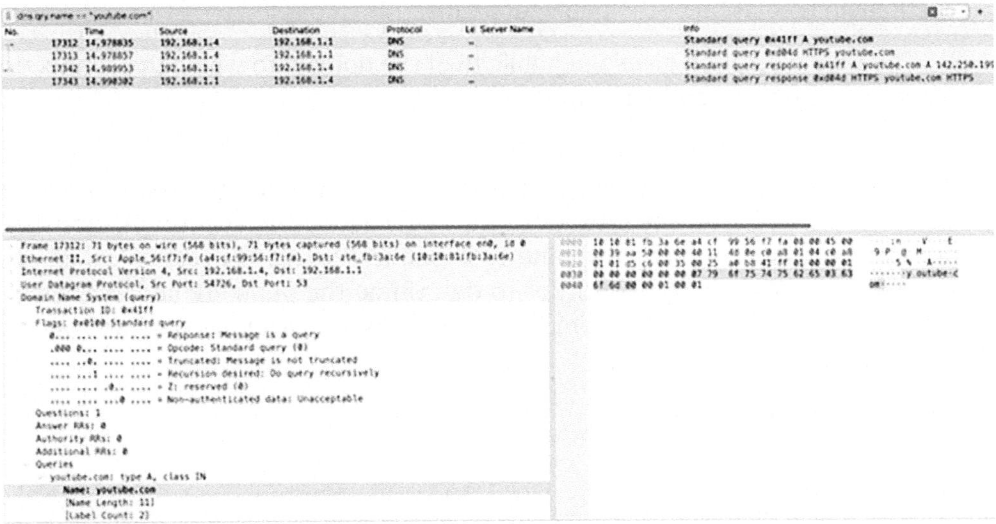

Figure 2.10: DNS Query *for* Youtube.com

The following is the response packet in packet no **17342**:

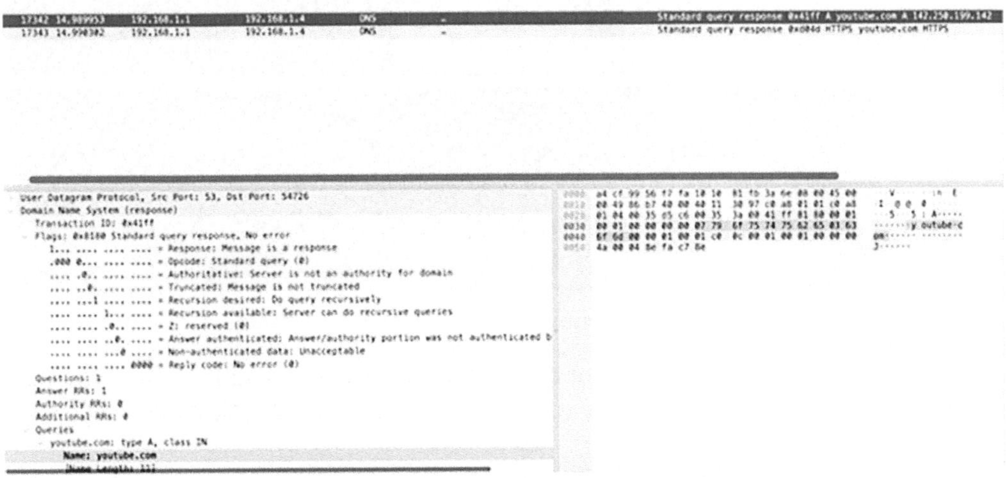

Figure 2.11: DNS Response *for* Youtube.com

If we follow the same preceding process by converting ASCII characters to hexadecimal, we get youtube= **79 6F 75 74 75 62 65** and com= **63 6F 6D 0A**.

We learnt the following steps when the Internet traffic is initiated from the endpoint machine.

1. The DNS resolution happens on the DNS server, which is configured on the endpoint machine.
2. The public DNS server is configured on the WIFI provider, which helps in the Domain resolution of the public domains.
3. The DNS resolution gives the public IP of the domain to which the connection is made from the endpoint machine.

In order to access the Internet, the endpoint machine should also have a public IP address. We saw that the endpoint machine had a private IP address in the range 192.168.x.x. The gateway to the Internet is the Wifi router. The Wifi router translates the private IP of the endpoint machine to a public IP. This process is called NAT (Network Address Translation). In order to determine the public IP address, we can type https://whatismyipaddress.com/ on the endpoint machine, and we get the following output:

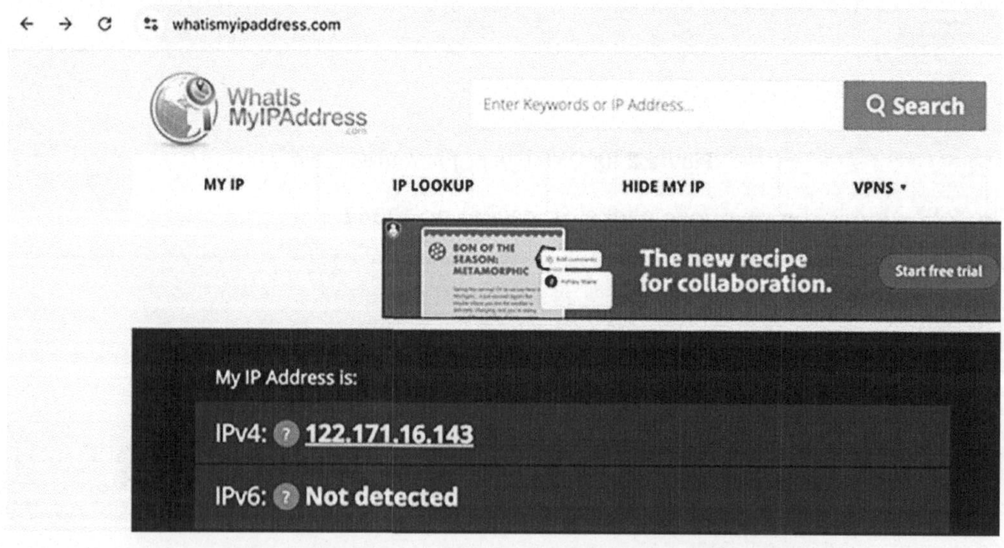

Figure 2.12: *Determining the Public IP of the Machine*

One would think that the public IP of **122.171.16.143** is not visible in the Wireshark capture. We saw the source IP of the endpoint machine as **192.168.1.4**.

Let us try to visualize the packet flow with the following network diagram:

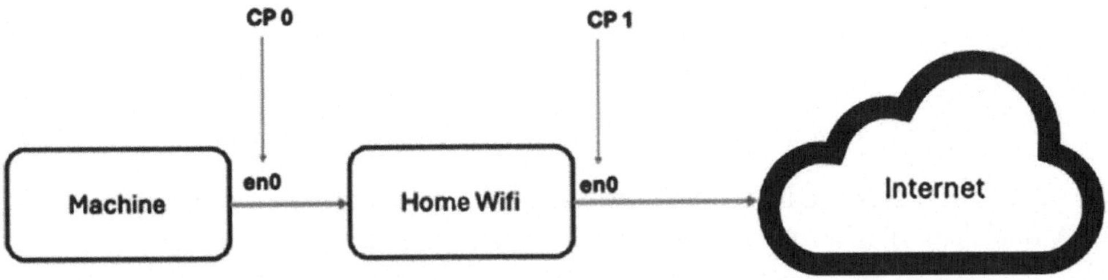

Figure 2.13: *Packet Flow when the Traffic leaves the Machine and reaches Internet*

We took the Wireshark capture on CP0, which is the nic for the endpoint machine from where the traffic was initiated. Had we taken the capture on CP1, which is the nic for the Wifi router, we could have seen the public IP of **`122.171.16.143`**. The Web Interface of the Wifi router does not give an option to take capture on CP1.

Let us look at the packet flow when the traffic is being initiated from the endpoint machine by focusing on different packet headers of the OSI layer, which we learnt.

We would try to analyze Wireshark for the traffic that was initiated to news18.com.

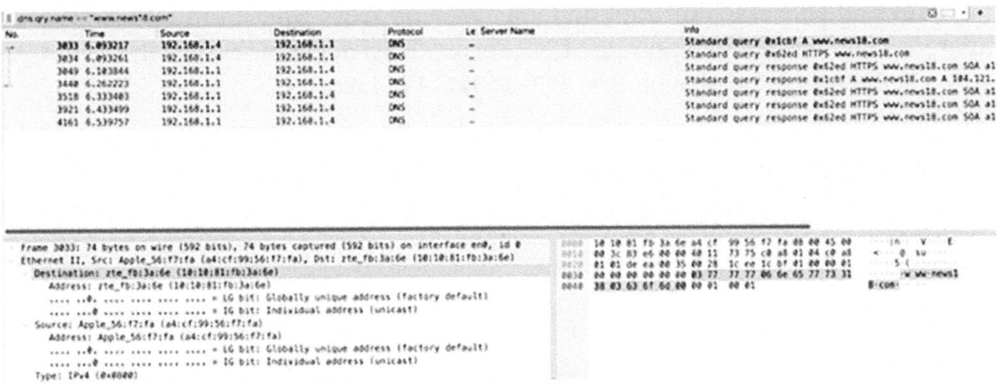

Figure 2.14: *Wireshark Filter for DNS Query*

The first address at the ethernet layer is the MAC address. This is the Data Link layer for the OSI model. MAC address stands for Media Access Control, which is a unique identifier assigned to the network Interface controller (NIC). The Ethernet layer would always consist of the source and destination MAC. The destination MAC would be of the WIFI router, and the source MAC would be of the endpoint machine from where the traffic is initiated. If we closely look at Pane 3, where the traffic bytes are shown, it starts with the Ethernet layer.

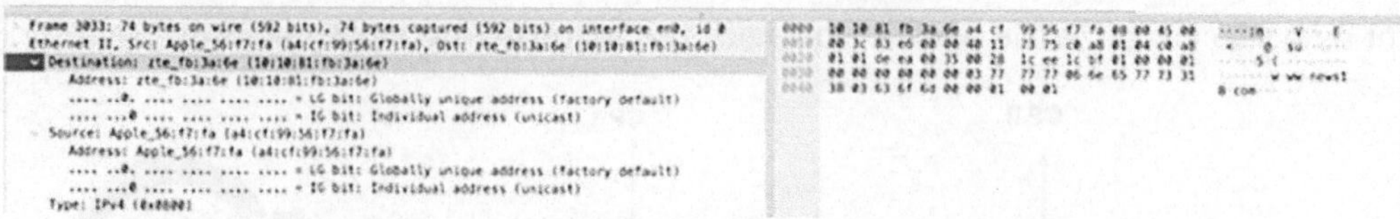

Figure 2.15: *Ethernet Layer showing the MAC Address*

The next Protocol is the Internet Protocol (IP) Layer. This is the Network Layer for the OSI Model. The IP layer provides the source and destination IP addresses.

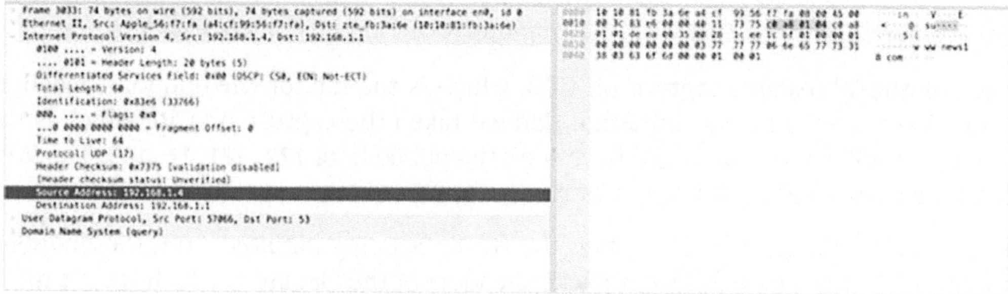

Figure 2.16: *IP Layer Information in Wireshark*

The source IP address is of the endpoint machine from where the DNS traffic was initiated, while the destination is the DNS Server. The Packet bytes on Pane 3 show the source IP address of the machine as **`192.168.1.4`** in hex.

The next layer is the Transport layer, which shows the User Datagram Protocol (UDP). Since this is DNS traffic, it generally works on the UDP protocol.

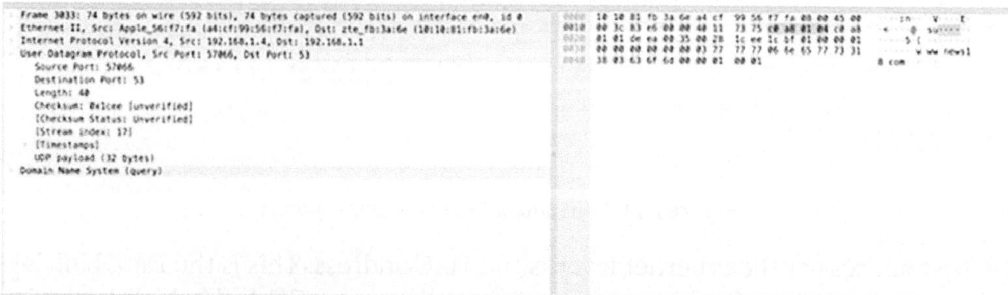

Figure 2.17: *Transport Layer showing DNS Query*

The UDP protocol provides information about the Source and Destination ports on which the traffic was initiated. Since it is DNS traffic, the destination port is **`53`** while the source port is **`57066`**. DNS traffic is always initiated on port **`53`**. The port range is generally between 0 and 65535.

We would now look at the DNS response packets from the DNS server.

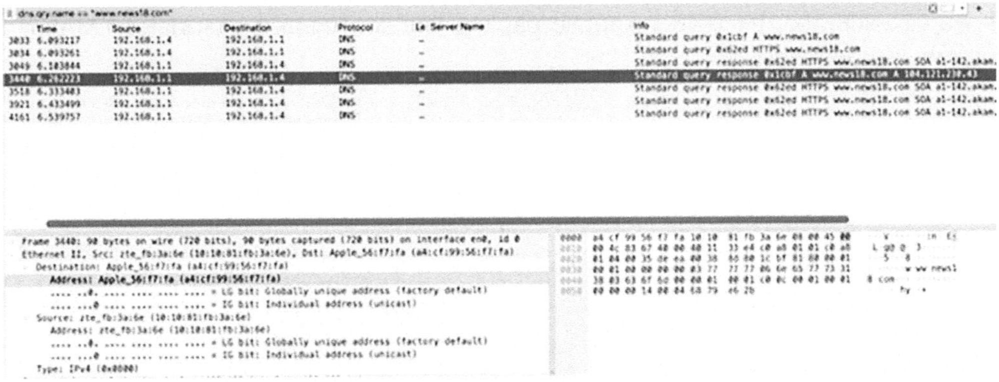

Figure 2.18: *Source and Destination MAC of the DNS Query*

Since the DNS reply is coming from the DNS server, the source MAC is of the Wifi router, and the destination MAC is of the endpoint machine.

The IP Protocol shows the Source IP of the DNS server, while the destination IP of the endpoint machine.

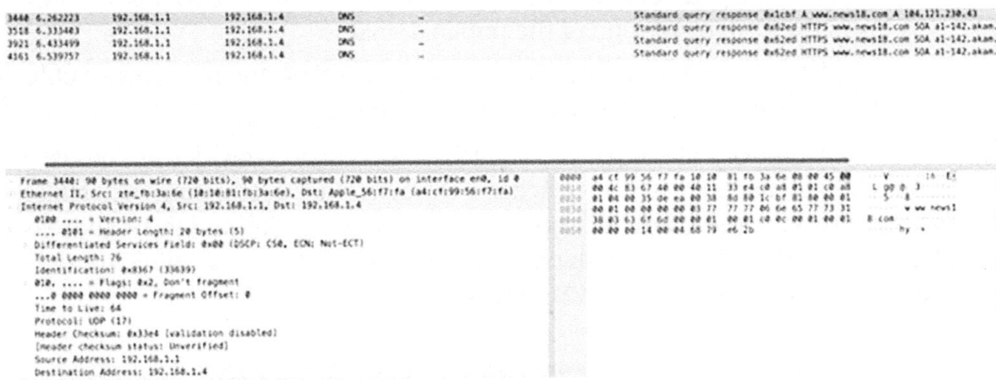

Figure 2.19: *Source and Destination IP of the DNS Query*

The Transport layer shows UDP protocol where the Source port is **`53`** and the destination port is **`57066`**.

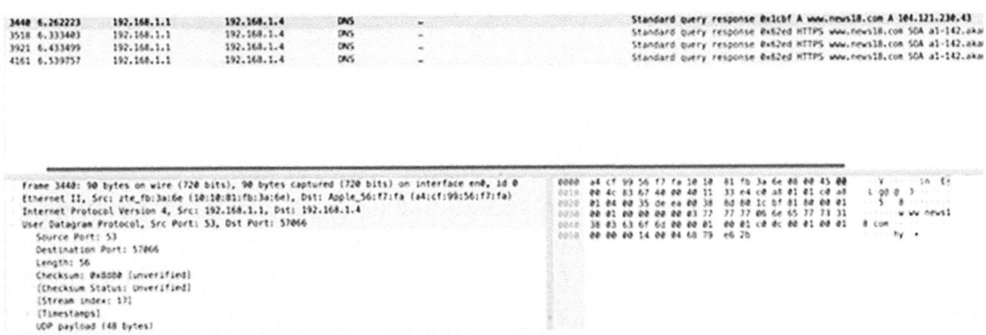

Figure 2.20: *Transport Layer Information of the DNS Query*

As we can see, for the DNS response packet, the source and destination MAC and ports would be reversed.

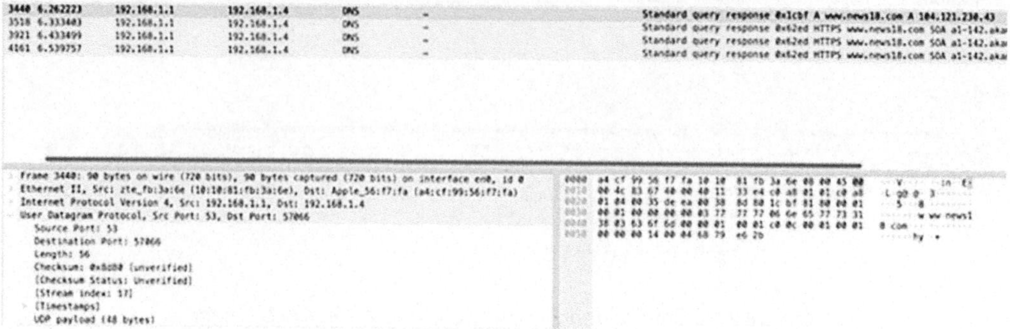

Figure 2.21: *Source and Destination MAC for the DNS Response*

We learnt the following:

- When the Internet traffic gets initiated, the first step is the DNS resolution.
- The DNS traffic gets forwarded to the DNS server, which is configured, which helps in the DNS resolution of the public domains.
- The Wifi router performs NAT for the source machine and provides a public IP for the machine to communicate with the Internet.

Till now, we have looked at the DNS packets in Wireshark. Now, let us look at the connection being made from the machine towards the destination news18.com. How do we filter out the traffic for news18.com? Since we know the IP address of news18.com from DNS response, which is `104.121.230.43`, we can filter out all the communication for IP address `104.121.230.43`.

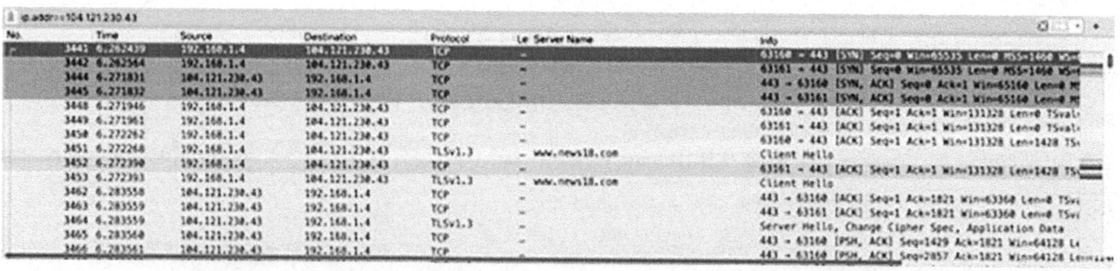

Figure 2.22: *Filtering Traffic on the News18.com IP Address*

This capture filter shows all the traffic initiated to the page news18.com. Let us look at each packet conversation along with the different packet headers.

The first packet is `TCP SYN` from the source machine. All the HTTPS connections are being made on TCP protocol, and for every new TCP connection, the initial TCP packet is `SYN`. `TCP SYN` is the initial control probe that the source machine sends to the destination server.

If we look at the details of the first packet, we can see the destination MAC is of the

Wi-Fi router and the source MAC is of the endpoint machine. Are you wondering if the destination MAC should be of the server where news18.com is hosted? Not really, because the gateway for the endpoint machine is the Wifi router, as a result, we would always see the destination MAC of the Wifi router.

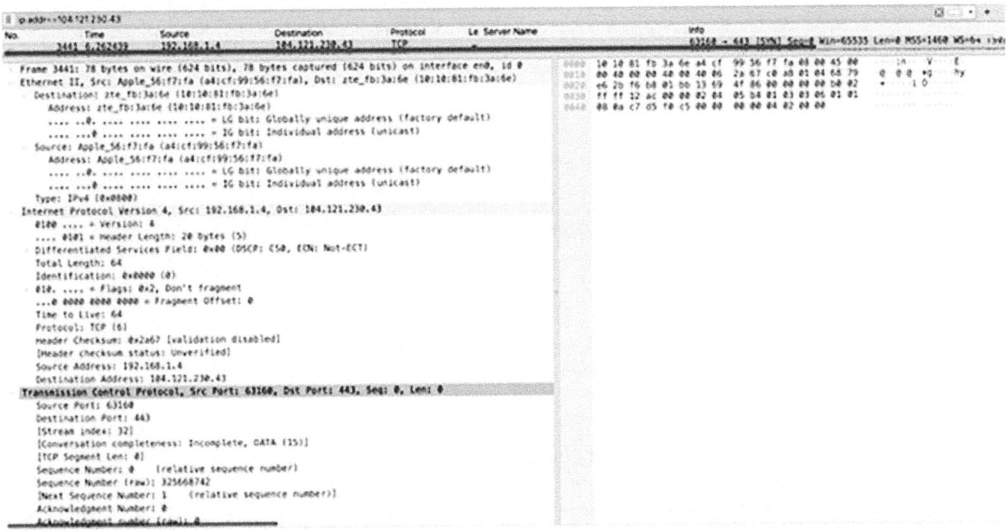

Figure 2.23: *Source and Destination Port for the Traffic initiated to news18.com*

As we can see, the source IP address is of the endpoint machine, while the destination IP is of news18.com. The source and destination ports are **63160** and **443**. For all HTTPS traffic, the TCP port is always **443**.

The server then responds with another control probe **SYN ACK**.

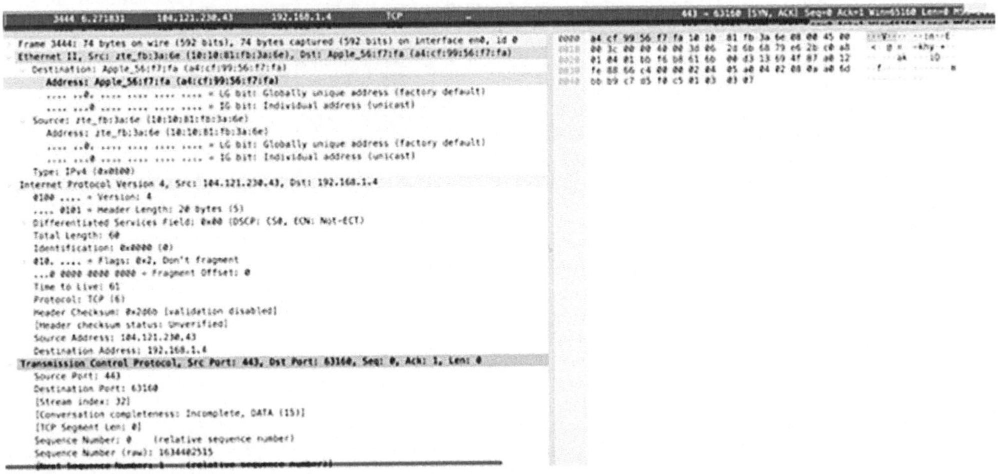

Figure 2.24: SYN *ack for the Traffic initiated to news18.com*

As we can see, the source port is **443** for **SYN ACK**, while the source IP is also of the new18.com server from where the response is coming. We can also see that the source MAC is of the WIFI router while the destination MAC is of the endpoint machine.

The endpoint machine acknowledges the **SYN ACK** with an **ACK** packet.

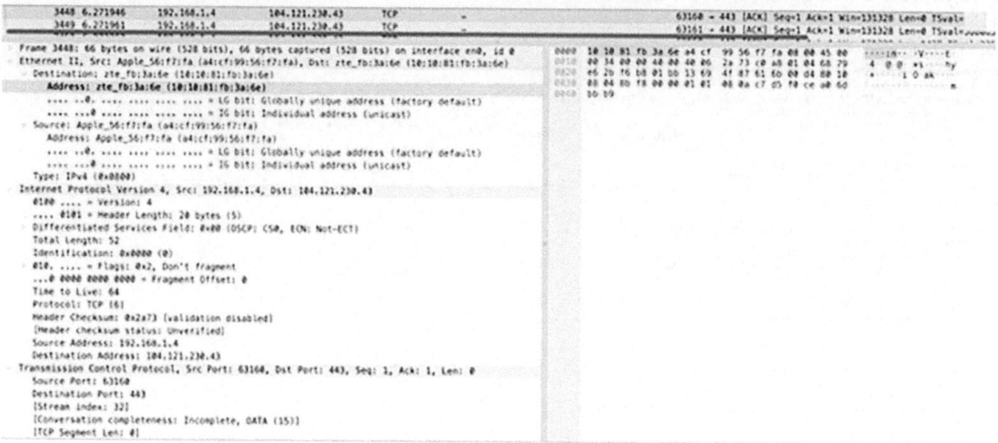

Figure 2.25: *ACK for the Traffic initiated to news18.com*

As we can see, the source IP is of the endpoint machine, while the destination IP is of the news18.com server.

Once the initial control connection of TCP is successful, the data connection starts. The first packet the client sends to the server is Client Hello as part of the SSL connection. Let us look at the details of the Client Hello packet in Wireshark.

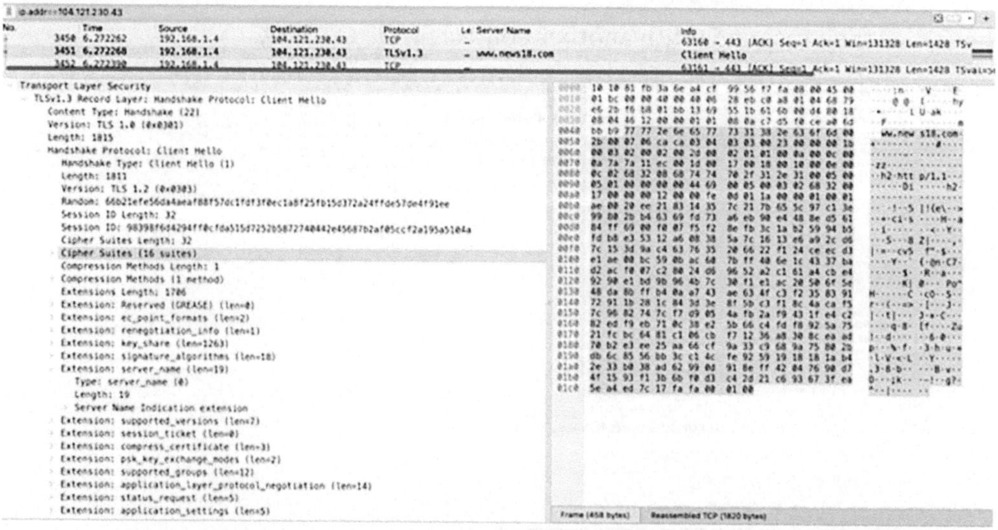

Figure 2.26: *Dissecting Client Hello Packet for Traffic initiated to news18.com*

The SSL handshake happens at the applications layer, and in Wireshark, we can look at the attributes of the Transport Layer Security, which is a version of SSL. The first information we can see is the TLS version, which is TLS 1.2. As part of TLS 1.2, the Server name indication is not **encrypted,** which gives the domain name of the server to which the traffic is initiated.

```
  > Elliptic curves point formats (1)
v Extension: renegotiation_info (len=1)
    Type: renegotiation_info (65281)
    Length: 1
  > Renegotiation Info extension
v Extension: key_share (len=1263)
    Type: key_share (51)
    Length: 1263
  > Key Share extension
v Extension: signature_algorithms (len=18)
    Type: signature_algorithms (13)
    Length: 18
    Signature Hash Algorithms Length: 16
  > Signature Hash Algorithms (8 algorithms)
v Extension: server_name (len=19)
    Type: server_name (0)
    Length: 19
  v Server Name Indication extension
      Server Name list length: 17
      Server Name Type: host_name (0)
      Server Name length: 14
      Server Name: www.news18.com
v Extension: supported_versions (len=7)
    Type: supported_versions (43)
    Length: 7
```

Figure 2.27: *Looking at the SNI Field for news18.com*

We then focus on the set of Cipher suites which are supported by the client as part of `TLS1.2`.

```
v Handshake Protocol: Client Hello
    Handshake Type: Client Hello (1)
    Length: 1811
    Version: TLS 1.2 (0x0303)
    Random: 66b21efe56da4aeaf88f57dc1fdf3f0ec1a8f25fb15d372a24ffde57de4f91ee
    Session ID Length: 32
    Session ID: 98398f6d4294ff0cfda515d7252b5872740442e45687b2af05ccf2a195a5104a
    Cipher Suites Length: 32
  v Cipher Suites (16 suites)
      Cipher Suite: Reserved (GREASE) (0xaaaa)
      Cipher Suite: TLS_AES_128_GCM_SHA256 (0x1301)
      Cipher Suite: TLS_AES_256_GCM_SHA384 (0x1302)
      Cipher Suite: TLS_CHACHA20_POLY1305_SHA256 (0x1303)
      Cipher Suite: TLS_ECDHE_ECDSA_WITH_AES_128_GCM_SHA256 (0xc02b)
      Cipher Suite: TLS_ECDHE_RSA_WITH_AES_128_GCM_SHA256 (0xc02f)
      Cipher Suite: TLS_ECDHE_ECDSA_WITH_AES_256_GCM_SHA384 (0xc02c)
      Cipher Suite: TLS_ECDHE_RSA_WITH_AES_256_GCM_SHA384 (0xc030)
      Cipher Suite: TLS_ECDHE_ECDSA_WITH_CHACHA20_POLY1305_SHA256 (0xcca9)
      Cipher Suite: TLS_ECDHE_RSA_WITH_CHACHA20_POLY1305_SHA256 (0xcca8)
      Cipher Suite: TLS_ECDHE_RSA_WITH_AES_128_CBC_SHA (0xc013)
      Cipher Suite: TLS_ECDHE_RSA_WITH_AES_256_CBC_SHA (0xc014)
      Cipher Suite: TLS_RSA_WITH_AES_128_GCM_SHA256 (0x009c)
      Cipher Suite: TLS_RSA_WITH_AES_256_GCM_SHA384 (0x009d)
      Cipher Suite: TLS_RSA_WITH_AES_128_CBC_SHA (0x002f)
      Cipher Suite: TLS_RSA_WITH_AES_256_CBC_SHA (0x0035)
```

Figure 2.28: *List of Cipher Suites supported as Part of Client Hello*

The next packet is Server Hello from news18.com, which decides on the Cipher suite to be used. Depending on the Server, it can either share the Server Certificate as part of Server Hello, or it does not share, as can be seen in the Server Hello packet from news18.com.

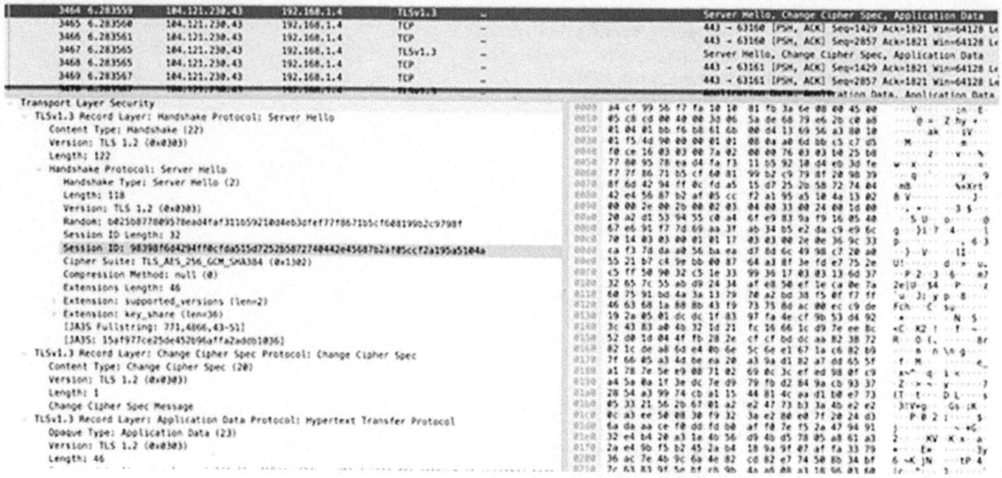

Figure 2.29: *Server Hello as Part of news18.com*

For some other Server, for example, **`cisco.webex.com`**, the Server Certificate is seen in Wireshark, as seen in *Figure 2.29.*

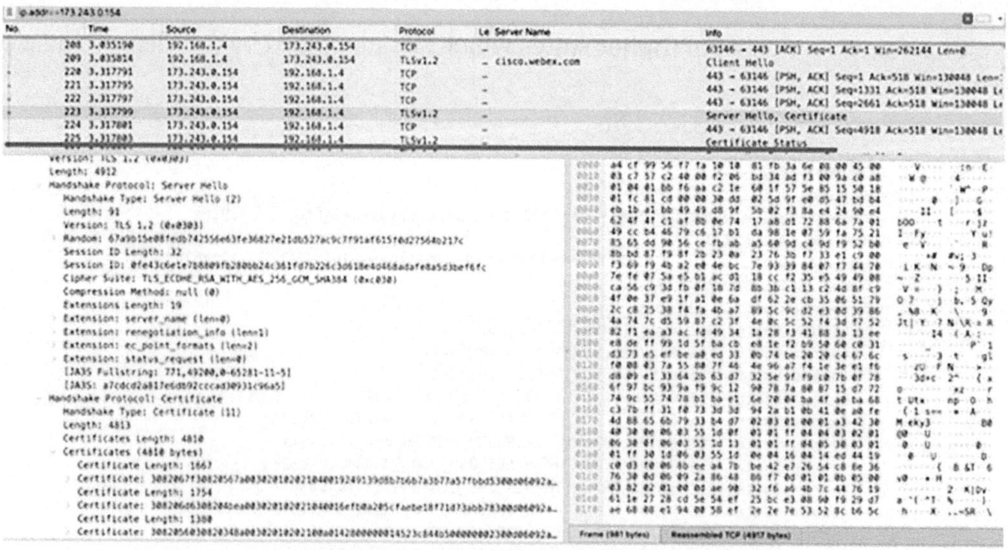

Figure 2.30: *Server Certificate as part of Server Hello*

All the data transfer between client and server would now be encrypted with the Cipher suite, which is negotiated between Client and Server.

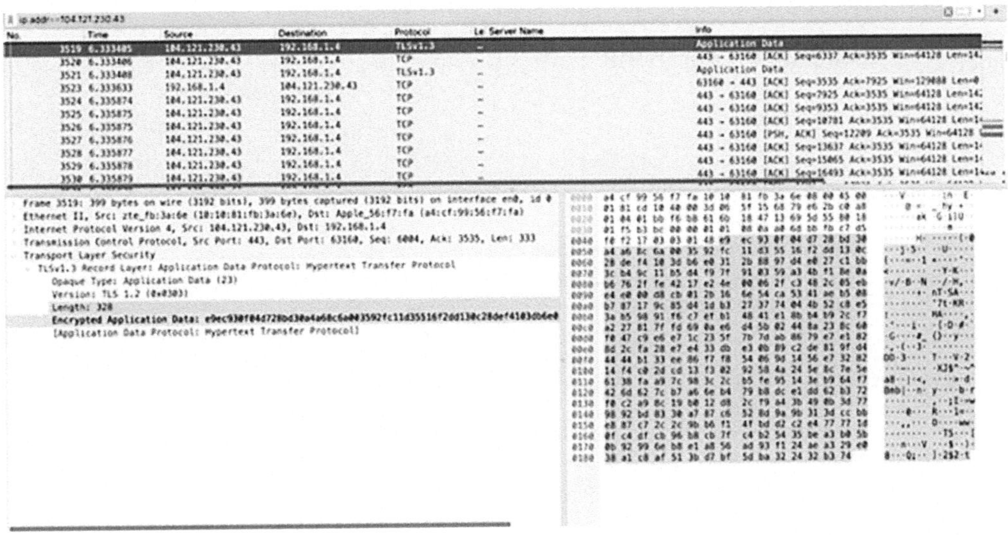

Figure 2.31: *Application Data being Encrypted*

Imagine there was some person in the middle who is sniffing the traffic between the Client and Server, they would not be able to view any transactions that are happening between the client and Server. This includes if the user is signing up on the Web page by entering personal credentials, and also confidential information in terms of the Personal Identity Number would be encrypted. This is one of the major differences between HTTP, where all the transactions are in clear text and not encrypted. In order to view the conversations, we need to have the private key where we can decrypt these conversations. Where do we get the key? The private key would be stored in the news18.com server securely, and unless the news18.com server infrastructure is infiltrated, the private key cannot be known. This means that none of the conversations that are happening over SSL can be traced until we get the private key from the server.

Let us try to view the Certificate when the user is initiating traffic to news18.com.

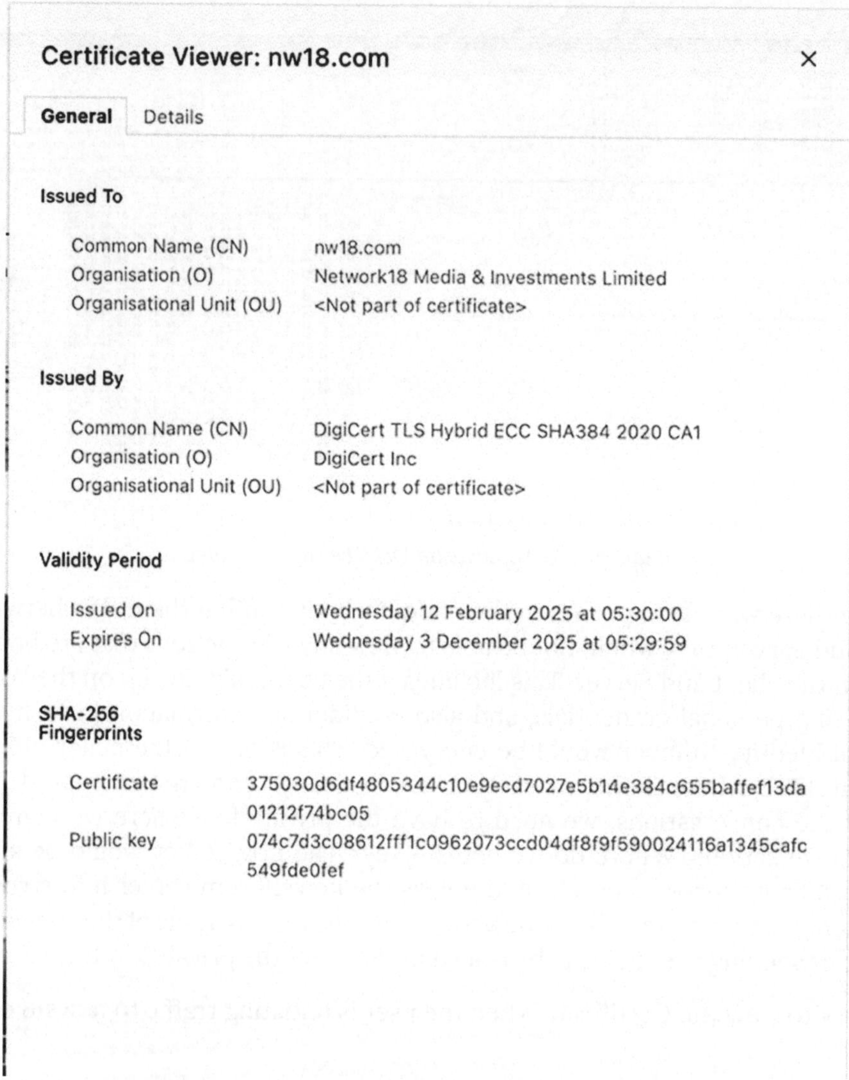

Figure 2.32: *Viewing the Certificate of news18.com*

As we can see, the public key is visible along with the Certificate, which can be exported.

We cannot decrypt the communication using a public key. The Certificate is generated using a private and public key pair. The public key is distributed to everyone on the Internet, but the private key is in the possession of the Server.

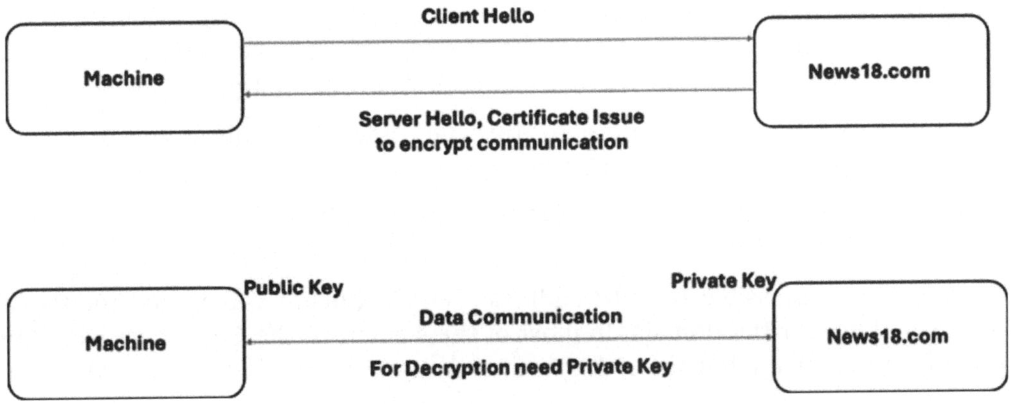

Figure 2.33: *Understanding the Public and Private Keys*

Once the private key is available, we can upload it to Wireshark for Decryption under `Wireshark` > `Preferences` > `Protocols` > `TLS` > `Browse` > `Pre-Master-Secret`.

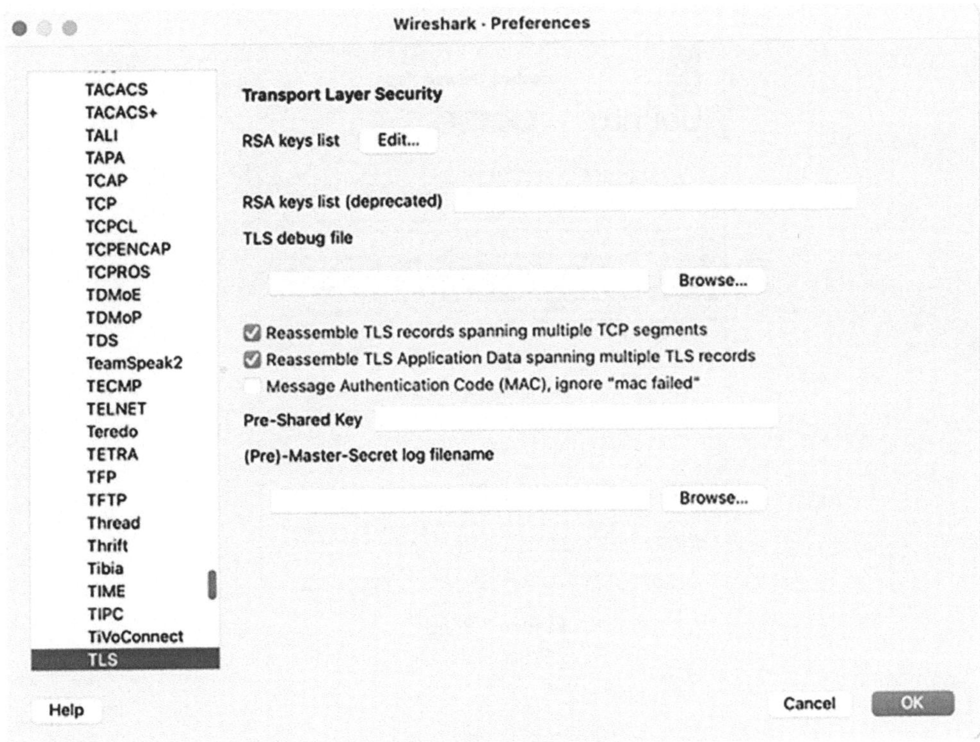

Figure 2.34: *TLS Protocol Options under Wireshark*

Analyzing practical SSL decryption: A Website has been hosted internally on https. The Website is hosted on the Apache server. The following are the reference links for setting up SSL on the Apache server and setting up the Apache server:

- https://www.arubacloud.com/tutorial/how-to-enable-https-protocol-with-apache-2-on-ubuntu-20-04.aspx.
- https://ubuntu.com/tutorials/install-and-configure-apache#3-creating-your-own-website

The website is accessible over IP address. The Certificate was issued for the IP address and not for the domain. In most of the scenarios, the Certificate would be issued for the domain, but since this is a lab setup, the Certificate is issued for the IP address.

The following is a sample page of the website. This is the default page of the Apache server. In the default page, we have added the Wireshark hyperlink along with the Wireshark image.

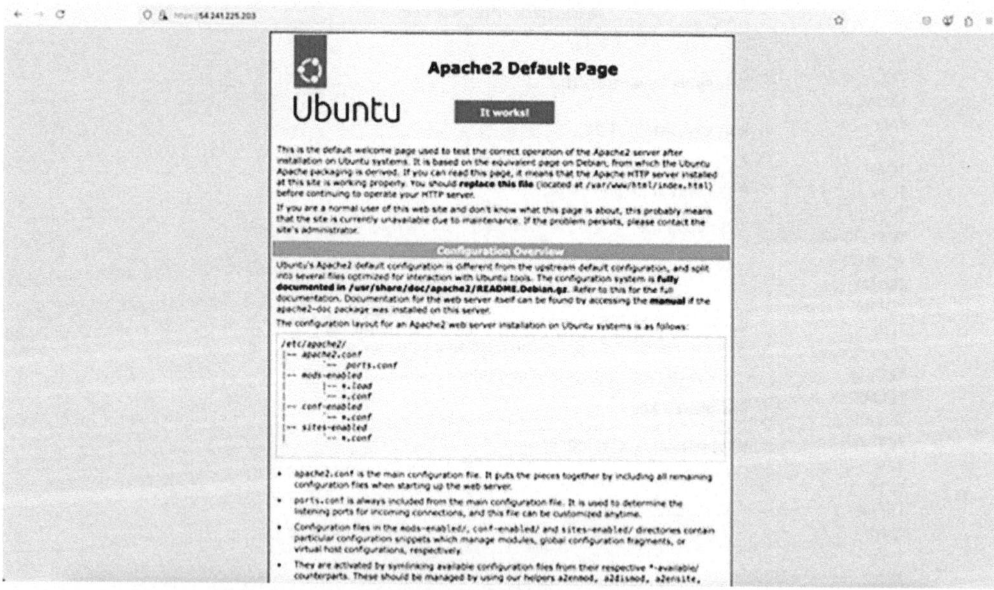

Figure 2.35(a)

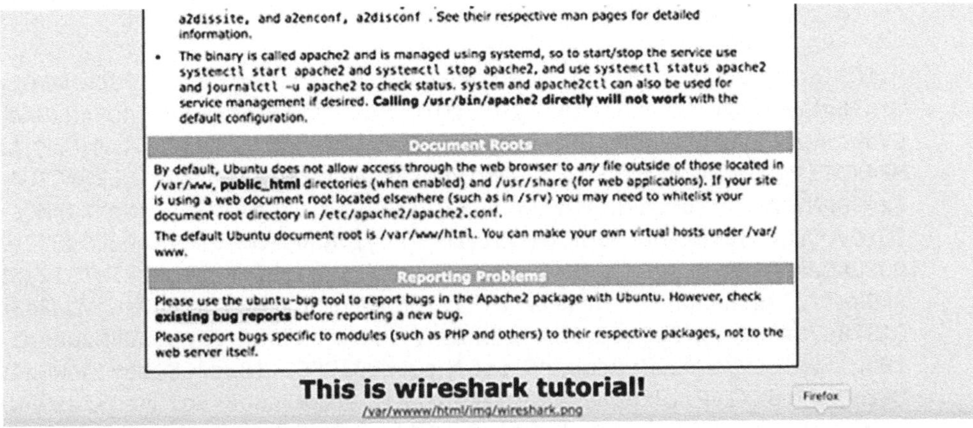

Figure 2.35(b)

Figure 2.35: *Apache Server Page in Lab*

Let us view the Certificate that has been issued.

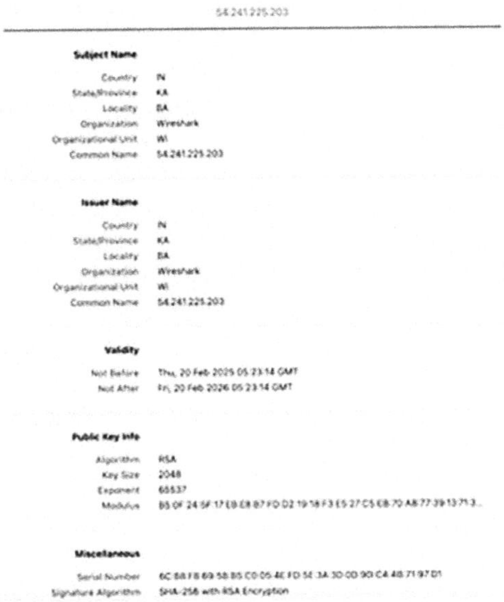

Figure 2.36: *Default Certificate Issued in Lab*

As can be seen, the Common name in the certificate is the IP address and not the domain name.

The following is the Certificate and the private key for the SSL certificate, which has been issued for the website:

```
root@ip-192-0-10-13:/etc/certificate# cat certificate.crt
-----BEGIN CERTIFICATE-----
MIIDSTCCAjECFGy4+GlbtcAFTv1eOj0NncRLcZfRMA0GCSqGSIb3DQEBCwUAMGEx
CzAJBgNVBAYTAklOMQswCQYDVQQIDAJLQTELMAkGA1UEBwwCQkExEjAQBgNVBAoM
CVdpcmVzaGFyazELMAkGA1UECwwCV2kxFzAVBgNVBAMMDjU0LjI0MS4yMjUuMjAz
MB4XDTI1MDIyMDA1MjMxNFoXDTI2MDIyMDA1MjMxNFowYTELMAkGA1UEBhMCSU4x
CzAJBgNVBAgMAktBMQswCQYDVQQHDAJCQTESMBAGA1UECgwJV2lyZXNoYXJrMQsw
CQYDVQQLDAJXaTEXMBUGA1UEAwwONTQuMjQxLjIyNS4yMDMwggEiMA0GCSqGSIb3
DQEBAQUAA4IBDwAwggEKAoIBAQC1DyRfF+vot/3SGRjz5SfF63CodzkTcTSl2N5L
7kDNkf/62xgtBbJNb7Kh1Hr0elVo0+k1Z76GQNmfMULbEBGNIDhPqDs6jVGw8s3n
QAS78c78tzEIwzg+JWQueOz1OmeZ4BkBSYFfkKnTEbaff5bR/QIasSBO6N2o6vwi
z0QgiIyhIeLtVsOl23ZyvcmB/r5+StElhzQLK97l7FQE+1BWd4G8llefIAoWHa4V
DYthOG8Re8XX1VP7iPfBEudwVNt1U2K9o7WklLBM1eB7poa8/EqIQsaQ3Z2S9FW/
Z/HW5hiHhEWXGauV/+b6aNbnUWFtlmBepfM20yJ0XxE4CMvPAgMBAAEwDQYJKoZI
hvcNAQELBQADggEBABgLhD9OLM2hMYkMLULC9fr3KMJM8vQzB2BeBd6c35/wN7bA
yVikmY23nM1l+60de7V/hnAMTZar8/Wu5c3XpoXpNjWvWq92IKqF6E2Jnn/PywZU
iu/UmcjmTOFEt/OUgWeK+MqWcx4HubQRSsx80v8F1HE767jlYn+YK4GGTBnMwCpG
6nav7EWCx3/1ajEkSeMeasfl01XfGD7q/oGkAAW0QDeX23ufg0jSquN6seG/YisW
lbKVQFakYy40AR4KqA157D3+/tJsf9/Ph0QPbiC0bzxOdpDwlHXy8GHfnmHM2tNq
C+l/jbEFHeSnT6Rfj6Uio/ooNILJDX3aJMRc3Fo=
-----END CERTIFICATE-----
root@ip-192-0-10-13:/etc/certificate# cat private.key
-----BEGIN ENCRYPTED PRIVATE KEY-----
MIIFLTBXBgkqhkiG9w0BBQ0wSjApBgkqhkiG9w0BBQwwHAQI2lPcPY9jf4wCAggA
MAwGCCqGSIb3DQIJBQAwHQYJYIZIAWUDBAEqBBCkv0IO8+0++8zg9ElLykR2BIIE
0BtIPm1ZqFrr5rW+9VQz7+nQ2oaM6mOrNK/s7YJfIx3F4/sCz0EtY1YqsF/18wrK
x5ZvdU2be0kXzuzzr7l2r5iStrZ2F7Op+gQh+z8QqiDPZhOCfmSbVuVh3GPYeJcI
odT1pL/nCJNN1SUfm3OKuzQroUUhSXsqiEhTbzl2enKj/ma/CDi5gHc2aIv3mlj9
6DTAWEPO9185nz4K3E41p4j6l4OODKHZaecQ4mPK+4bwWG2AMITsAd5LeSThV2NX
CckLscVUHebY/9BEB/lgKxKe7W9cptoiy9AOcwwz/uh8LtrfPkBBmX8mq+TG4LJK
B4Nc4Ny9DNxgaibmGwdQkQ49IlE8/MToTgYiwcYk9ckknuayOr8eyL79GRVynni8
KhsOborMlsVJYZ6AnJJZgAoTQc2mEgnM+tV5KYxchnc2gc+UVM9N9kjBJTwTguSz
6aSjcN0Dg7jNiS2qlaYT9KHfujjzvEaya9wcN9uDQY9SqJ7t9c926l4J75NF8cwH
yZ3DmL1BQcHv65PbNbzLXCrzc7hrCvmVMbAbyitKOFZPhackwqGLh9H3zhqho9zK
hOx71cz7WOLvTpTDkxtGZ3nuWvO6J/2LZGyyqfSLCeRS6lizABZ6J5ir9QabVYfb
cLuQjfflr/vnfbxTLOtIMAi95tqlDeIlEc1+jwluyWOGob+hwixRO5yXZUprwuw6
3BTLjsEiAQSaKyto0UbB0L5ZGlVHq5dUsTva+kjIuKlMwPa/7GPAvk0zuBUBbNfv
Sr9UVy9U0xXf4aKlbdQVo/cKloMcRr8CuB5pWQyXu1BkimeBffzLbn09lbw0c1Os
MFLKiED4wcvdK8TBFMOf7KTUle7N5jhHvU5dOyB8cg3s3rqc2KxqzfL2aAREdRPu
a6qEhhInm7+GSdwfXj5ucKB4LLV7QQIXyuhedR8hCUi3z92zT6z9VDxS/2YK3NEm
og3DlLZIme2FYA44MT3QwAfudlo6oL/nybWTwC6Xiq5ujHhJvZApyguAv35LABAJ
1w1b3OvkGo9oK3cUVjpEKyRUYhbVmYVuA3J/S/OSoy5M1lxmLalK1RXPTLkmPk1w
xnwTlv892lvfxF+FiCj7Ao8eZJr8vEETNPd2oZ04UX7GBx46RIFehJF1e4nqk+41
iP3HuPwu+5OhukwI5iTYMVvINe2QCH+1gRMsC8jkjdSgqo1Ab9F0sRK4RpAZfZJP
crm4kK0psebddm7u3uEq5lLHL8+Eb0GtwVq15u1e+Tv60qUIkdTH53N4tL24sMia
XvzYrz4/7U2vJnRnDdo26umKqKOFfd2HgY8nwE2dkRQ3rIL6quk2SG/w+Q7fMPKZ
yituKq29b4cJG1oYD8i4te/zTjhMj/bN4rzw5ASEoyi9z7x88arZRdjHPJEYyaK/
```

```
XnxNgQsg8eVSzLHb8LM6n6iPD0xKxjk0RA3P8ZvnpUID/HFwwwAf2+7GoVv3axu/
ouHPLWelmW6i1Egrn1r5pKSI3ONnlHdq2ml+H/YdvSsnC/NvlYA8xlnaN66rbQvh
aNKTidW8YLhe9MVKRfGIYiz2eeM1fdJY7Ik3O7ClBlSiqxqaiHLAAHXExCQEmCVK
8Sr8rvTJsjGy3l43rpCzf52rRuY8jAySDdEpKtme6UX+
-----END ENCRYPTED PRIVATE KEY-----
```

We have learnt that for SSL communications, the Wireshark capture shows encrypted data, and we need the private key for the decryption of the encrypted conversations.

We would now decrypt the communications between Client and Server on Wireshark. Since this is a server hosted in the lab, we have access to the server CLI where the Certificate and the key are stored. **As an attacker, one would need to brute-force the Infrastructure to get access to the private key**.

While setting up this Apache server, it was configured for the TLS protocol. The following are the steps that are performed as part of the TLS handshake:

1. The initial handshake between Client and Server decides the TLS version, which is communicated as part of Server Hello.
2. Cipher suites are being communicated.
3. Authentication of Server identity via server public key and SSL certificate digital signature.
4. **Pre-master secret is derived by the client and sent to the server to compute master secrets.**

What is a Pre-master key?

The client generates a 48-bit pre-master secret and shares it with the server. The client encrypts the pre-master secret using the server's public key obtained from the server certificate. The server decrypts the message using the server's private key. The client and the server use the pre-master secret to produce symmetric keys to secure further communication.

Once we go under **`Wireshark`** > **`Preferences`** > **`Protocols`** > **`TLS`**, we click **`edit`** and put the Private key, which we have obtained from the Apache server.

Figure 2.37: *Option to Add the Private Key*

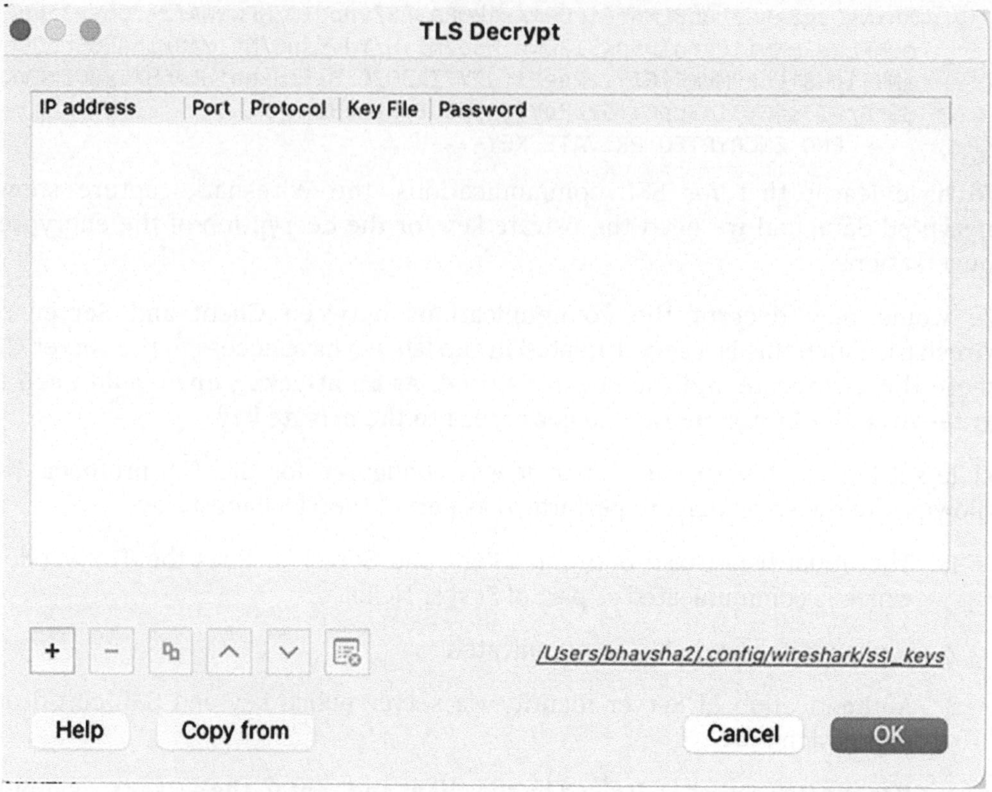

Figure 2.38: *TLS Preferences for entering the Private Key*

We click the '+' icon and enter the details.

1. **`IP address`:** IP address of the Apache server, that is, **`54.241.225.203`**
2. **`Port`: `443`**
3. **`Protocol`:** TLS
4. **`Key File`:** Reference the private key file from the Apache server.
5. **`Password`:** Passphrase while generating the key request

Figure 2.39: *Entering the Private Key in the Wireshark*

The next section is to store the debug file for all the TLS decryption messages on Wireshark. This is optional, but it is a kind of logging for all the decryption messages. It is always a best practice to have the logging configured to trace back the Communication happening between the Client and the Application.

Figure 2.40: *Referencing the Debug File*

The next section is important, where we reference the pre-master secret. With TLS 1.3 this is mandatory to provide the debug file which consists of Pre-master Secret which is generated randomly. Only referencing the Private key from the Server would not result in successful Decryption and we would also need Pre-Master Secret messages to successfully decrypt the transactions between the User and the Server. This Pre-Master Secret would always be generated when the traffic is initiated from the Client to the Application which works on TLS.

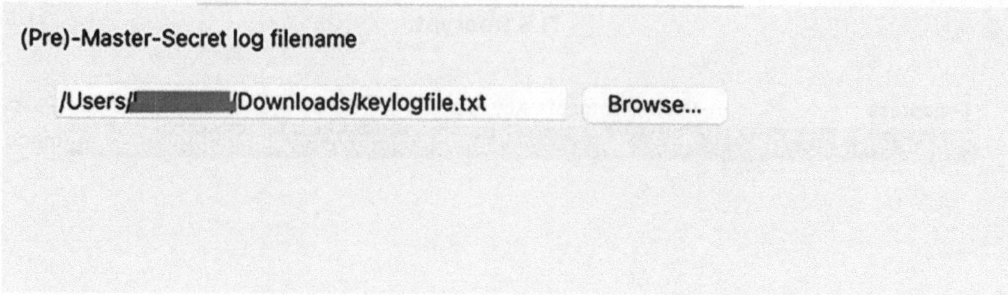

Figure 2.41: *Referencing the Key Log File which consists of Pre-shared Master Secret*

Let us try to look at the **`keylog`** file contents.

```
CLIENT_RANDOM
5b9825568fc475fe021f15b8281279420eff5db6f97380986076229e1ea61178
a74d335f9b31e5f11a321e1b061d862580fb1c52713adbbb13359adcd7297fb44f243b1e
39acfd86926f72da556efd7c

CLIENT_RANDOM
1f6db99144b9b2c9810e625d7f3c56f869a4278e5b2124f02871baf6420b78fc
03d61983e236a5b7a95b46f48fd7421542b8d308e5181fb68b5c85cecbfe2d08047f9974
e5eef201fda0951c1473fefd

CLIENT_HANDSHAKE_TRAFFIC_SECRET
73a113be0fde5b679ca078d6deb441a3c0f79de7b1d1353e4f6a636975efe3a3
bd5725bba54d20f777c450230c8b079af357f87c8c9aa4e1f59c1fbd23ef6939

SERVER_HANDSHAKE_TRAFFIC_SECRET
73a113be0fde5b679ca078d6deb441a3c0f79de7b1d1353e4f6a636975efe3a3
bf189675e60cd79ea52ebde98462147047dd8997b0bc259192be655e759ecc6e
```

Figure 2.42: *Contents of Keylog File*

This file gives the client and the server a random secret that has been generated while the traffic was being initiated to the Apache server **`54.241.225.203`**

How do we generate the Pre-Master Secret Log file?

The following is the reference link to generate the Pre-Master Secret Log file:

https://wiki.wireshark.org/TLS

We initiate the traffic to the Apache server **`54.241.225.203` and log the file by setting up the environment variable as mentioned in the preceding link.**

Let us try to look at the logs when the Pre-master secret log file is not referenced.

This teaches us that the Pre-master secret is important in decrypting the communication.

Once we have referenced the Pre-master secret key file along with the private key in the RSA keys list, we will now check the traffic decryption to the Apache server **54.241.225.203** on Wireshark.

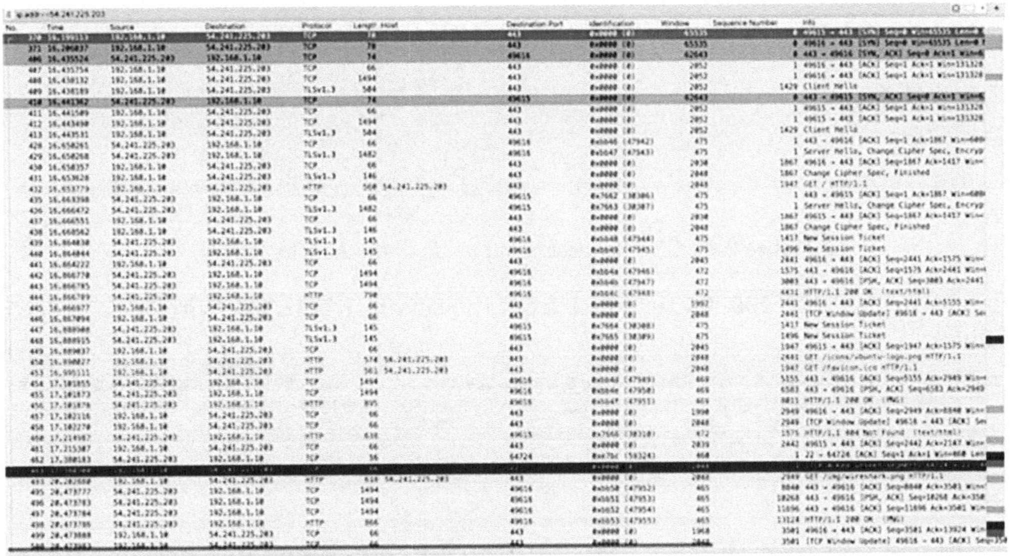

Figure 2.43: *Traffic Decryption to the Apache Server* **54.241.225.203**

We can now see that there are no Application data messages that are encrypted. We can see there is an HTTP GET request, which is decrypted.

On the bottom, we can see the Decrypted TLS messages header.

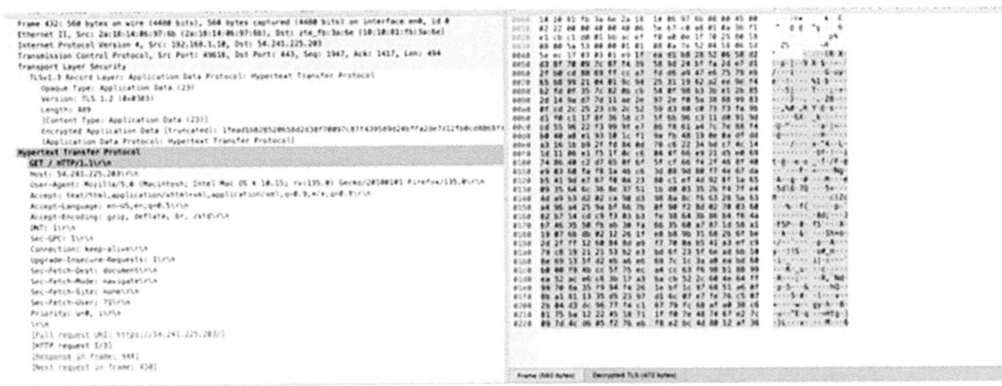

Figure 2.44: *Decrypted TLS Messages Header*

If we look at the packet no **493**, we can see the request was being made to **/img/wireshark.png**

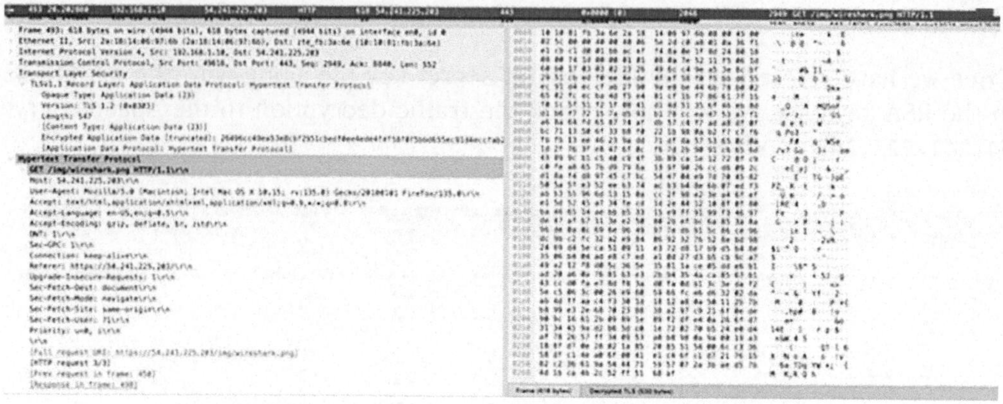

Figure 2.45: *GET Request being made to the Apache Server*

The following is the **200 OK** response from the server, where the Wireshark image is visible:

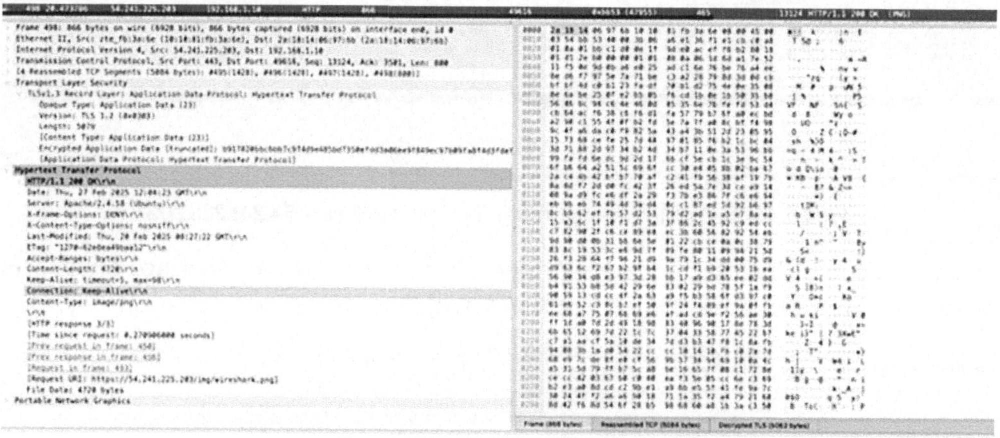

Figure 2.46: HTTP 200 OK *from Apache Server*

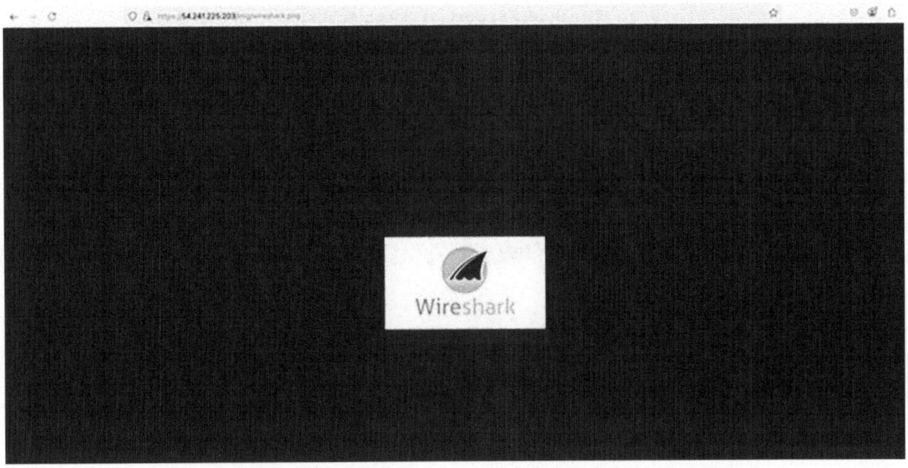

Figure 2.47: *Apache Server UI showing Wireshark Image*

We can export the same PNG file from Wireshark by going under **`File`** > **`Export Objects`** > **`Http`**

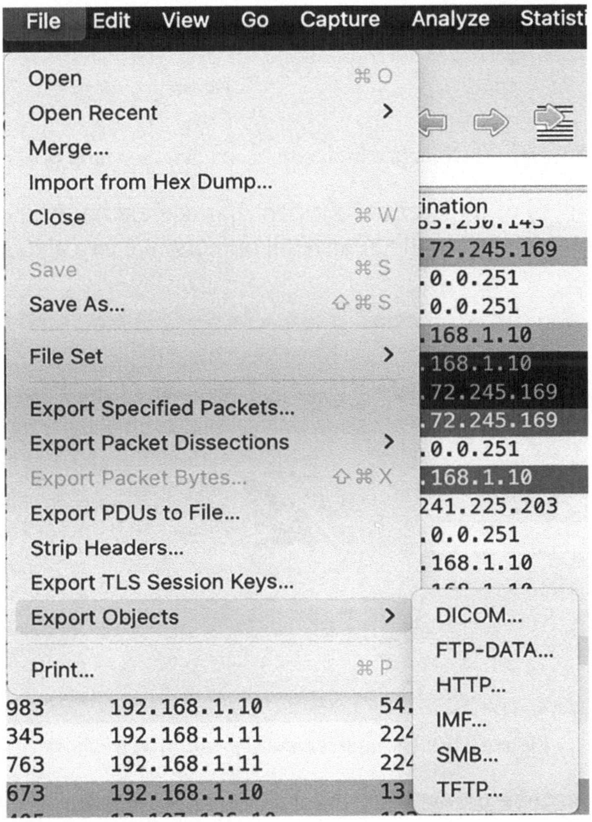

Figure 2.48: *Option in Wireshark to export the PNG File*

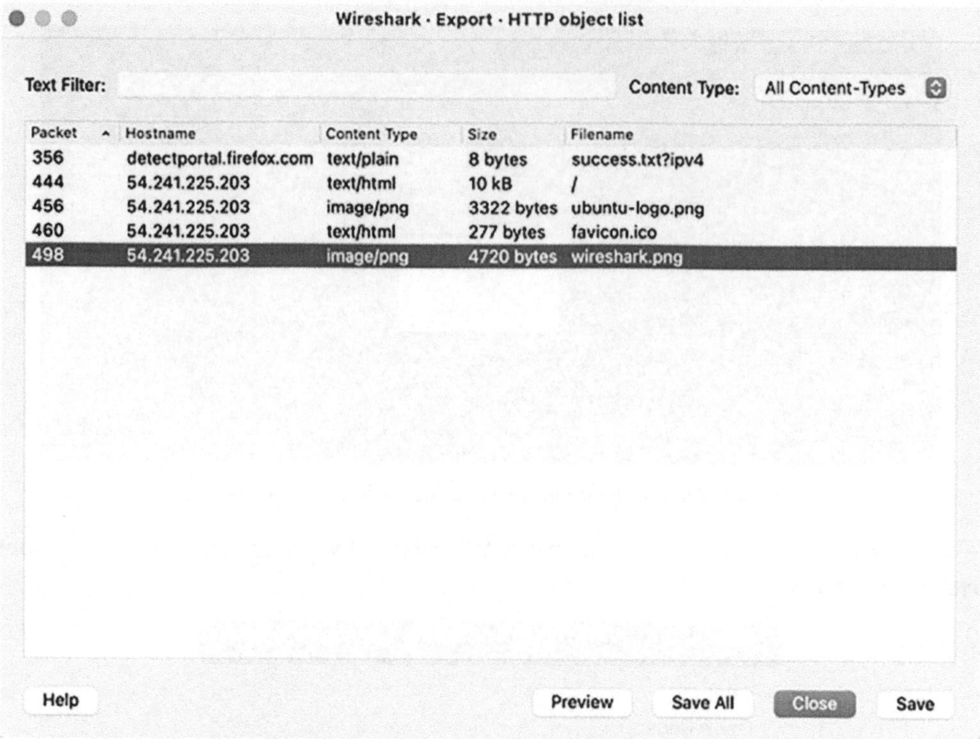

Figure 2.49: *Different Objects which can be exported as part of HTTP Request*

It shows all the objects of different file types that are exchanged over HTTP. We can either save each object individually or save all objects. We can also preview the objects and view the image.

Figure 2.50: *Using Preview Option in Wireshark*

Applying remote capture using Wireshark: The captures that we took till now were on the client machine from where the traffic was initiated. This can be verified by looking at the source of the traffic from which **TCP SYN** was initiated as follows:

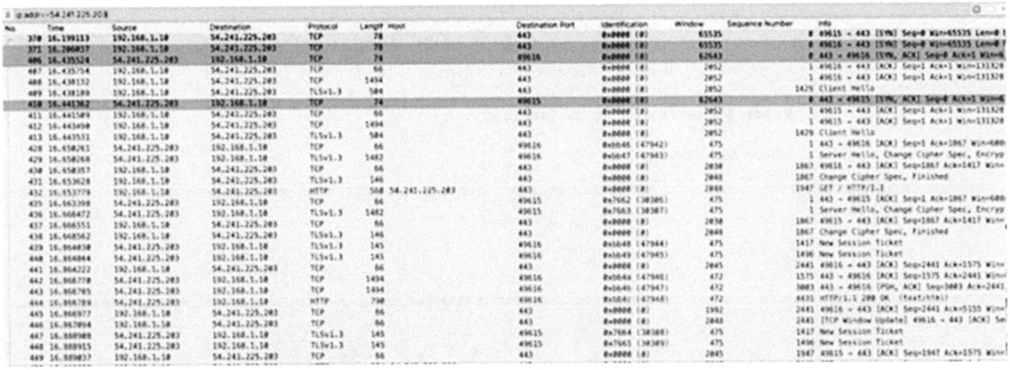

Figure 2.51: *Remote Capture Using Wireshark*

Wireshark has added another utility where we can take remote server captures. In this case, we would take captures on the Apache server where we have hosted our Web page.

Click and select **`'SSH remote capture:sshdump'`**.

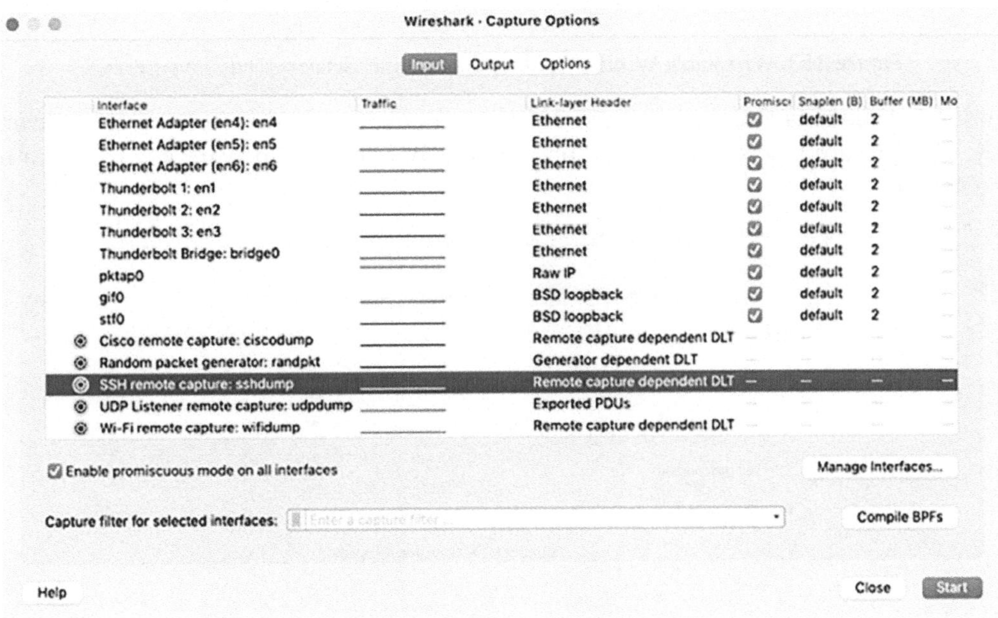

Figure 2.52: *Option to take Remote Capture*

Enter the remote server address as **54.241.225.203.**

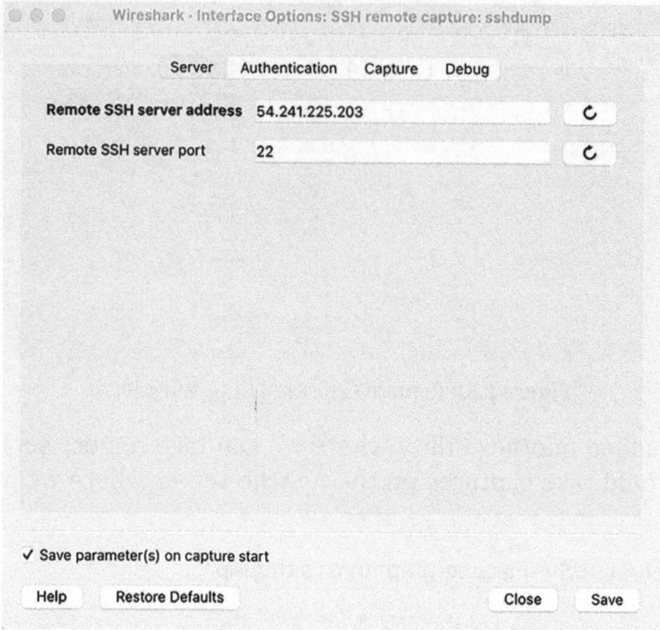

Figure 2.53: *Wireshark Window where Remote SSH Server IP can be entered*

Under **Authentication**, enter the username as **ubuntu** and reference the private key. This private key is not the SSL private key, but the SSH private key to log in to the server.

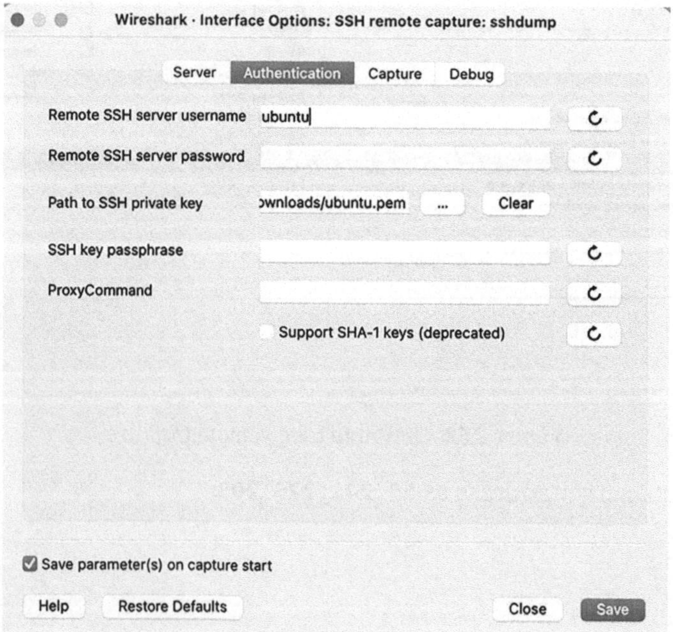

Figure 2.54: *Providing the Authentication Parameters for the Remote Server*

Under **`Capture`** options, make sure to enable the **`capture privilege on the remote machine`** as **`sudo`**.

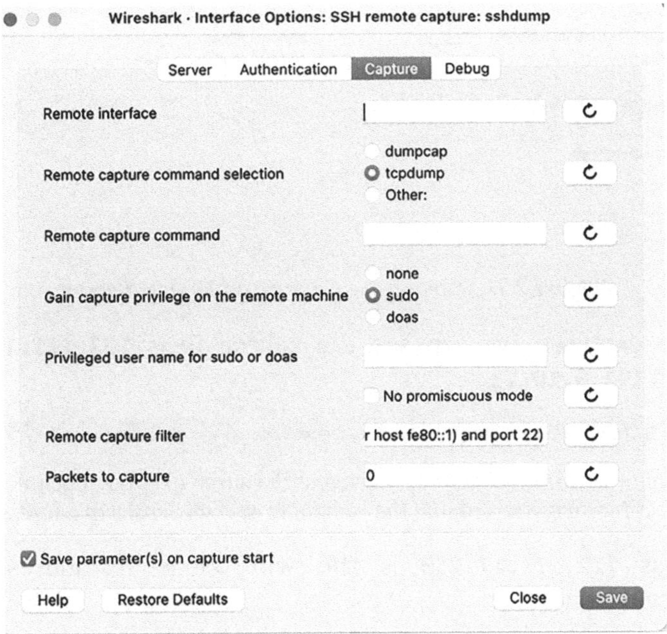

Figure 2.55: *Capture Options on the Remote Server*

Under the **`Debug`** section, we can reference the **`file for logging`**.

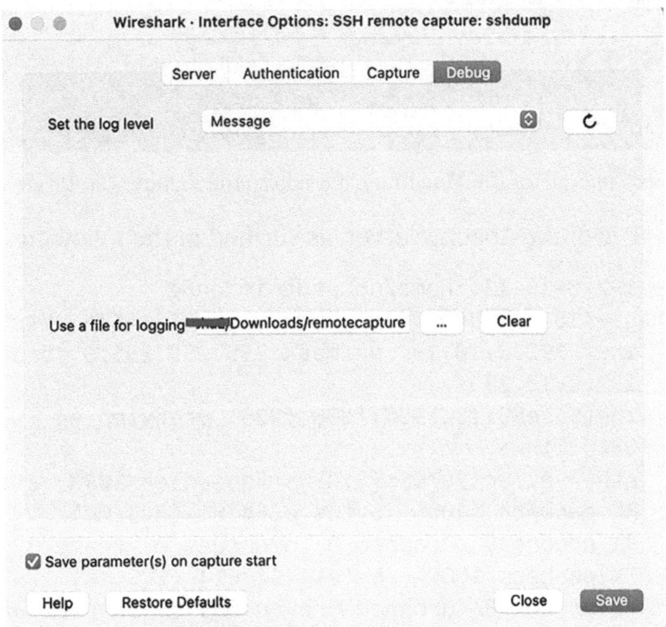

Figure 2.56: *Enable Logging*

Once all the settings are saved for Remote capture, we can click **`Start`**, as shown in *Figure 2.56*.

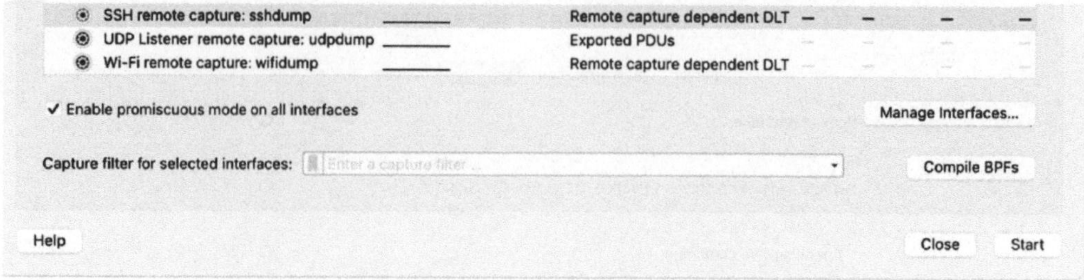

Figure 2.57: *Starting the Capture on Remote Server*

Looking at the captures, we can see the source IP is **`122.171.17.250`** and the destination IP is **`192.0.10.13`**.

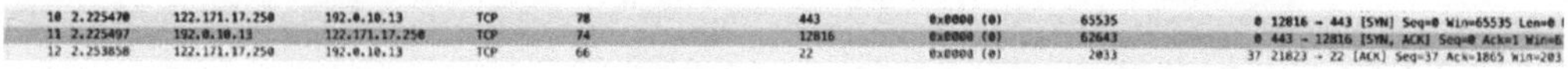

Figure 2.58: *Remote capture successfully started with source ip of the machine from where the capture was started and the remote is Apache Server ip address*

The IP address **`122.171.17.250`** is the wifi public IP address, as seen in whatsmyipaddress.com

Figure 2.59: *Public IP of the Machine from where the Remote Capture was started*

The destination IP is of the Apache server, as verified in the following:

```
root@ip-192-0-10-13:/home/ubuntu# ifconfig
enX0: flags=4163<UP,BROADCAST,RUNNING,MULTICAST>  mtu 9001
        inet 192.0.10.13  netmask 255.255.255.0  broadcast
        192.0.10.255
        inet6 fe80::8c:9dff:fe08:f225  prefixlen 64  scopeid
        0x20<link>
        ether 02:8c:9d:08:f2:25  txqueuelen 1000  (Ethernet)
        RX packets 24096  bytes 8364781 (8.3 MB)
        RX errors 0  dropped 0  overruns 0  frame 0
        TX packets 16094  bytes 1923614 (1.9 MB)
        TX errors 0  dropped 0 overruns 0  carrier 0  collisions
        0
```

The remote capture, which we took, is similar to taking **tcpdump** on the Apache server locally.

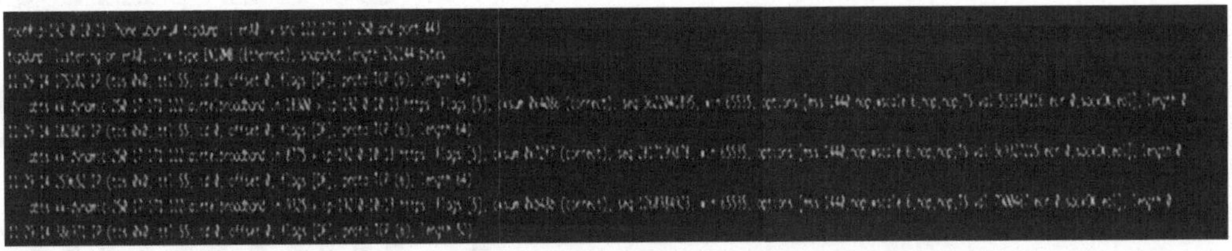

Figure 2.60: *TCPdump on the Remote Server*

Conclusion

We looked at how the Internet traffic works at home and what the different stages of the packet flow are from an OSI layer perspective. We then set up a private Web Server Apache on which we visualized SSL Decryption and Encryption. We also learnt how to enable remote server captures on Wireshark. The next chapter is about SSL and Certificate Chaining. We also learnt that with TLS 1.3 that we need Random Secret generated in real time for decrypting the communication between the Client and the Server. This also helps in safeguarding the Communication between the Client and the Server if the Private key is leaked. If the attacker is able to acquire the Private key the Pre-Shared Master Secret is still required which means the attacker needs to get access to the client machine because the Pre-shared Master Secret would be different for different requests initiated from the Client Machine.

CHAPTER 3
SSL and Certificate Chaining

Introduction

This chapter highlights the evolution of the traffic handshake between the client and server from HTTP to HTTPS. This chapter talks about how the encrypted transaction is achieved between the client and the server. The essential components of the SSL and how the trust is established between the client and the server, and most importantly, how it becomes difficult for an attacker to sniff the communication between the client and the server.

Structure

In this chapter, we will cover the following topics:

- Introducing HTTP Transaction
- Functioning of SSL
- Dissecting an SSL Conversation in Wireshark
- Analyzing SSL Certificate

Introducing HTTP Transaction

With the Internet penetration increasing, malware attacks are also rising, it becomes important to have the traffic handshake between the client and the server encrypted. Following is a Wireshark snippet for the application traffic, which works on port 80 (http):

As seen, the traffic is not encrypted, and all the transactions are visible between the client and server.

Figure 3.1: *Sample application on port 80*

The modern browsers do alert for the application access which works on HTTP by labeling "**`Not secure`**". Let us deep dive into the Wireshark snippet, which was taken while the client was accessing the application. The Wireshark capture was taken on the client machine while the application was being accessed.

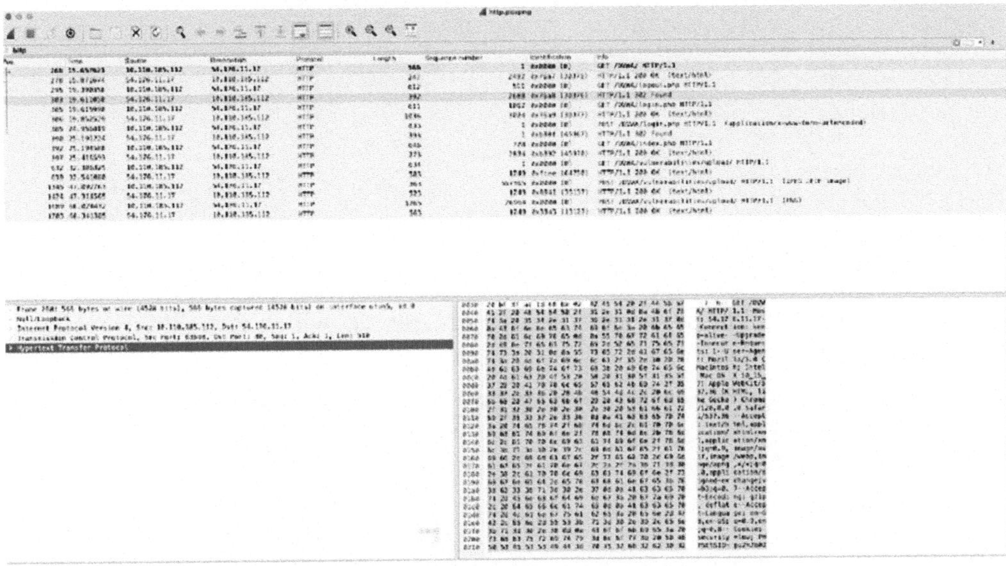

Figure 3.2: *Wireshark Trace showing all the Packets for HTTP*

The above traffic shows all the HTTP transactions happening between the client and the server **`54.176.11.17`**. We have a filter in Wireshark named **`"http"`**. Let us analyze the packets and determine what information can be determined. Since each HTTP request has GET and POST methods, where a GET request means the user is trying to fetch something from the application server, and POST, where the client is trying to push some request to the application server.

As seen in packet **`268`**, the client machine initiated a GET request with the URI / DVWA.

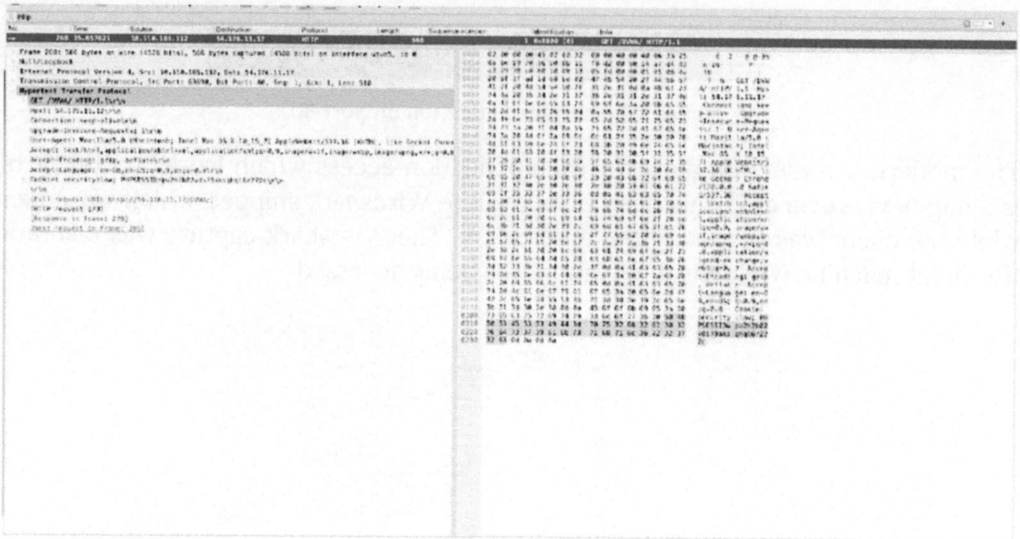

Figure 3.3: *Wireshark Trace showing GET Request initiated to the Website*

As seen in packet **278**, the server responds with **200 OK**, which gives the HTML page contents of what the page offers.

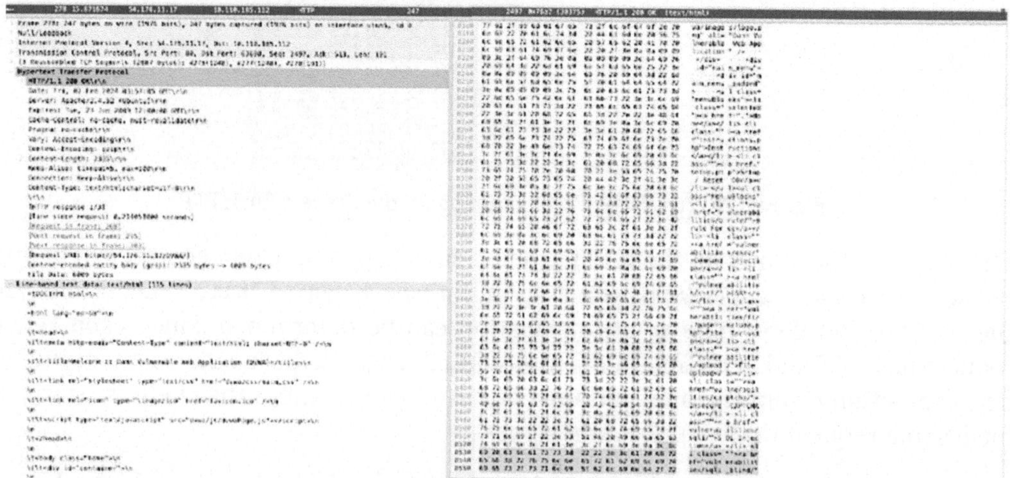

Figure 3.4: *HTTP Response for GET Request*

Since it is an application server, which would require some login, we will look at the post request from the client, because in a POST request, the client enters some information on the server.

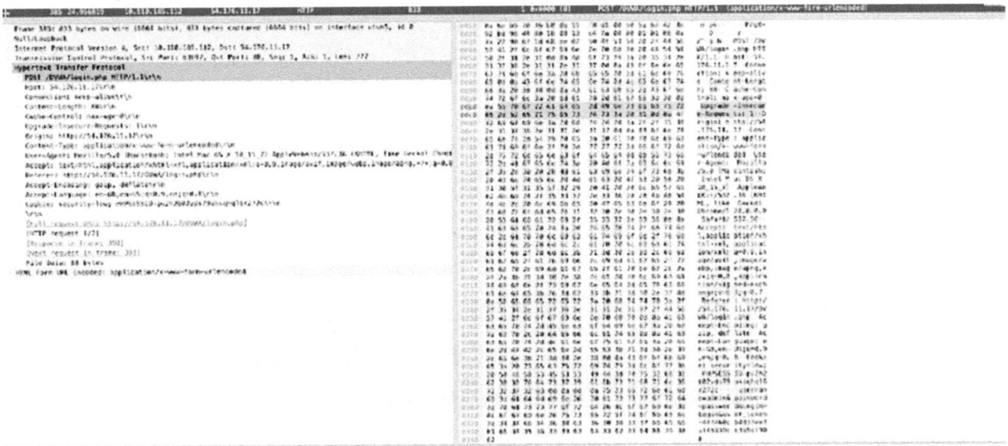

Figure 3.5: *POST Request to the Website*

```
65 3a 20 73 65 63 75 72  69 74 79 3d 6c 6f 77 3b   e: secur ity=low;
20 50 48 50 53 45 53 53  49 44 3d 70 75 32 68 32    PHPSESS ID=pu2h2
62 30 32 76 64 73 37 39  61 6b 73 71 68 71 6c 36   b02vds79 aksqhql6
72 32 37 32 63 0d 0a 0d  0a 75 73 65 72 6e 61 6d   r272c··· ·usernam
65 3d 61 64 6d 69 6e 26  70 61 73 73 77 6f 72 64   e=admin& password
3d 70 61 73 73 77 6f 72  64 26 4c 6f 67 69 6e 3d   =passwor d&Login=
4c 6f 67 69 6e 26 75 73  65 72 5f 74 6f 6b 65 6e   Login&us er_token
3d 34 34 66 34 36 30 63  36 30 38 33 37 65 65 66   =44f460c 60837eef
61 66 34 35 38 33 39 63  63 33 62 39 64 66 39 30   af45839c c3b9df90
62                                                 b
```

Figure 3.6: *Wireshark Trace which shows the User entering Details on the Website*

As seen in *Figure* 3.6 snippet, the username and password are visible, which the user entered, which is username= **`admin`** and password as **`password`**. This is confidential information that is beneficial for untrusted actors to log in to the application server. This is one of the reasons why all the applications now have security enabled with https port 443. As seen in the packet capture, all the information is available in plaintext, and confidential information can be traced.

If we look carefully at other packets, we can also determine that a PNG and a JPEG image were being uploaded. Looking at packet no **1689**, we can see the PNG file was being uploaded. We can extract the entire PNG file by selecting the PNG header, as shown in *Figure* 3.7.

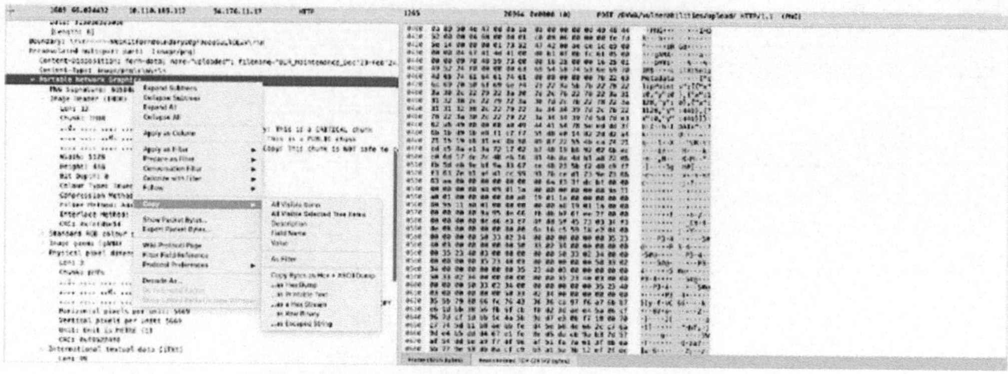

Figure 3.7: *Extracting the PNG File from the Wireshark Trace*

We can also see the name of the file, as shown in *Figure 3.8*.

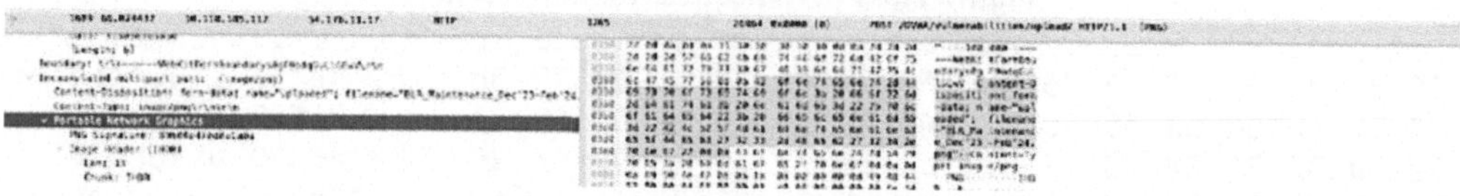

Figure 3.8: *Looking at the File Name in the Wireshark Trace*

By looking at the Conversation for Websites working on port 80 which was clear text it highlights if someone Sniffing the traffic can always understand the contents of the transaction happening between the User and the Application. This highlights the importance of having an encrypted channel between the User and the Application in the form of Secure channel called Secure Socket Layer (SSL).

Functioning of SSL

SSL encrypts the data that is transmitted over the web. As we saw, the data transferred over HTTP is plaintext; even if someone is able to sniff the communication, it would be difficult to intercept, as the communication is encrypted.

SSL also initiates an authentication process called handshake between two devices (client and server) to ensure both devices are really who they claim to be.

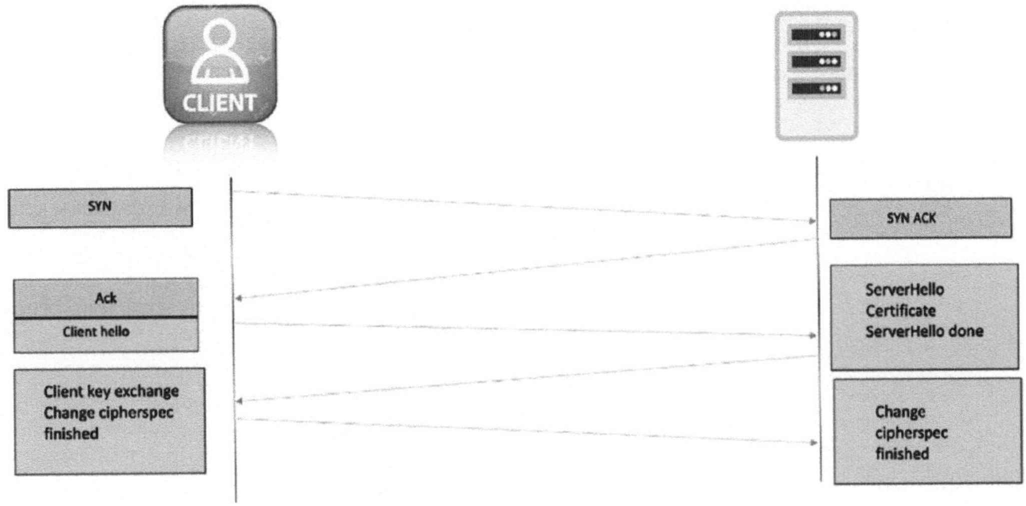

Figure 3.9: *SSL Handshake Flow*

As seen in *Figure* 3.9 handshake process, the important element in the entire transaction is the Certificate. As we have our identities (PAN or Aadhaar), which are issued by the Government of India to different Citizens, similarly, there is a list of third-party Certificate authorities that issue Certificates to different applications, which are hosted on the Internet. Following is the link for trusted Certificate Authorities https://developer.visa.com/pages/trusted_certifying_authorities.

A Certificate authority can validate the digital entity on your behalf, and the same Certificate authority can also issue cryptographic keys. These cryptographic keys help in encrypting the transaction between the Client and Server so that no third party can view the transaction.

SSL is a communication protocol that creates secure communication between the client and the server. SSL was introduced in 1995, and it had a few vulnerabilities that were being mitigated by TLS. A few of the vulnerabilities in SSL were the popular **Heartbleed** vulnerability.

What was the vulnerability?

The Heartbleed bug was a critical vulnerability(CVE-2014-0160) found in the OpenSSL library. For a secure connection that uses TLS, it sends a heartbeat message to determine if the peer (connection) is alive or not. The heartbeat message works like an echo command. If a text is being entered as part of the echo command, it outputs the same text. For example, echo "*Wireshark*" would give the output of Wireshark.

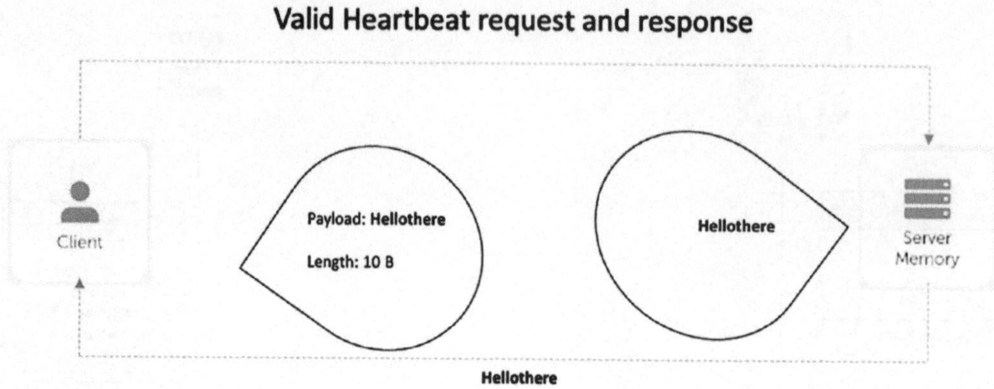

Figure 3.10: *Typical Flow of a SSL Handshake*

The following figure shows how the Heartbleed attack is being executed. As can be seen, the message buffer is increased to a maximum limit of 64B.

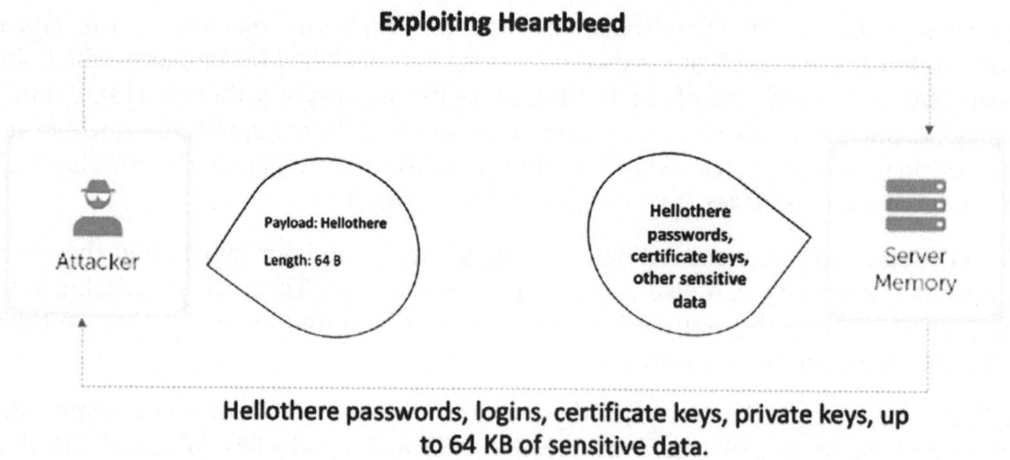

Figure 3.11: *Exploiting the SSL Flow*

Let us look at the **capture**, which shows the TLS handshake that we discussed.

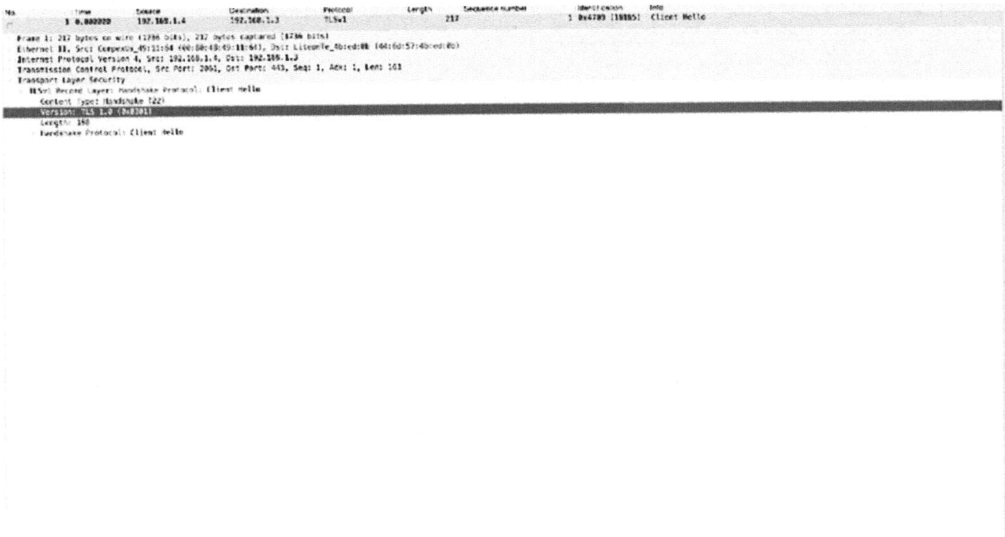

Figure 3.12: *Wireshark Trace showing the TLS 1.0 Version of SSL*

As seen in *Figure* 3.12, the capture shows the TLS version, which is **`1.0`**. Let us look at other parameters from the **`Client Hello`**.

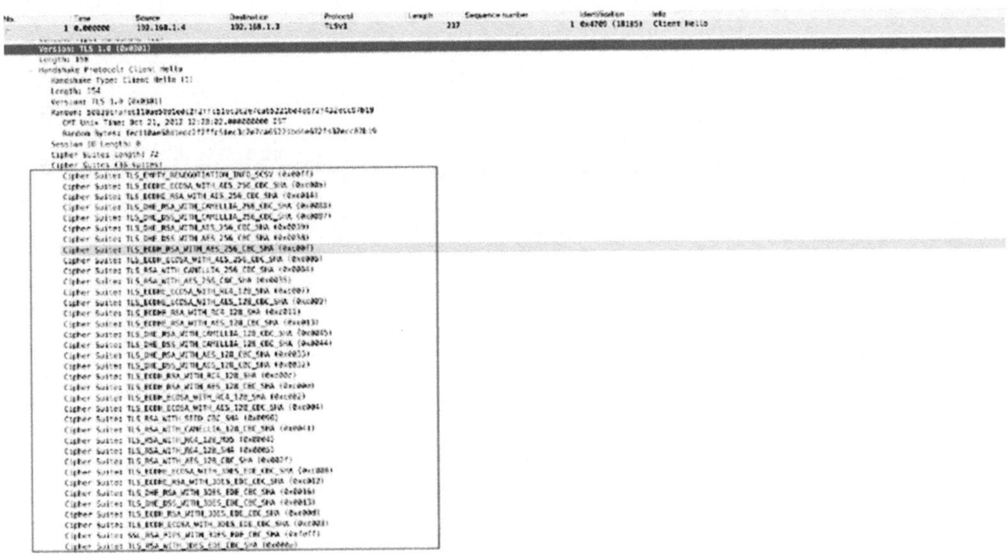

Figure 3.13: *Viewing the Client Hello Parameters*

In *Figure* 3.13, Wireshark shows the list of ciphers supported by the Client. Next is the Server name identification field. This field shows the hostname requested by the client. This is the domain name that the client requests, that is, the site which the client enters in the browser, for example, google.com or facebook.com. Here in the capture, the hostname is **`bawmashbij`**, which is a test server.

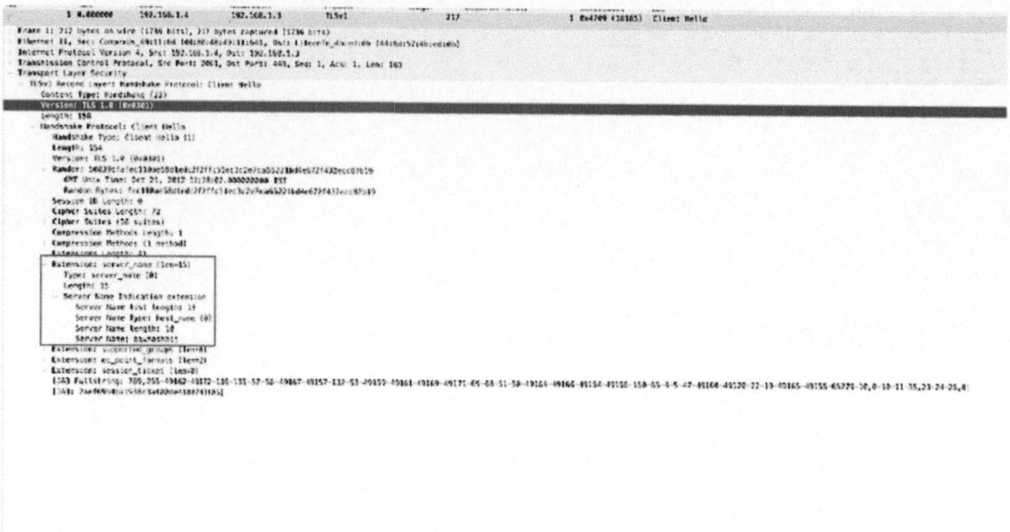

Figure 3.14: *Verifying the Server Name as part of the Client Hello*

Now, let us check on how the data is encrypted. If we remember the captures that we analyzed for HTTP, we can see that the data was in plain text. Let us now look at how SSL/TLS helps in encrypting the data.

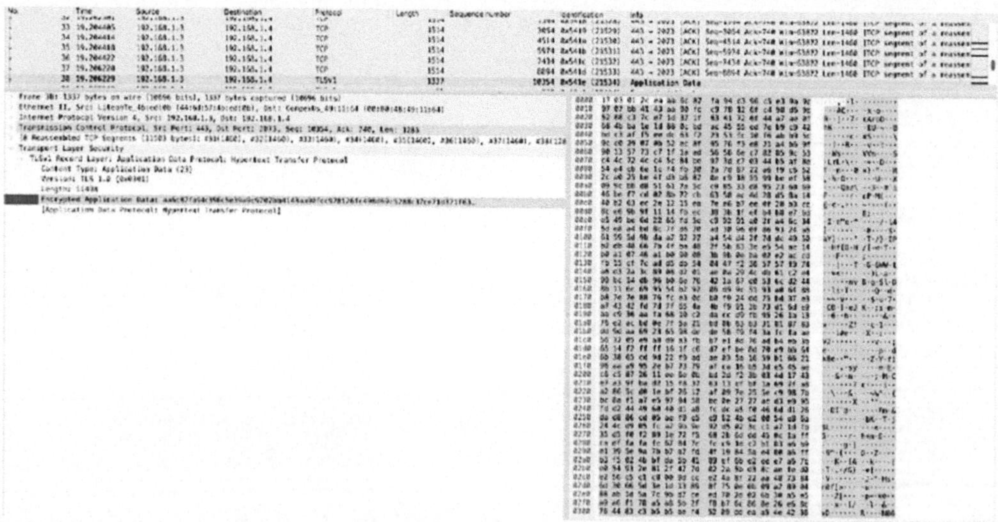

Figure 3.15: *Looking at the Data Portion of the Website being accessed by the User*

As seen in *Figure* 3.15, the application data is encrypted and is not available in plaintext. Now, let us understand how the data gets encrypted.

Encryption

Encryption means hiding the original message. When we enter the credentials while we log in to any system, for example, it can be our machine, or when we log in to our email accounts, the password entered on screen is not visible. Similarly, in order to transfer the messages between client and server in an encrypted way, SSL/TLS is used.

- **Public Key:** The public key is given by the application server, and this gets derived from the certificate that the application server is using. This certificate is issued by Certificate Authorities. Taking the analogy of the password, imagine the password gets shared from the client to the server. The password gets encrypted by this public key.
- **Private key:** In order to decrypt the password that is shared by the client, it can only be done with the private key. The application server only has the private key. Thus, even if there is a main-in-middle to sniff the messages between the client and the server, it would not be able to read the message, as it would not have the private key. As a result, the application servers are always behind a Web Application firewall to protect themselves against DDOS attacks from attackers.
- **Authentication:** The certificate, which is issued by the Certificate Authority, gets verified by browsers like Chrome or Firefox to validate that it is the web server that it claims to be. The way they verify is by matching the certificate ID with the issuer of the certificate.
- **Digital Signature:** A digital signature is the issuing authority's number. Whenever the certificate is provided to the application server by the Certificate Authority, it provides a unique number. The application server generates a new unique number, which the Browser verifies with the Certificate Authority to verify that the certificate has not been changed in the path.

All these components are part of the RSA(Rivest- Shamir - Adleman) algorithm. The traffic would be encrypted and in the form of Public and Private Keys.

In order to mitigate Public and Private Key pair Vulnerability seen in RSA, TLS was introduced, which has evolved from TLS1.0, TLS1.1, TLS1.2, and currently, TLS1.3.

Let us look at the flow of TLS1.2 and TLS1.3.

TLS 1.2

Step 1 - Client Hello

The handshake starts with the Client Hello message from the client browser. The message includes

a. `TLS version`

b. `28-byte random number( Client Random)`

c. `List of Cipher Suites`

Step 2 - Server Hello

After receiving **`Client Hello`**, the server starts preparing **`Server Hello`**

a. It checks if the TLS version is a valid one.

b. It saves the **`Client Random`** and puts it aside.

c. It generates another 28-byte random number (Server Random)

d. It picks a preferred cipher suite from the list. TLS recommends using ECDHE(Ephemeral Elliptic-curve Diffie-Hellman) as the key exchange algorithm. The suggested Cipher Suite is **`TLS_ECDHE_RSA_WITH_AES_256_GCM_SHA384`**

e. It adds a server Certificate to prove its identity.

f. With ECDHE, it puts the key exchange algorithm parameters to message

g. A signature encrypted with the Server's Private key is attached for additional identity verification.

The Key Exchange Algorithm (ECDHE) parameters are as follows:

- Curve Type
- Named Curve
- Public Key
- Signature algorithm
- Signature

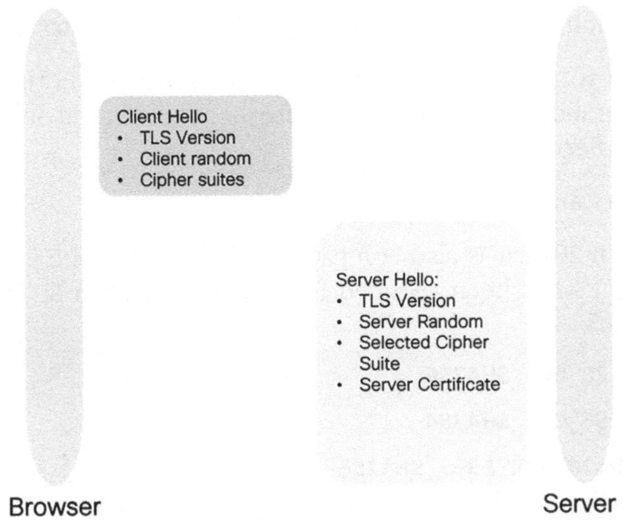

Figure 3.16: *Parameters as part of Client and Server Hello*

Step 3 - Client Key exchange and generating the Pre-master Secret

This step is all about the browser, where it performs following actions:

- It verifies the server identity with the server Certificate.
- It also verifies the signature in the key exchange algorithm parameters.
- The Browser creates a public key and adds it to the key exchange parameters.

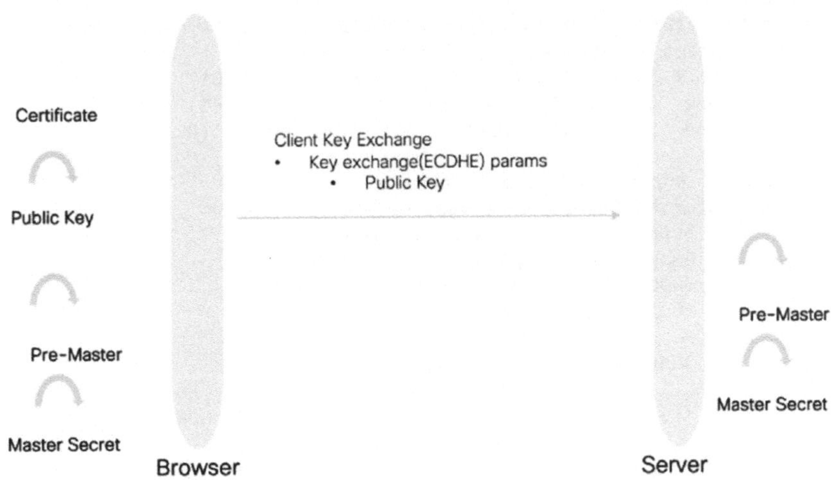

Figure 3.17: *TLS Handshale Flow*

The steps can be summarized as follows:

1. Server (Key Exchange Params)(Step 2) + Client (Key Exchange Params)(Step 3) = Pre-Master

2. Client Random(Step 1) + Server Random (Step 2) + Pre-Master = **Master Secret**

The Master Secret is not the session key for communication. Both Client and Server will use a Psuredo-random function to generate more keys based on the master secret, such as Client and Server Session keys.

Let us try to understand how **TLS 1.3** works.

TLS 1.3 came out in 2018. It is also compatible with TLS 1.2. The list of Cipher suites supported in TLS 1.3 has been reduced from 37 in TLS1.2 to 5. The list of ciphers supported in TLS 1.3:

- **`TLS_AES_128_GCM_SHA256`**
- **`TLS_AES_256_GCM_SHA384`**
- **`TLS_CHACHA20_POLY1305_SHA256`**
- **`TLS_AES_128_CCM_SHA256`**
- **`TLS_AES_128_CCM_8_SHA256`**

Since the Cipher Suites have been reduced to a single **`Client Hello`** and **`Server Hello`** packet, all the extensions can be sent in one message.

The following is an example of **`Client Hello`** for TLS 1.3:

```
Handshake Protocol: Client Hello
  Version: TLS 1.2 (0x0303)
  Random:
d06068b9b0a6a451949f02b55683dfcceecf95d49cbd4e9e273f8f3f453462ea
  Cipher Suites (27 suites)
        Cipher Suite: TLS_AES_128_GCM_SHA256 (0x1301)
        Cipher Suite: TLS_AES_256_GCM_SHA384 (0x1302)
        Cipher Suite: TLS_CHACHA20_POLY1305_SHA256 (0x1303)
  ...
  Extension: supported_groups (len=12)
        Supported Groups (5 groups)
            Supported Group: x25519 (0x001d)
            Supported Group: secp256r1 (0x0017)
            Supported Group: secp384r1 (0x0018)
            Supported Group: secp521r1 (0x0019)
  Extension: key_share (len=107)
        Key Share extension
            Client Key Share Length: 41
            Key Share Entry: Group: x25519, Key Exchange length: 32
            ...
  Extension: supported_versions (len=11)
        Supported Versions length: 10
        Supported Version: TLS 1.3 (0x0304)
        Supported Version: TLS 1.2 (0x0303)
        Supported Version: TLS 1.1 (0x0302)
        Supported Version: TLS 1.0 (0x0301)
```

Figure 3.18: *Client Hello Example of* TLS 1.3

- Supported_groups is for supported named curves, such as **P-256** and **X25519**. **X25519** is a high-performance curve
- **Key_share** is for client public key params

The following is an example of **Server Hello**:

```
Handshake Protocol: Server Hello
    Version: TLS 1.2 (0x0303)
    Random:
b0a37492143def6d4959205dfe6fd620d93baa7ba89e1593e8cb60d6497537d4
    ...
    Cipher Suite: TLS_AES_128_GCM_SHA256 (0x1301)
    ...
    Extension: supported_versions (len=2)
        Supported Version: TLS 1.3 (0x0304)
    Extension: key_share (len=36)
        Key Share extension
            Key Share Entry: Group: x25519, Key Exchange length: 32
            Group: x25519 (29)
            Key Exchange:
105aaf79c1f424cdc9352723a4dea7db65568a229c091d3fd8a700da883bd15e
6
```

Figure 3.19: *Server Hello Example of* TLS 1.3

In the supported version Server confirms using TLS1.3.

Key Share has selected named curve and key exchange parameters.

- Client Key share + Server Key Share = Pre-Master
- Client random + Server random + Pre-Master = **Master Secret**

One of the differences in Server Hello in TLS 1.3 is that it is encrypted.

While receiving the **Client Hello**, the Server has all the required parameters for generating the master secret, including :

- Client Key Share
- Server Key Share
- Client Random
- Server Random

The Server generates the master secret, encrypts the **Server Hello**, and finally sends it to the client.

Let us look at how to view the certificate for google.com.

Figure 3.20: *Verifying the Certificate of Google.com*

Open the lock icon, which means that the site supports HTTPS. Then click the **`Connection is secure`** arrow as shown in *Figure 3.21*.

Figure 3.21: *Browser shows Connection is Secure*

Then click **`Certificate is valid`**.

Figure 3.22: *Validating the Certificate of Google.com*

Now one can see the Certificate details such as the Issuer and the expiry of the certificate. As can be seen, the public key of the certificate is also available. The certificate was issued by Google Trust Services.

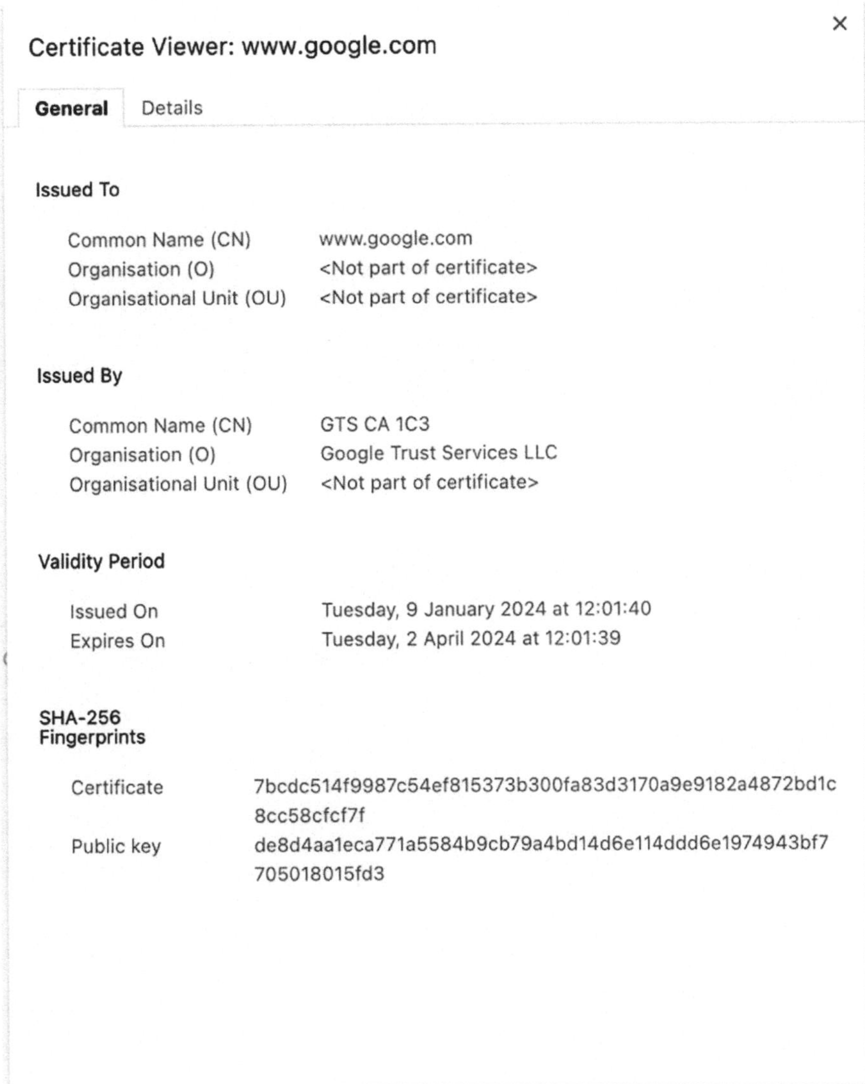

Figure 3.23: *Verifying Certificate of Google.com*

One can also download the certificate by clicking **`export`** on the Chrome browser, as seen in *Figure* 3.24.

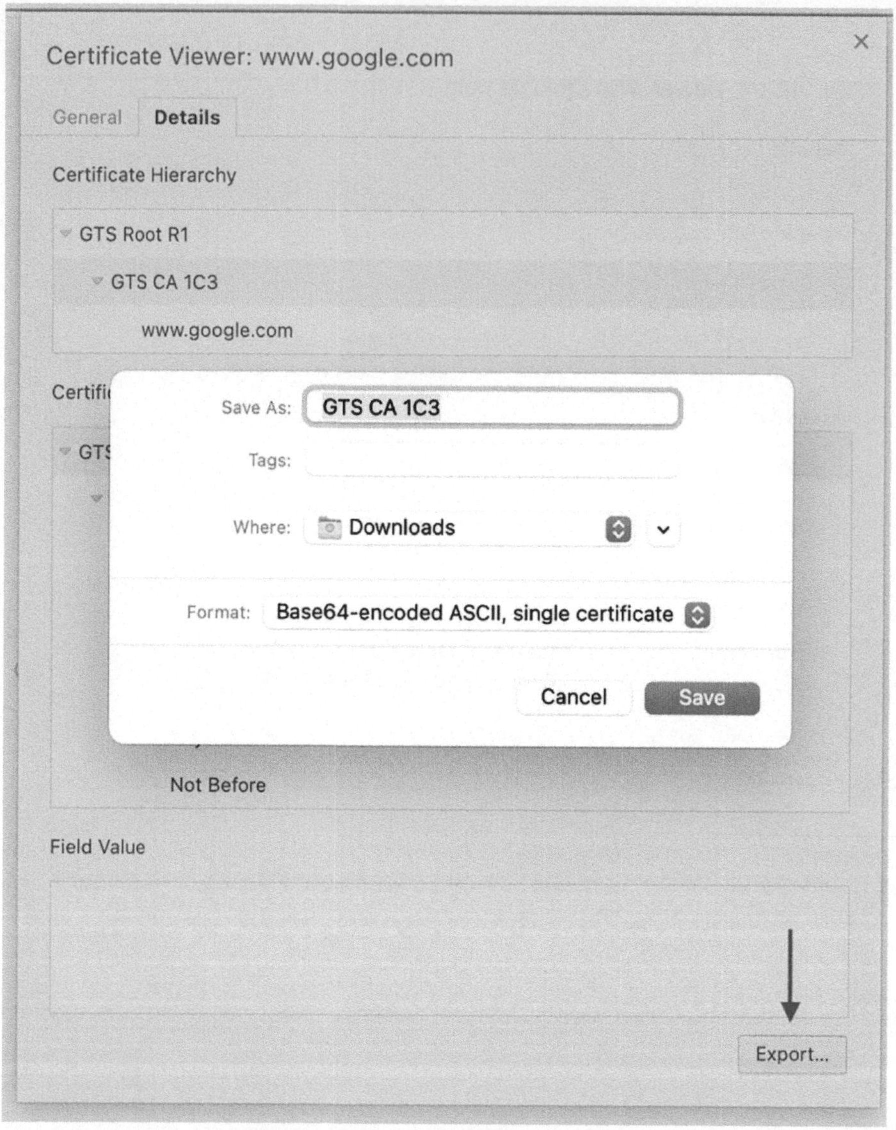

Figure 3.24: *Exporting the Certificate*

Conclusion

We understood the disadvantage of the plaintext traffic between the client and server. We visualized the plaintext traffic of HTTP in Wireshark and how the application data can be seen by any attacker who is between the Client and Server. We then understood the SSL protocol and how TLS was being developed due to vulnerabilities in SSL. The next chapter explores how the Enterprise network is evolving.

CHAPTER 4
Evolving Network Architecture

Introduction

This chapter will focus on how the Enterprise network is evolving and the different Security controls that are in place. We will take captures on different Network endpoints in the Enterprise Network and see how the traffic is getting routed and Secured. We will also take a look at the Network Architecture of **Secure Service Edge** and how the traffic flow is routed from the endpoint through an agent.

Structure

In this chapter, we will discuss the following topics:

- Typical Enterprise Network
- Zero Trust Architecture

Typical Enterprise Network

In the previous chapters, we looked at how the Internet traffic was routed from the home machine through the home Wi-Fi provider.

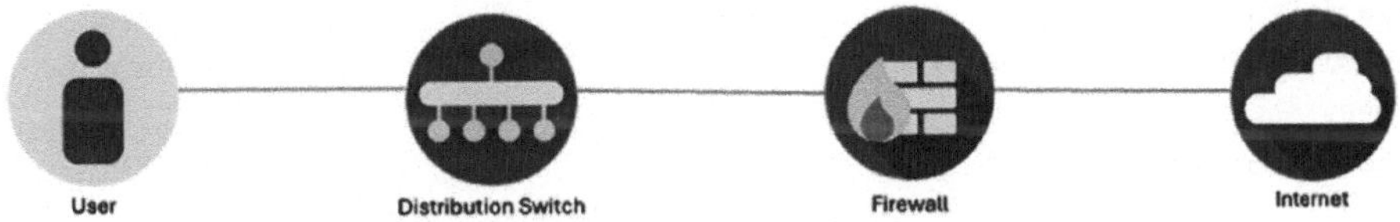

Figure 4.1: *Typical Enterprise Network Diagram*

A typical Enterprise Network consists of a Distribution switch where most of the endpoints get connected. Different VLANs are created on the Distribution switch as different LAN Segments are created to isolate the traffic and also enforce security controls depending on the LAN segments. All the Internet traffic has a default route from the Switch towards the Firewall. The Firewall then applies appropriate URL filtering, Layer 7 Inspection, and also restricts traffic to specific websites. We would verify and visualize this on Wireshark.

Let us look at the Lab which we have set up on AWS. The Windows server setup has 2 NICs, one NIC is used for Management, while the other NIC is used for data traffic.

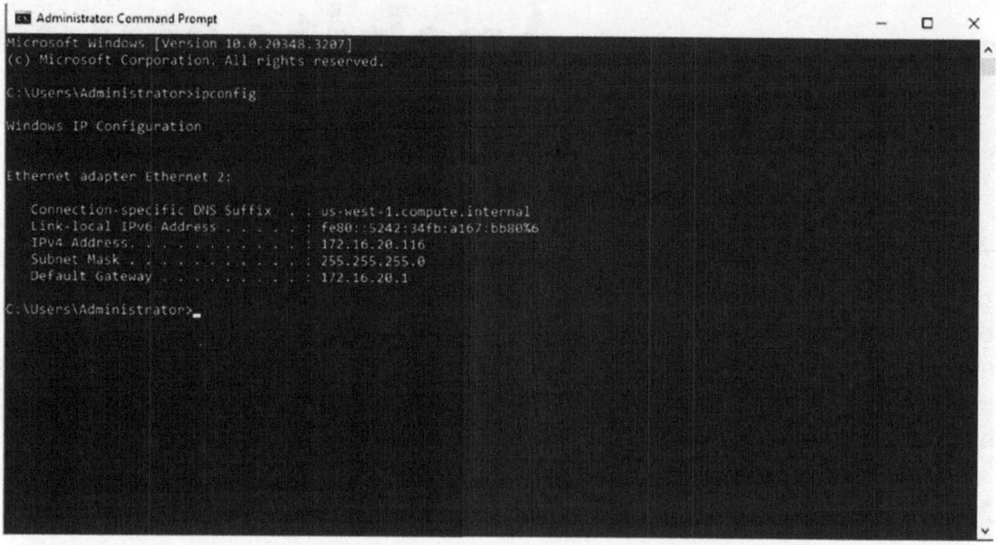

Figure 4.2: *IP Address of the Windows Server*

The first NIC is used to RDP into the Windows server machine, while the second NIC is used to initiate data traffic. The Windows server machine IP address is 172.16.20.116, while the gateway is the VPC Switch of AWS.

Let us log in to the Secure firewall (Cisco Next-gen Firewall), and following is the CLI, which shows different interfaces that are configured:

```
Interface                 Name                    Security
Management0/0             management               0
TenGigabitEthernet0/0     inside                   0
TenGigabitEthernet0/1     outside                  0
firepower# show int ip br
firepower# show int ip brief
Interface                 IP-Address      OK? Method Status        Protocol
Internal-Control0/0       127.0.1.1       YES unset  up            up
Internal-Control0/1       unassigned      YES unset  up            up
Internal-Data0/0          unassigned      YES unset  down          up
Internal-Data0/0          unassigned      YES unset  up            up
Internal-Data0/1          169.254.1.1     YES unset  up            up
Internal-Data0/2          unassigned      YES unset  up            up
Management0/0             203.0.113.130   YES unset  up            up
```

```
TenGigabitEthernet0/0      172.16.20.221    YES CONFIG up                    up
TenGigabitEthernet0/1      192.0.30.157     YES DHCP   up                    up
```

The inside interface is Te0/0, and the outside interface is Te0/1.

In order to manage the Windows server from outside, the following routing has been configured, where to manage the Windows server from the Internet, the public IP is specified to point to the Internet gateway, while the rest of the traffic should be routed through the firewall.

Figure 4.3: *Routing Configuration on AWS Infra*

Here, **`122.171.23.156`** is the public IP, while the NIC ID **`eni-08316df9632f6a260`** is the Inside interface of the Secure Firewall.

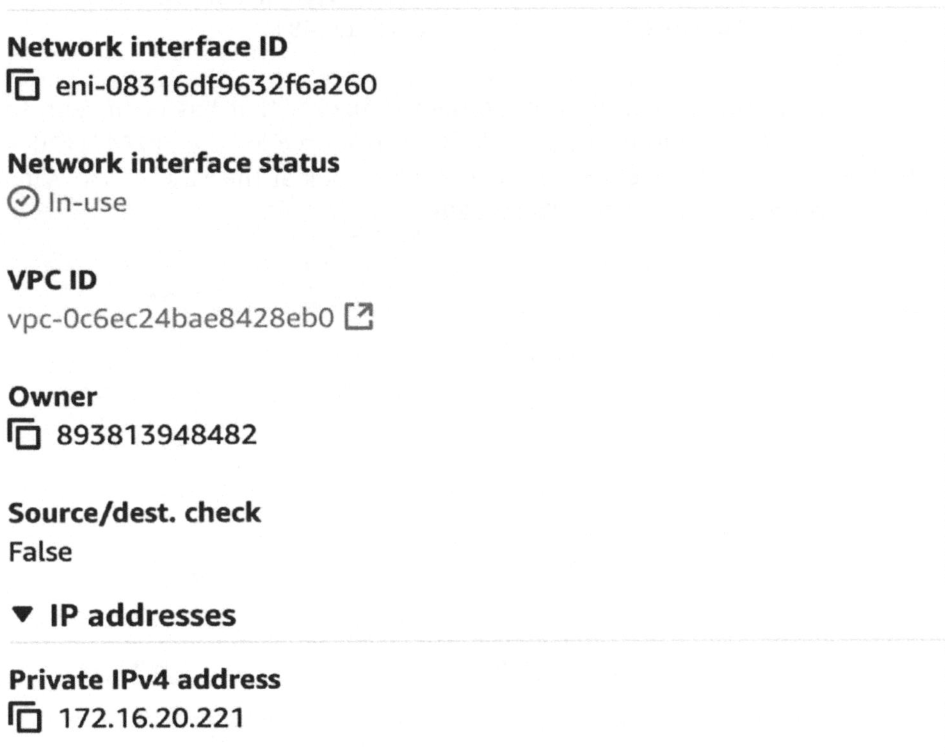

Figure 4.4: *Viewing NIC Information in AWS Infra*

We initiated some Web Traffic from the Windows server machine, and let us take some network traces on the Firewall (Secure Firewall of Cisco) for the traffic initiated from the Windows Server. The network trace is taken using the following command:

```
cap capi interface inside match ip any any

capi - is the capture name
Interface inside - mentions the network trace is taken on inside
interface
ip any any - Filter to capture all traffic

firepower# show cap capi packet-number 1 detail


   1052 packets captured

   1: 04:37:46.968806 0264.1f2d.46f9 02a6.ad70.9fe1 0x0800 Length: 66
      172.16.20.193.50102 > 184.28.149.157.443: SWE [tcp sum ok]
1132452420:1132452420(0) win 62727 <mss 8961,nop,wscale 8,nop,nop,
sackOK> (DF) [tos 0x2,ECT]  (ttl 128, id 13448)
1 packet shown
```

As can be seen in the packet, it is the initial **SYN** packet that has been sent. Let us try to trace the source and destination MAC. The source MAC is **0264.1f2d.46f9**, and the destination MAC is **02a6.ad70.9fe1**. If we look at the MAC of the Windows machine, it shows a value of **0255.504a.025f**

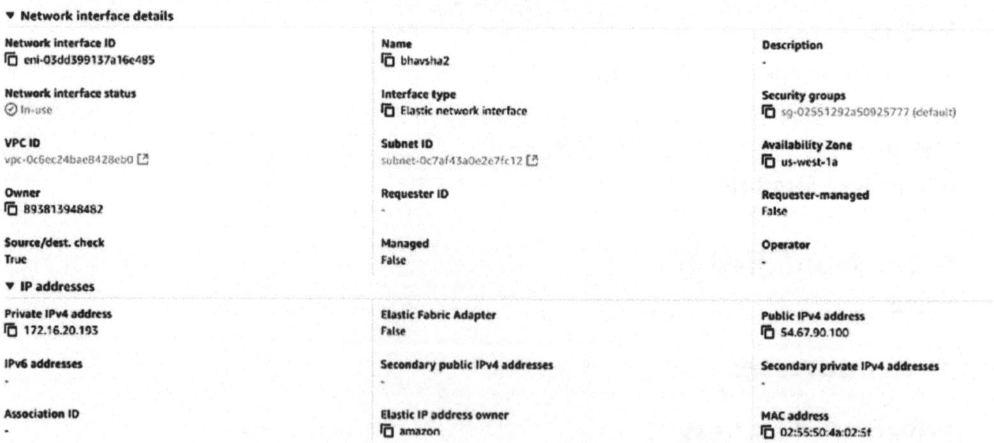

Figure 4.5: *NIC Details of the Windows Server Machine in AWS*

If the traffic is initiated from the machine, the source MAC should be of the machine, right? The trace is being taken on the Firewall, which is receiving the traffic from the Windows machine.

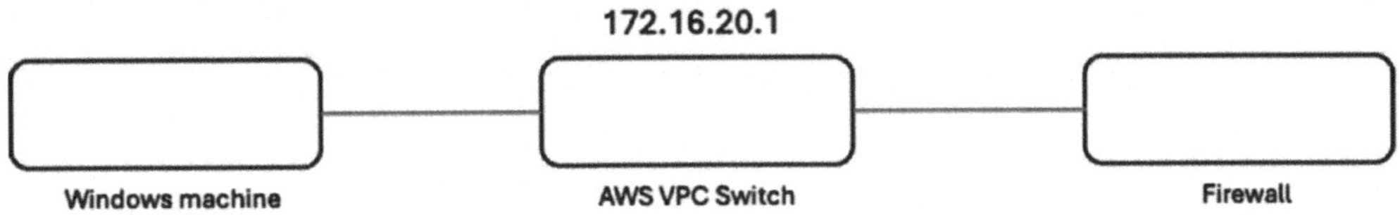

Figure 4.6: *Looking at how the Windows Machine is connected to Firewall*

The source MAC **0264.1f2d.46f9** is of the AWS VPC Switch. We can also verify by checking the ARP entries on the firewall as follows:

```
firepower# show arp
        inside 172.16.20.1 0264.1f2d.46f9 41
        inside 172.16.20.193 0255.504a.025f 6967
        outside 192.0.30.1 0294.cf10.5343 41
```

The destination MAC **02a6.ad70.9fe1** is of the Firewall Inside interface, which can be verified as follows:

```
firepower# show interface tenGigabitEthernet 0/0 detail
Interface TenGigabitEthernet0/0 "inside", is up, line protocol is up
  Hardware is net_ena, BW 10000 Mbps, DLY 10 usec
    Auto-Duplex(Full-duplex), Auto-Speed(10000 Mbps)
    Input flow control is unsupported, output flow control is
    unsupported
    MAC address 02a6.ad70.9fe1, MTU 1500
    IP address 172.16.20.221, subnet mask 255.255.255.0
```

Looking at packet number **2**, we see **SYN ACK** being sent from the application. In this case, google.com was browsed from the Windows machine.

```
firepower# show cap capi packet-number 2 det

1052 packets captured

    2: 04:37:46.970576 02a6.ad70.9fe1 0255.504a.025f 0x0800 Length: 66
       184.28.149.157.443 > 172.16.20.193.50102: S [tcp sum ok]
750253391:750253391(0) ack 1132452421 win 64240 <mss 1380,nop,
nop,sackOK,nop,wscale 7> (DF) (ttl 56, id 0)
1 packet shown
```

As can be seen, the source IP is **184.28.149.157,** which is google.com IP, and the source MAC is of the Inside interface of the firewall, while the destination MAC is of the actual Windows machine from where the request was initiated.

Finally, the **ACK** packet is received from the Windows machine as follows:

```
firepower# show cap capi packet-number 3 detail

1052 packets captured

   3: 04:37:46.970774 0264.1f2d.46f9 02a6.ad70.9fe1 0x0800 Length: 54
      172.16.20.193.50102 > 184.28.149.157.443: . [tcp sum ok]
1132452421:1132452421(0) ack 750253392 win 1024 (DF) (ttl 128, id
13449)
```

The following is the Logging from the Firewall, which confirms the traffic is being received from the Windows machine:

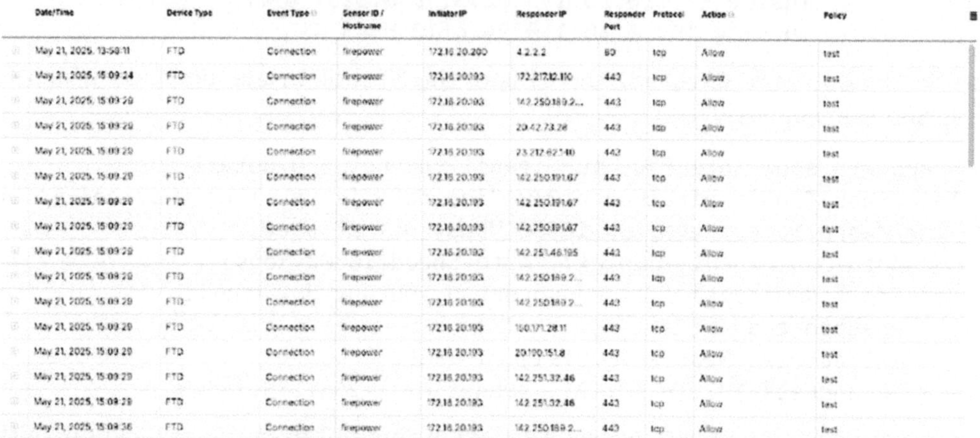

Date/Time	Device Type	Event Type	Sensor ID / Hostname	Initiator IP	Responder IP	Responder Port	Protocol	Action	Policy
May 21, 2025, 13:50:11	FTD	Connection	firepower	172.16.20.200	4.2.2.2	80	tcp	Allow	test
May 21, 2025, 15:09:24	FTD	Connection	firepower	172.16.20.193	172.217.12.110	443	tcp	Allow	test
May 21, 2025, 15:09:29	FTD	Connection	firepower	172.16.20.193	142.250.189.2...	443	tcp	Allow	test
May 21, 2025, 15:09:29	FTD	Connection	firepower	172.16.20.193	20.42.73.28	443	tcp	Allow	test
May 21, 2025, 15:09:29	FTD	Connection	firepower	172.16.20.193	23.212.62.140	443	tcp	Allow	test
May 21, 2025, 15:09:29	FTD	Connection	firepower	172.16.20.193	142.250.191.67	443	tcp	Allow	test
May 21, 2025, 15:09:29	FTD	Connection	firepower	172.16.20.193	142.250.191.67	443	tcp	Allow	test
May 21, 2025, 15:09:29	FTD	Connection	firepower	172.16.20.193	142.250.191.67	443	tcp	Allow	test
May 21, 2025, 15:09:29	FTD	Connection	firepower	172.16.20.193	142.251.46.195	443	tcp	Allow	test
May 21, 2025, 15:09:29	FTD	Connection	firepower	172.16.20.193	142.250.189.2...	443	tcp	Allow	test
May 21, 2025, 15:09:29	FTD	Connection	firepower	172.16.20.193	142.250.189.2...	443	tcp	Allow	test
May 21, 2025, 15:09:29	FTD	Connection	firepower	172.16.20.193	150.171.28.11	443	tcp	Allow	test
May 21, 2025, 15:09:29	FTD	Connection	firepower	172.16.20.193	20.190.151.8	443	tcp	Allow	test
May 21, 2025, 15:09:29	FTD	Connection	firepower	172.16.20.193	142.251.32.46	443	tcp	Allow	test
May 21, 2025, 15:09:29	FTD	Connection	firepower	172.16.20.193	142.251.32.46	443	tcp	Allow	test
May 21, 2025, 15:09:36	FTD	Connection	firepower	172.16.20.193	142.250.189.2...	443	tcp	Allow	test

Figure 4.7: *Viewing Logs on the Firewall*

Following is the rule that has been configured. The source zone is the Inside interface, while the outside zone is the Outside interface. Currently, everything is being allowed on the Firewall.

Ideally Firewall would not allow all the traffic and would have restrictions on the kind of applications and different URLs that can be allowed. For the Firewall to perform these deep Inspections, it should perform SSL decryption, as all the traffic would be initiated on port **443**. The following is the rule that has been created to decrypt all traffic on the Firewall:

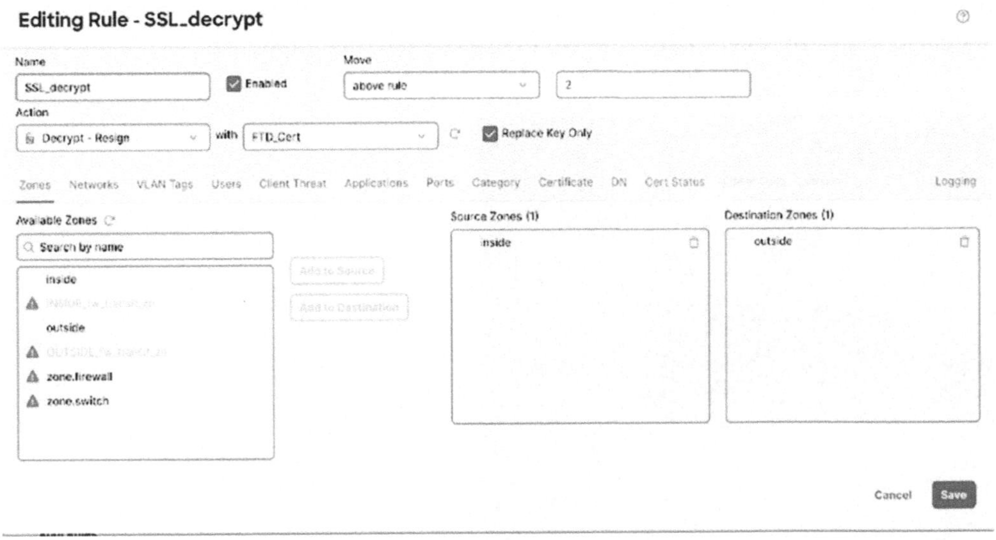

Figure 4.8: *SSL Decrypt Rule on Firewall*

The Cert name is **`FTD_cert`**, which was generated on the Firewall using the following parameters:

Figure 4.9: *Details of the cert used in Firewall for Decryption*

Let us verify if the Certificate is getting applied. We initiated traffic to ibnlive.com, and we can see that the Certificate that we created is getting applied.

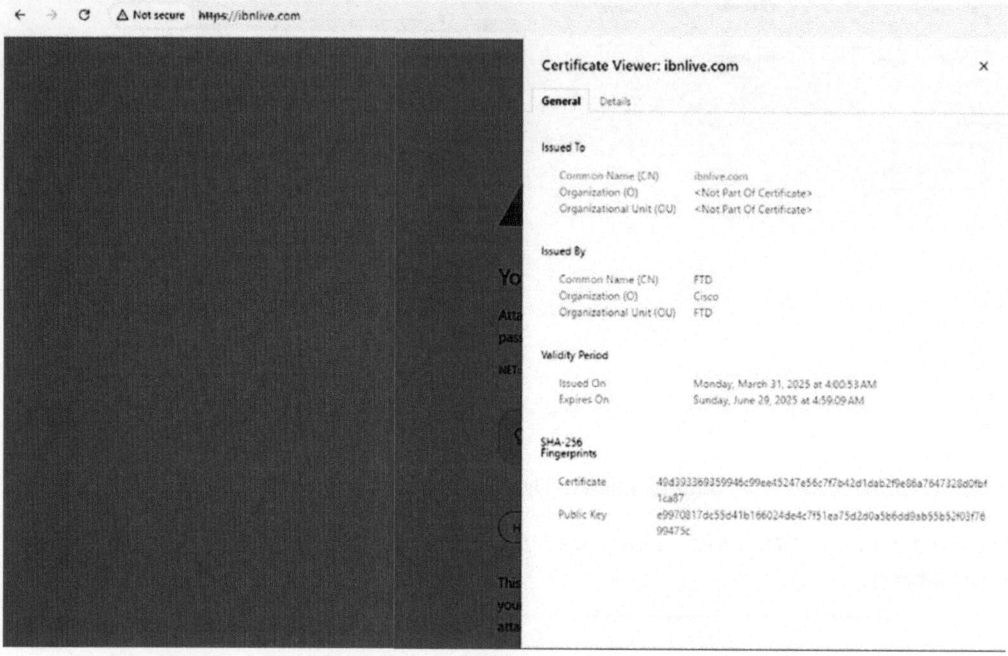

Figure 4.10: *Viewing the Certificate on the Chrome Browser when the Traffic is initiated to ibnlive.com*

Note: *The reason it shows Not Secure is because the Certificate generated on the firewall is not imported into the Trusted store of the Machine. All Self Signed Certificates should be imported to the Trusted Certificate Store.*

Let us configure a policy to block google.com. As seen in *Figure* 4.11, we have configured a rule to block Google.com by configuring a category-based rule. Google.com comes in the Search engines category, and it is referenced in the rule. For Next-Gen Firewall, we have Categories defined for different URLs, and this can also be found at the Cisco link https://talosintelligence.com/reputation_center/lookup?search=google.com

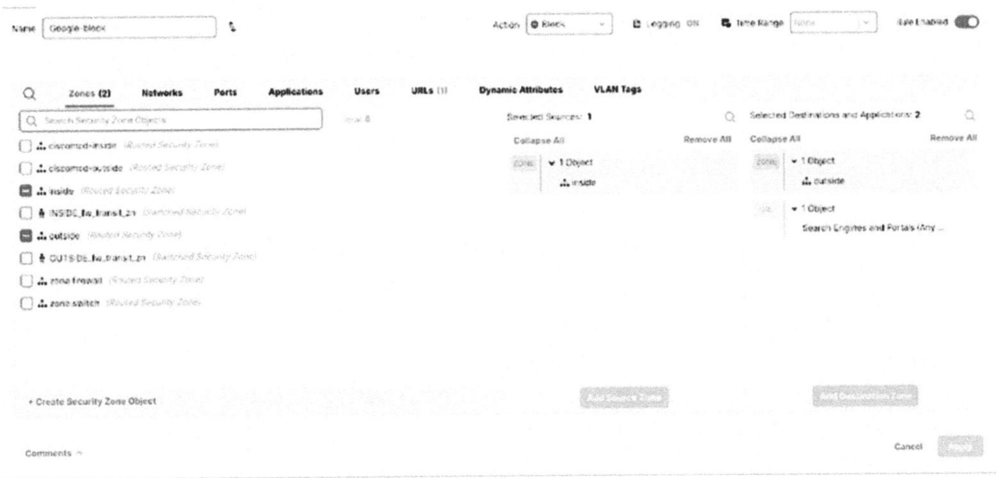

Figure 4.11: *Creating Rule in Firewall to block google.com*

If we take the capture on the Firewall, we can see an **`RST`** packet (packet number **`163`**) being sent from the Firewall, as the rule is configured to block the request to google.com.

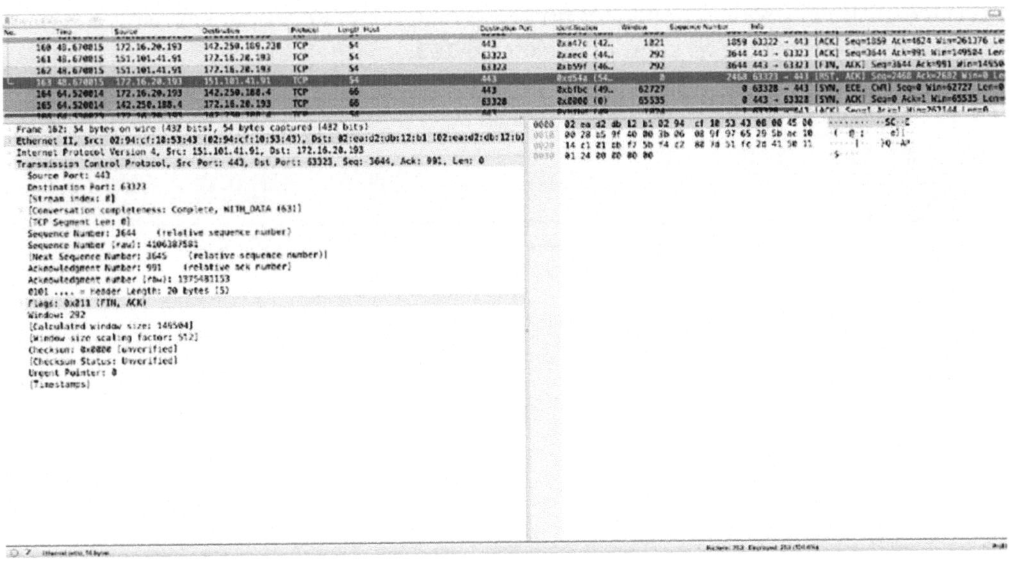

Figure 4.12: *Looking at the Wireshark Trace when google.com was browsed*

If we see the source MAC, it is of the AWS Internal Switch **`0294.cf10.5343`** of the outside interface. Since the Firewall is inspecting the traffic between the Client and

Server, it would send the Reset packet back to the client. The Reset packet is an indication that the rule is configured to block the request to Google.com.

```
firepower# show arp
        inside 172.16.20.1 0264.1f2d.46f9 26
        inside 172.16.20.193 0255.504a.025f 6921
        outside 192.0.30.1 0294.cf10.5343 26
```

The destination MAC is of the outside interface of the Firewall, as follows:

```
firepower# show interface te0/1
Interface TenGigabitEthernet0/1 "outside", is up, line protocol is up
  Hardware is net_ena, BW 10000 Mbps, DLY 10 usec
    Auto-Duplex(Full-duplex), Auto-Speed(10000 Mbps)
    Input flow control is unsupported, output flow control is
    unsupported
    MAC address 02ea.d2db.12b1, MTU 1500
    IP address 192.0.30.157, subnet mask 255.255.255.0
```

The Reset packet is then sent to the User machine, as we see in packet no **163**. As seen in *Figure* 4.13, the Source MAC is **0264.1f2d.46f9**, which is the AWS internal Switch MAC for the Inside Interface, and the destination MAC is that of the Inside interface of the Firewall. The packet no **163** is **Ack** of the Reset packet, which is being initiated by the Firewall, as seen in packet no **162**.

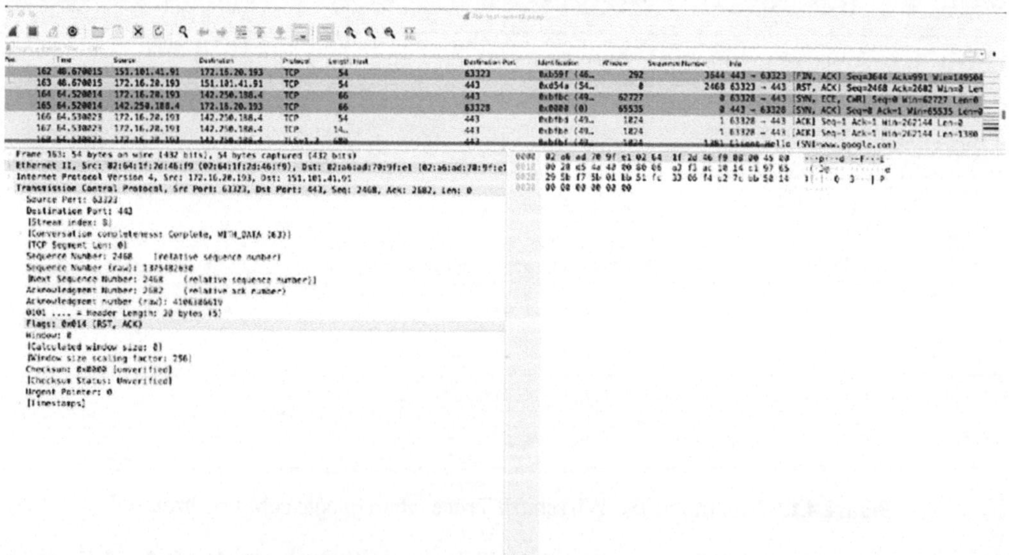

Figure 4.13: *Reset Packet initiated by the Firewall*

Let us analyze the capture that we have taken on the end machine and the Firewall. If we remember from the previous chapters, we configured the **SSLKEYLOGFILE** environment variable for tracking the session keys for decrypting the TLS traffic.

Next-Gen firewalls have the inherent capability of decrypting the traffic as they have a dedicated module for encrypting and decrypting the traffic.

As seen in *Figure* 4.14, **ftd-test-snort1.pcap** is taken on the Firewall and **traffic.pcap** is taken on the end machine at the same time:

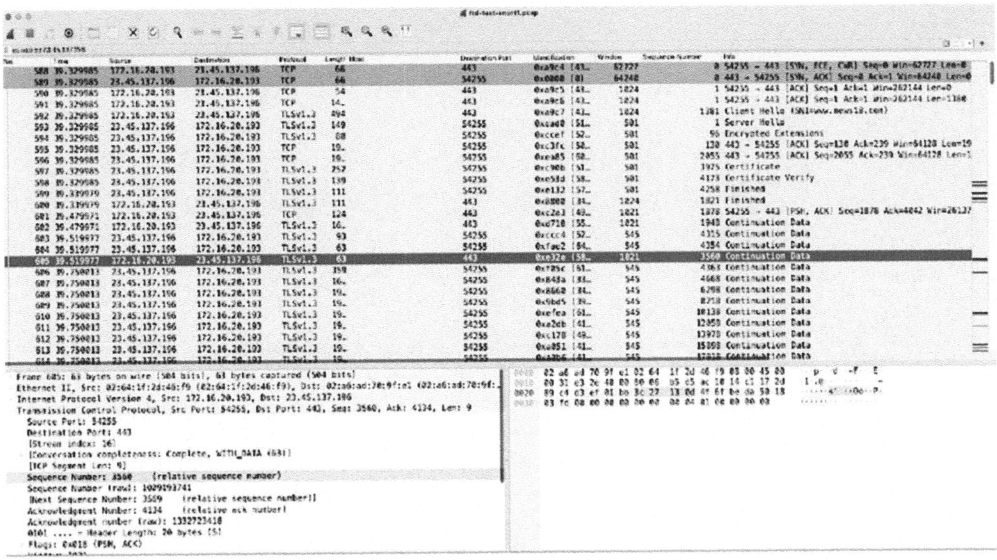

Figure 4.14: *Looking at the Capture taken on the Firewall*

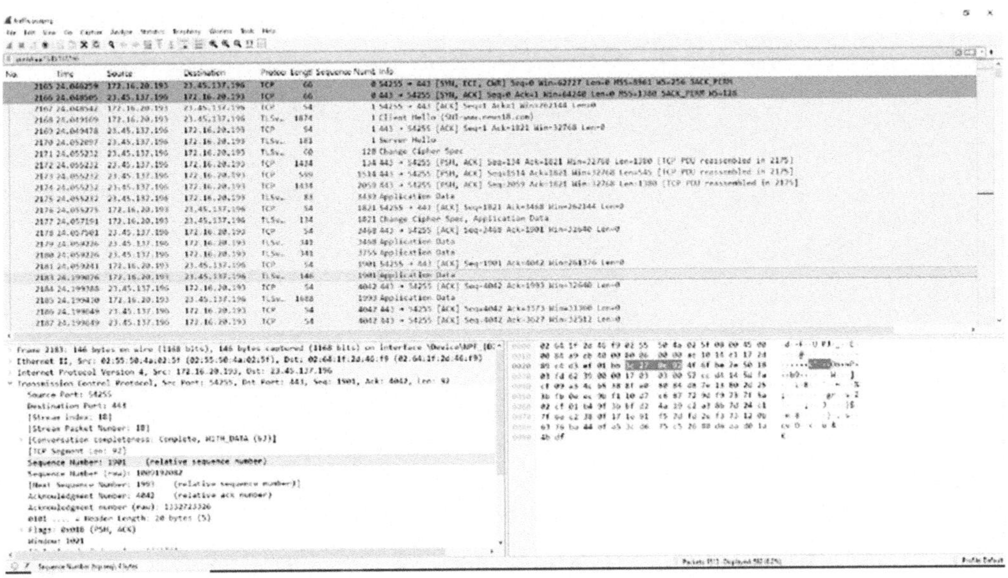

Figure 4.15: *Looking at the Capture taken on the Windows Server*

In both captures, we have filtered by the IP address of news18.com. The capture was taken when the traffic was initiated to this domain. How did we know the IP address of news18.com? We used the filter of **`tls.handshake.extension.type==0`**, which looks for all the packets which has SNI information.

Let us look at the **`Client Hello`** packet, which is initiated from the user machine, and compare it with the capture taken on the Firewall.

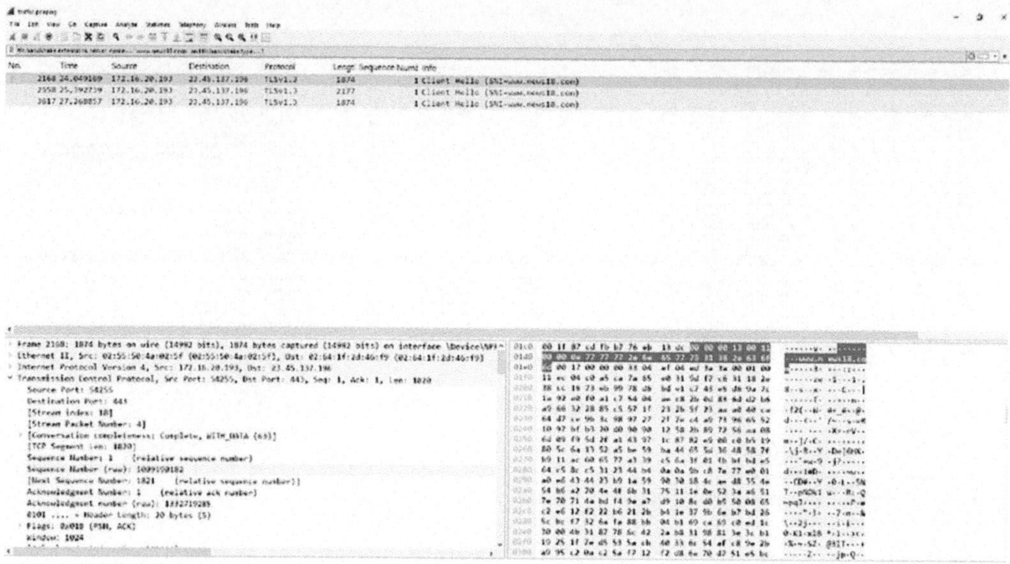

Figure 4.16: *Client Hello Packet when Traffic was initiated to news18.com*

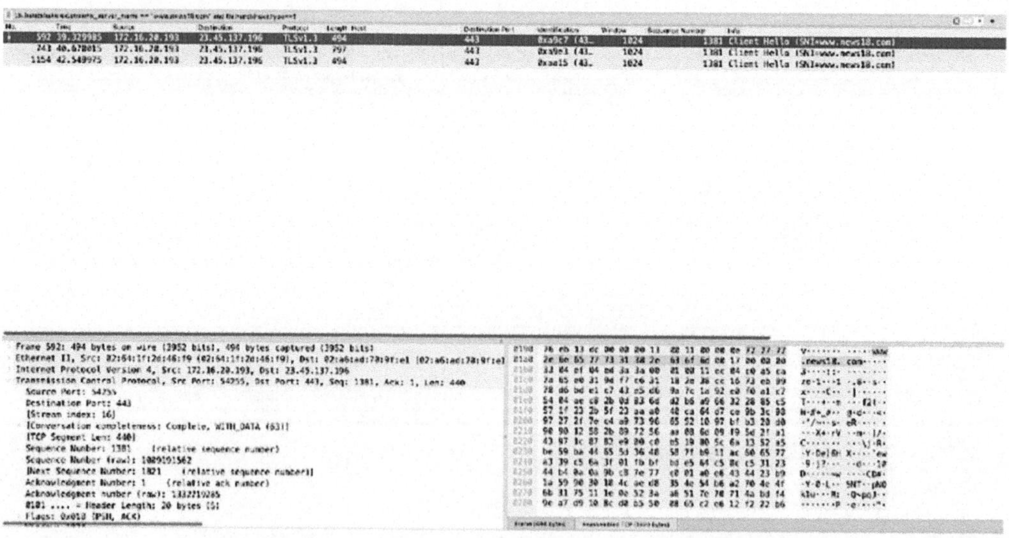

Figure 4.17: *Client Hello Packet as seen on Firewall Capture*

As can be seen, the source MAC on the capture taken on the user machine is of the user machine, while on the Firewall capture, it is of the AWS Internal Switch, which is forwarding the traffic to the Inside interface of the Firewall. Similarly, the destination MAC on the user machine capture is of the AWS Internal Switch, while on the Firewall capture, it is of the Inside interface of the Firewall. If we look at the capture taken on the Firewall, we see the actual Certificate shared by the new18. com. This is because the capture taken on the Firewall is decrypted, and we see the actual Certificate shared by news18.com.

All the traffic is decrypted from packet number **604**, as can be seen, which is coming from the application server news18.com.

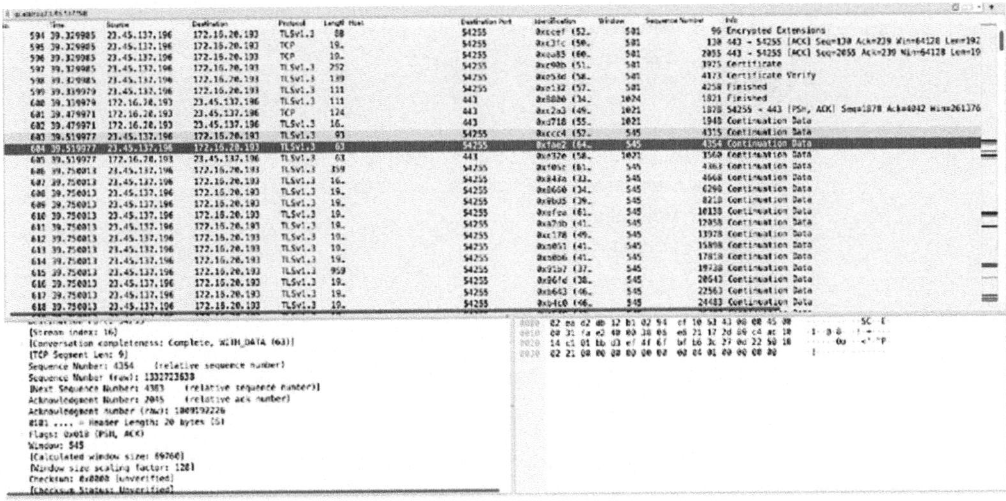

Figure 4.18: *Decrypted Traffic seen on Firewall Capture*

Note: *Since we have access to the Firewall, we can take captures and we can decrypt them. In the next section, we will look at other scenarios where it would not always be possible to take a decrypted capture on the Firewall or a Proxy.*

Zero Trust Architecture

As users are working from home post-COVID, the existing Security Controls that are applied at the Branch or the Headquarters Data Center using the Firewalls should also be enforced for users who are roaming, that is, changing their locations. In order to enforce the Security controls for the Roaming users, we install a Security agent which would Sync the Policies from the Controller, which is SaaS (Software as a Service). The Controller is a Cloud Proxy that would inspect all the policies initiated from the User and would restrict the traffic or allow it depending on the Policy configured. The agent enforces the Security Policy as close to the user and also follows the user.

As seen in *Figure* 4.19, we have the **`Secure client`** from Cisco installed on the user's machine, which would encrypt all the Web traffic.

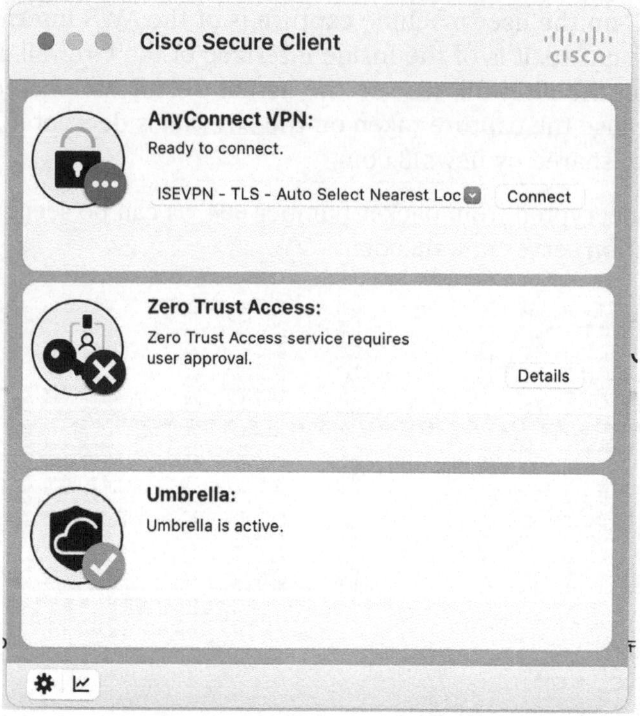

Figure 4.19: *Cisco Secure Client(Agent)*

The **`Umbrella`** Module is responsible for inspecting all the Internet traffic. We have configured a rule to block all traffic to google.com, and we can see the following block page:

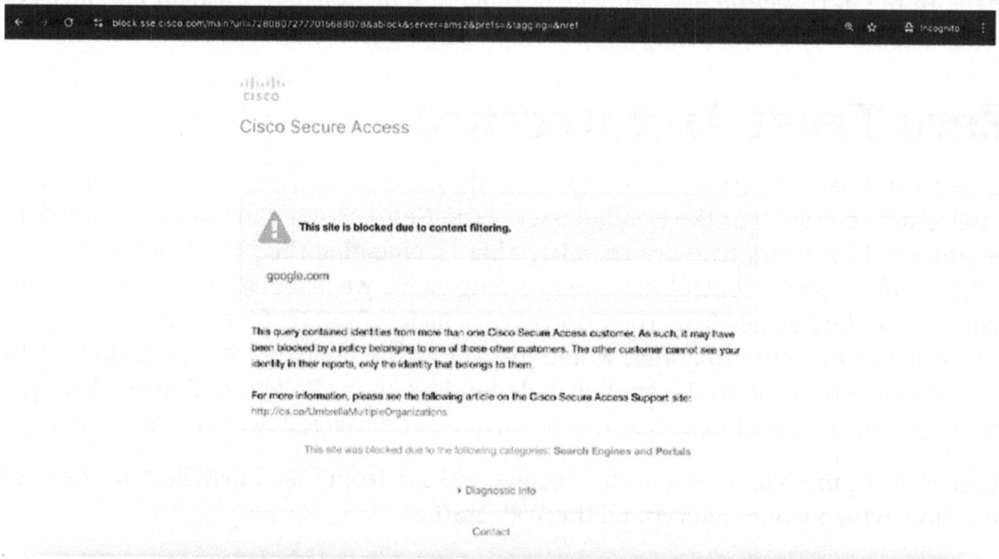

Figure 4.20: *Block Page while the User is trying to access google.com*

If we look the Certificate, we can see the following Certificate, which is issued by the Cloud Proxy:

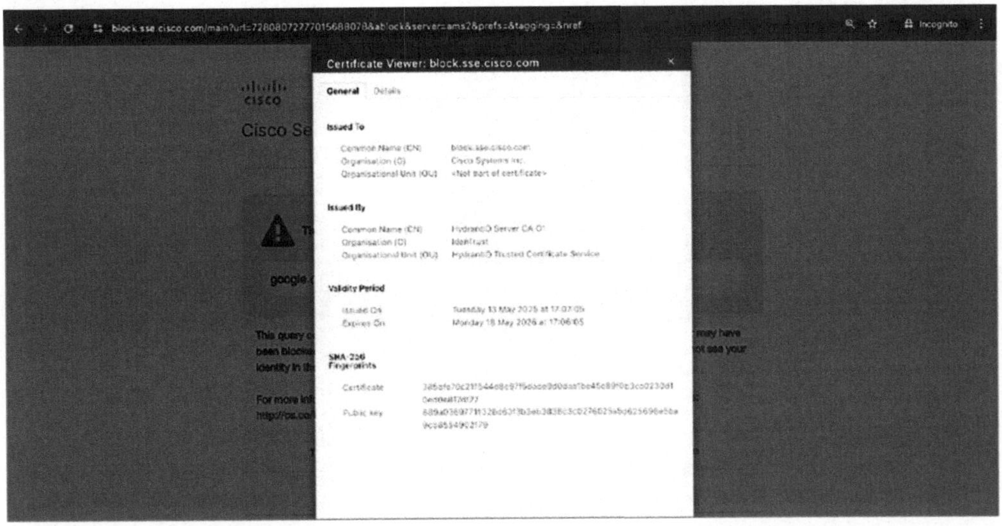

Figure 4.21: *Viewing Certificate Details for the Block Page Issues by Cisco Secure Access*

Let us look at the capture when the traffic is initiated with the agent installed.

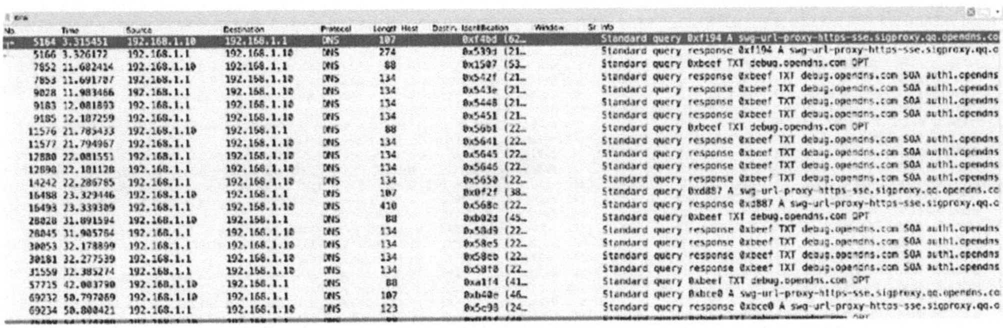

No.	Time	Source	Destination	Protocol	Length	Identification	Info
5164	3.315451	192.168.1.10	192.168.1.1	DNS	107	0xf4bd (62…	Standard query 0xf194 A swg-url-proxy-https-sse.sigproxy.qq.opendns.co
5166	3.326172	192.168.1.1	192.168.1.10	DNS	274	0x539d (21…	Standard query response 0xf194 A swg-url-proxy-https-sse.sigproxy.qq.o
7852	11.682414	192.168.1.10	192.168.1.1	DNS	88	0x1507 (53…	Standard query 0xbeef TXT debug.opendns.com OPT
7853	11.691707	192.168.1.1	192.168.1.10	DNS	134	0x542f (21…	Standard query response 0xbeef TXT debug.opendns.com SOA auth1.opendns
9028	11.983466	192.168.1.1	192.168.1.10	DNS	134	0x543e (21…	Standard query response 0xbeef TXT debug.opendns.com SOA auth1.opendns
9183	12.081893	192.168.1.1	192.168.1.10	DNS	134	0x5448 (21…	Standard query response 0xbeef TXT debug.opendns.com SOA auth1.opendns
9185	12.187259	192.168.1.1	192.168.1.10	DNS	134	0x5451 (21…	Standard query response 0xbeef TXT debug.opendns.com SOA auth1.opendns
11576	21.785433	192.168.1.10	192.168.1.1	DNS	88	0x56b1 (22…	Standard query 0xbeef TXT debug.opendns.com OPT
11577	21.794967	192.168.1.1	192.168.1.10	DNS	134	0x5641 (22…	Standard query response 0xbeef TXT debug.opendns.com SOA auth1.opendns
12880	22.081551	192.168.1.1	192.168.1.10	DNS	134	0x5645 (22…	Standard query response 0xbeef TXT debug.opendns.com SOA auth1.opendns
12898	22.181128	192.168.1.1	192.168.1.10	DNS	134	0x5646 (22…	Standard query response 0xbeef TXT debug.opendns.com SOA auth1.opendns
14242	22.286785	192.168.1.1	192.168.1.10	DNS	134	0x5650 (22…	Standard query response 0xbeef TXT debug.opendns.com SOA auth1.opendns
16488	23.329446	192.168.1.10	192.168.1.1	DNS	107	0x0f2f (38…	Standard query 0xd887 A swg-url-proxy-https-sse.sigproxy.qq.opendns.co
16493	23.339309	192.168.1.1	192.168.1.10	DNS	410	0x568c (22…	Standard query response 0xd887 A swg-url-proxy-https-sse.sigproxy.qq.o
28028	31.891594	192.168.1.10	192.168.1.1	DNS	88	0xb02d (45…	Standard query 0xbeef TXT debug.opendns.com OPT
28045	31.905764	192.168.1.1	192.168.1.10	DNS	134	0x58d9 (22…	Standard query response 0xbeef TXT debug.opendns.com SOA auth1.opendns
30053	32.178899	192.168.1.1	192.168.1.10	DNS	134	0x58e5 (22…	Standard query response 0xbeef TXT debug.opendns.com SOA auth1.opendns
30181	32.277539	192.168.1.1	192.168.1.10	DNS	134	0x58eb (22…	Standard query response 0xbeef TXT debug.opendns.com SOA auth1.opendns
31559	32.385274	192.168.1.1	192.168.1.10	DNS	134	0x58f8 (22…	Standard query response 0xbeef TXT debug.opendns.com SOA auth1.opendns
57715	42.083790	192.168.1.10	192.168.1.1	DNS	88	0xa1f4 (41…	Standard query 0xbeef TXT debug.opendns.com OPT
69232	50.797869	192.168.1.10	192.168.1.1	DNS	107	0xb40e (46…	Standard query 0xbce0 A swg-url-proxy-https-sse.sigproxy.qq.opendns.co
69234	50.800421	192.168.1.1	192.168.1.10	DNS	123	0x5c93 (24…	Standard query response 0xbce0 A swg-url-proxy-https-sse.sigproxy.qq.o

Figure 4.22: *Viewing the Capture taken on the End Machine when Traffic was initiated to google.com*

If we look at the response of the **DNS** query in *Figure* 4.23, the IP address is **98.130.21.18**.

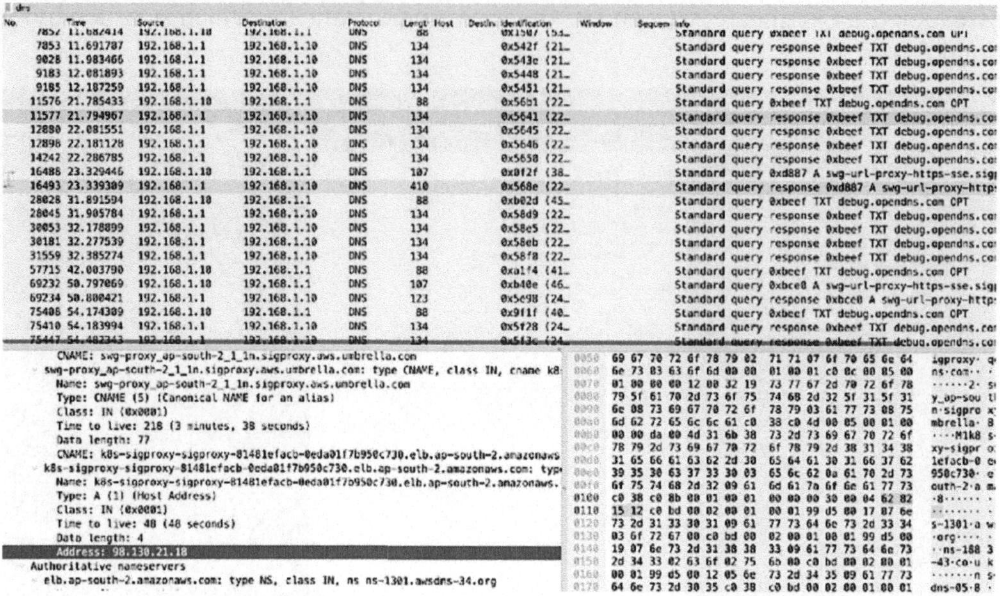

Figure 4.23: *DNS Response IP Address for the DNS Query*

Let us filter the capture with IP address **98.130.21.18**, and we see the following output:

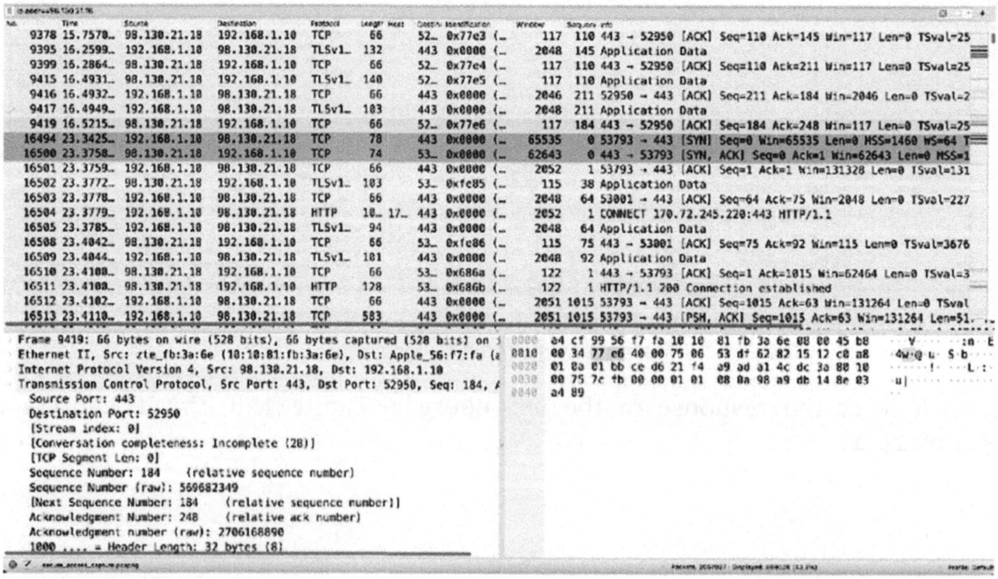

Figure 4.24: *Filtering the Wireshark Trace by the DNS Server IP Address*

As we see, there is an HTTP connect request to **170.72.245.220**, which is the actual application IP address. Here, the traffic was initiated to Webex.com. This is called an Explicit proxy mode, where all the traffic is tunneled into the proxy, and then the proxy makes a connection request. We can see the HTTP connect is successful, and then the proxy forwards all the traffic to the actual application traffic by enforcing all the rules that are configured. This is one of the fundamental differences between the firewall and the proxy. In firewall captures, we did not see HTTP connect mode, but in proxy, it tunnels all the traffic. The other difference is that the firewall forwards the user traffic to the actual application, while in an explicit proxy, it is the proxy that interacts with the actual application. In summary, with a proxy, there are two connections: one between the user machine and the proxy, and the other between the proxy and the application server. One of the most fundamental difference in Proxy processing the traffic, is that it creates two connections one from the client to the Proxy and the other from the Proxy to the Application.

Conclusion

We started with the essential components of an Enterprise Network. We looked at the traffic flow across the Network by applying captures at several hops. We also understood the Network Infrastructure of AWS, where the Lab was hosted. We then looked at the Zero Trust Architecture, where an agent was deployed on the end machine, and how the traffic was secured. One major difference to note with Zero Trust Architecture is that with the user roaming, that is, whether in the Enterprise Network or Outside Enterprise Network, the same security controls get applied. The next chapter is on Wireshark.

CHAPTER 5

Introduction to Wireshark

Introduction

This chapter moves deeper into using Wireshark skills in analyzing the network traffic and will also practically show a **Covert Channel** attack. This chapter looks into the essential attributes of Wireshark, which would help in understanding the traffic patterns for different protocols.

Structure

In this chapter, we will cover the following topics:

- Understanding Wireshark attributes
- Filtering in Wireshark
- Exporting Packets in Wireshark
- Covert Channel Attack
- Types of Covert Channel Attack
- Analyzing Covert Channel Attack in Wireshark

Understanding Wireshark attributes

Before analyzing traffic on Wireshark, it needs data. As we see in different programming languages, it accepts input on which the programming algorithm runs and provides an output. Similarly, Wireshark needs an input on which it can capture traffic and provide us with data for different OSI layers, which we studied in previous chapters. Most importantly the Wireshark captures the traffic at the Physical layer. Wireshark can capture the traffic in real time.

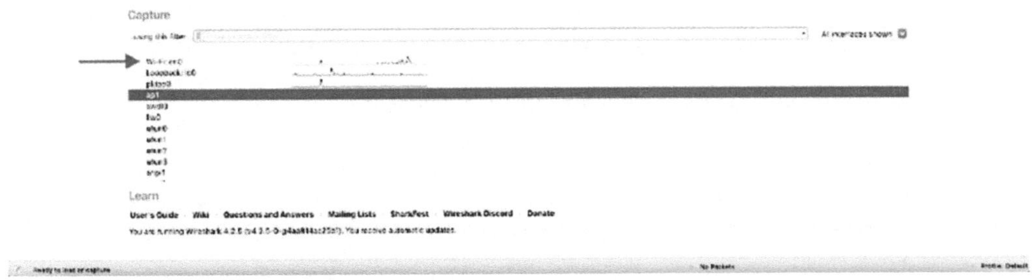

Figure 5.1: *Wireshark - It shows the capture*

Figure 5.1 shows when you launch Wireshark. It shows the capture points in the form of different interfaces from where the traffic can be shown on Wireshark.

The first interface is the Wifi interface where the machine is connected.

Since a Mac is being used, we can verify on the CLI whether it is the Wi-Fi interface.

```
en0: flags=8863<UP,BROADCAST,SMART,RUNNING,SIMPLEX,MULTICAST> mtu 1500
    options=6460<TSO4,TSO6,CHANNEL_IO,PARTIAL_CSUM,ZEROINVERT_CSUM>
    ether 6e:71:b5:79:39:35
    inet6 fe80::1804:d589:29b9:1d72%en0 prefixlen 64 secured scopeid
    0xe
    inet 192.168.1.4 netmask 0xffffff00 broadcast 192.168.1.255
    nd6 options=201<PERFORMNUD,DAD>
    media: autoselect
    status: active
```

It can be seen that the IP address of this interface is **`192.168.1.4`**.

What are the other Interfaces?

The second interface is **`Loopback lo0`**

```
lo0: flags=8049<UP,LOOPBACK,RUNNING,MULTICAST> mtu 16384
    options=1203<RXCSUM,TXCSUM,TXSTATUS,SW_TIMESTAMP>
    inet 127.0.0.1 netmask 0xff000000
    inet6 ::1 prefixlen 128
    inet6 fe80::1%lo0 prefixlen 64 scopeid 0x1
    nd6 options=201<PERFORMNUD,DAD>
```

This interface is like the virtual interface, which would be available on all the endpoints. The other interface is ap1, which would be used if the machine is being used as the Access Point.

```
ap1: flags=8863<UP,BROADCAST,SMART,RUNNING,SIMPLEX,MULTICAST> mtu 1500
    options=6460<TSO4,TSO6,CHANNEL_IO,PARTIAL_CSUM,ZEROINVERT_CSUM>
    ether 5e:40:11:1d:3b:f9
    nd6 options=201<PERFORMNUD,DAD>
```

```
media: autoselect (none)
status: inactive
```

How do we select the Interface and start capturing the data?

Select the interface you want to use and double-click it.

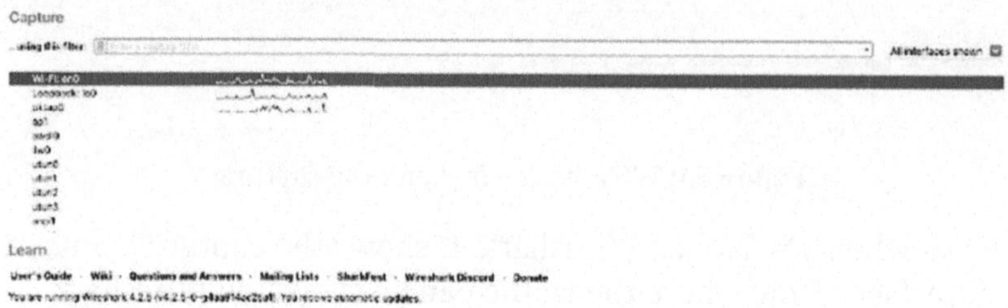

Figure 5.2: *Selecting the Interface on Wireshark to start Capture*

Once the Wi-Fi interface is selected, it captures the traffic in real time as follows:

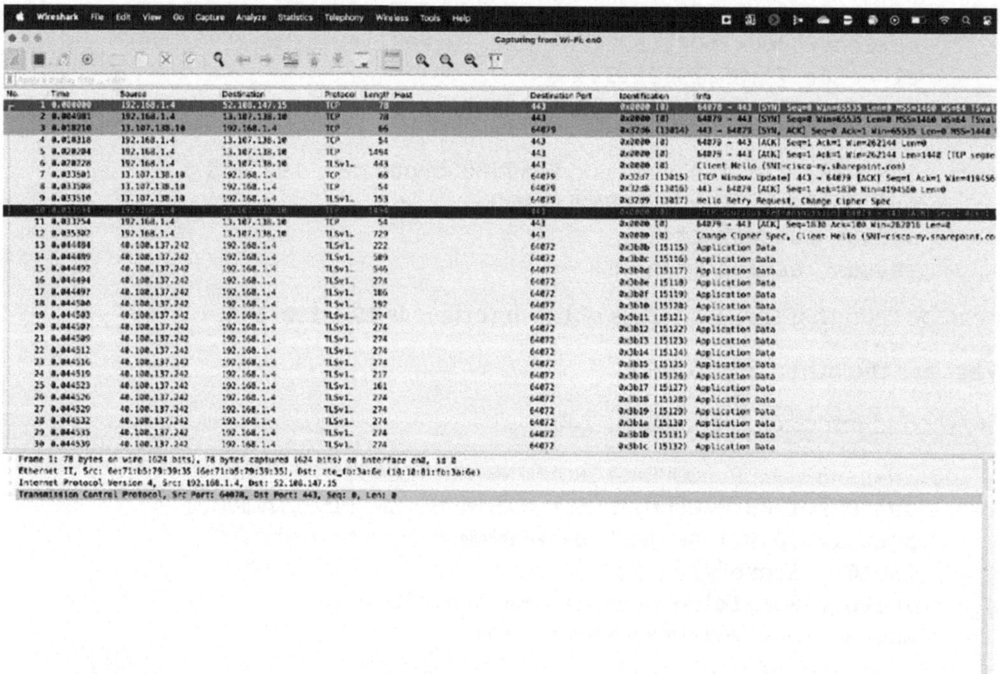

Figure 5.3: *Traffic being captured shown on the Interface selected in the Wireshark*

On the top left, there are 3 important icons:

This is to start the capture in real time

This is to stop the capture

This is to restart the capture. Similar to refresh, where the previous capture points would be lost

One can also select the default interface for the capture shown as follows. `Wireshark` > `Preferences` > `Capture`

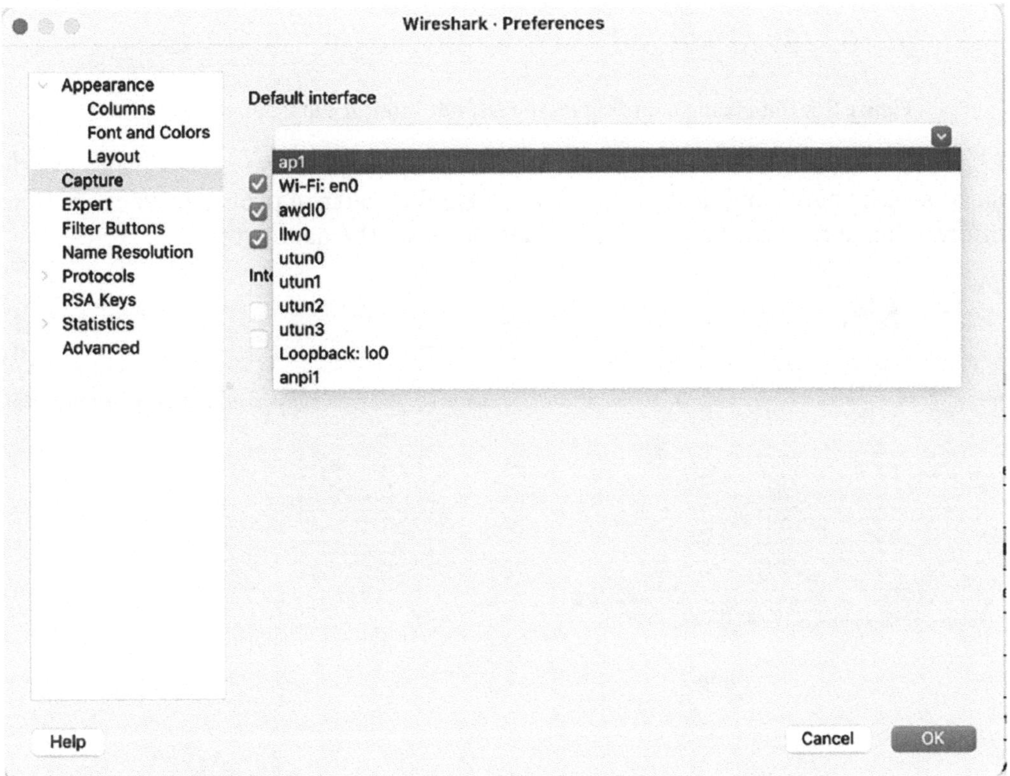

Figure 5.4: *Configuring the Default Interface of Machine in Wireshark to capture*

The following diagram shows how the data is being shown on Wireshark:

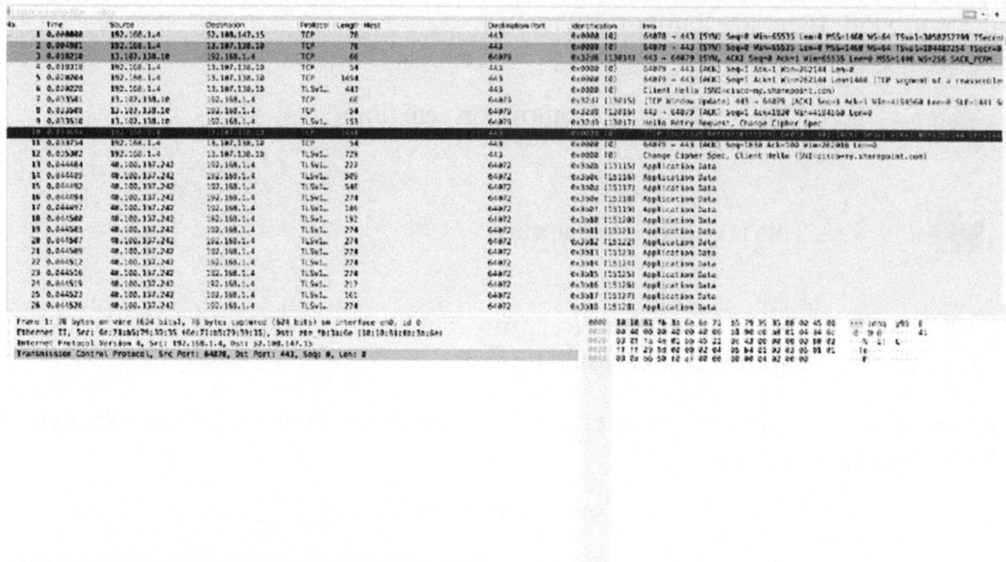

Figure 5.5: *Data being captured on the Default Interface which was configured*

If one can visualize, there are 3 panes as seen in *Figure* 5.5. The first pane shows the packets with source and destination IP and also the **Layer 4** protocol. **Pane 2** shows different headers at the OSI layer, and **pane 3** shows the data bytes.

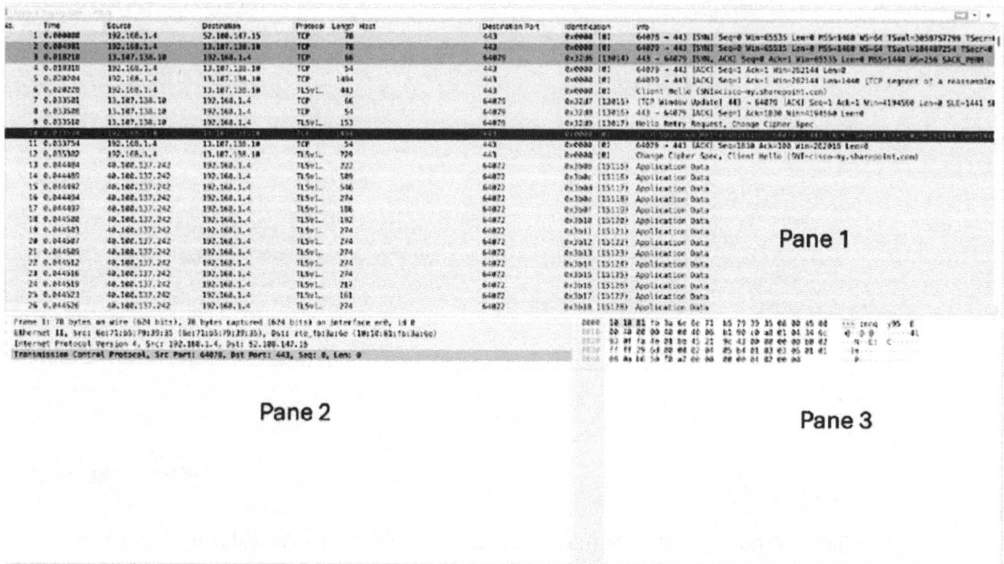

Figure 5.6: *Default Layout of the Wireshark Pane*

Can this visualization of the panes be modified? The answer is yes.

Depending on the OS, the options would change. In MAC, it is under **`Wireshark`** > **`Preferences`** > **`Appearance`** > **`Layout`**.

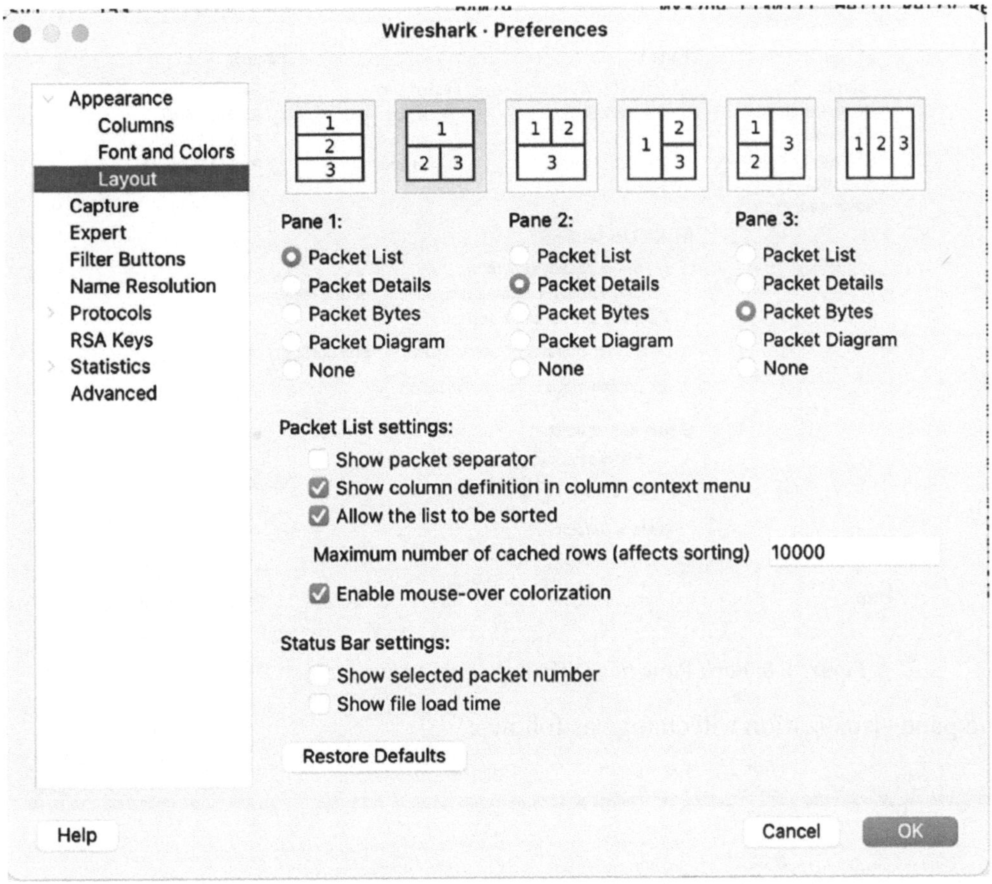

Figure 5.7: *Modifying the Layout Pane of Wireshark*

As can be seen, all Panes list different data that can be shown. **`Pane 1`** shows a list of all packets with all the headers. **`Pane 2`** shows packet details under each header, while **`Pane 3`** shows the data in bytes under the TCP/UDP header. Let us try to select the Packet diagram for Pane 3.

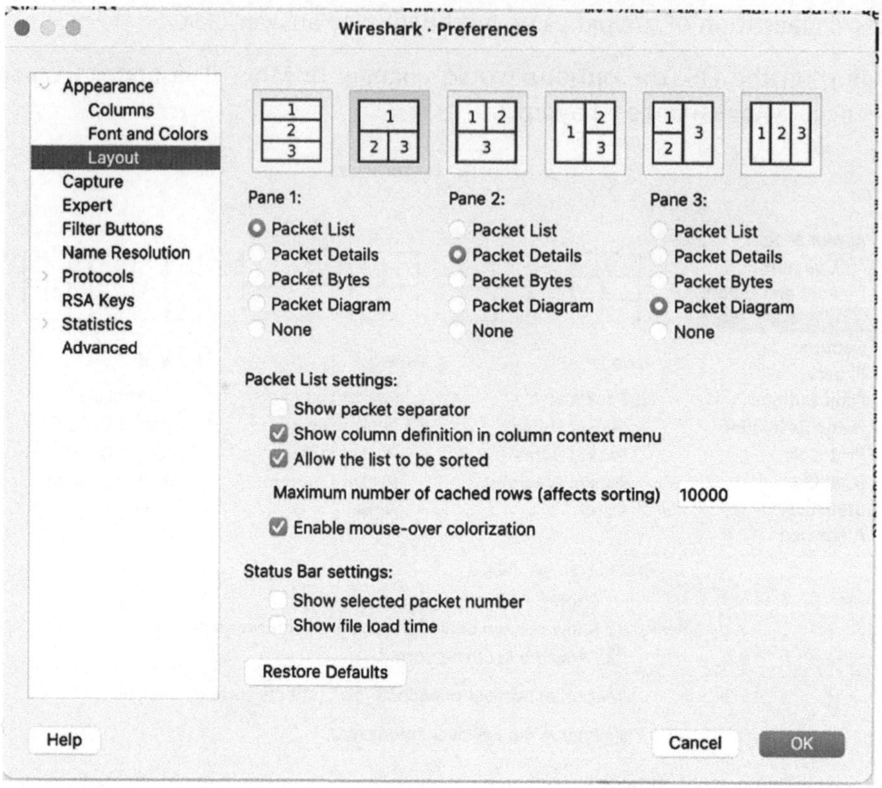

Figure 5.8: *Each Pane has Different Options from which We can select*

The pane visualization will change as follows:

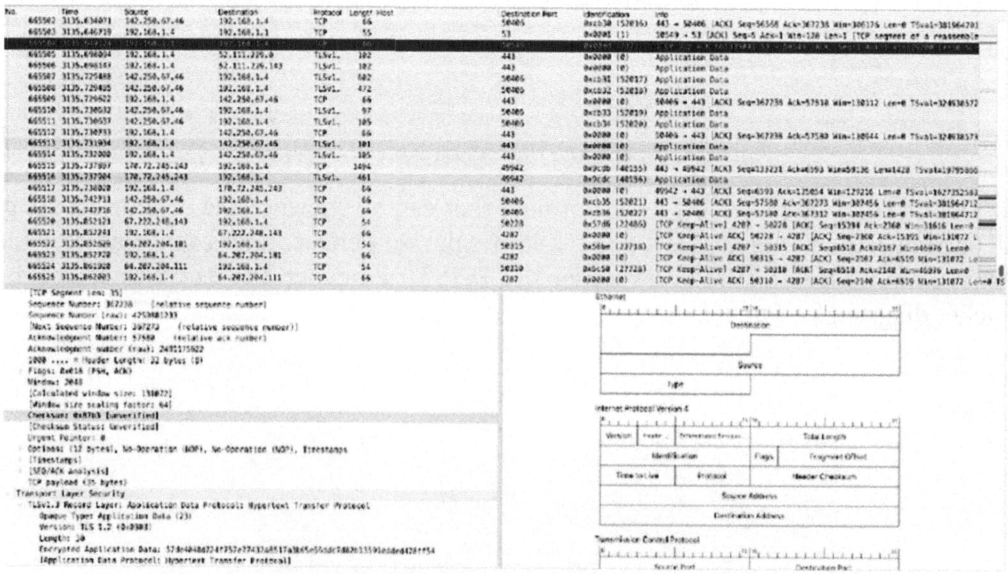

Figure 5.9: *Wireshark Layout after the Default Layout is being modified*

One can hover on the Packet diagram Pane by clicking the **`Source Port`**, for example, which would then show the Source port information in the Packet header in **`Pane 2`**, as follows:

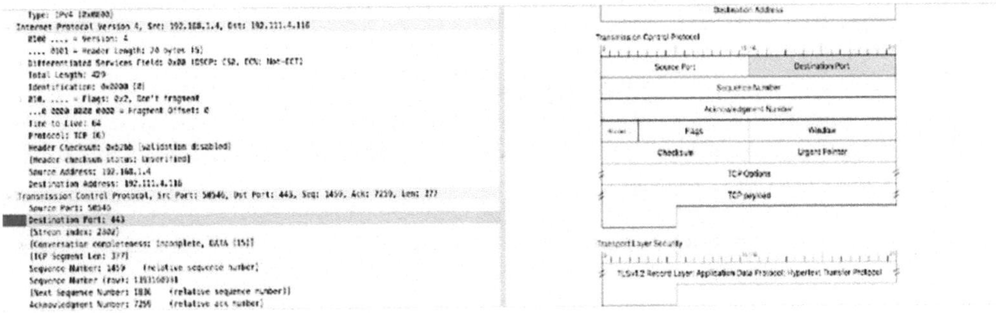

Figure 5.10: *Hovering over the Destination Port in Pane 3 shows the value of Destination Port in Pane 2*

Looking at the Wireshark Panes, we can see there are different color formats for different packets. As seen in *Figure* 5.11, some packets are shown in **red**. If we look closely, the packets in red **`are TCP Spurious Retransmission`** and **`TCP Dup ACK`**.

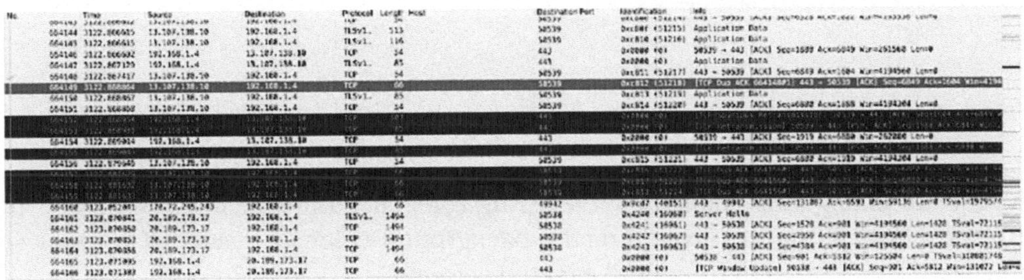

Figure 5.11: *Visualizing the Wireshark Traces*

We can modify the coloring rules under **`View`** > **`Coloring Rules`**

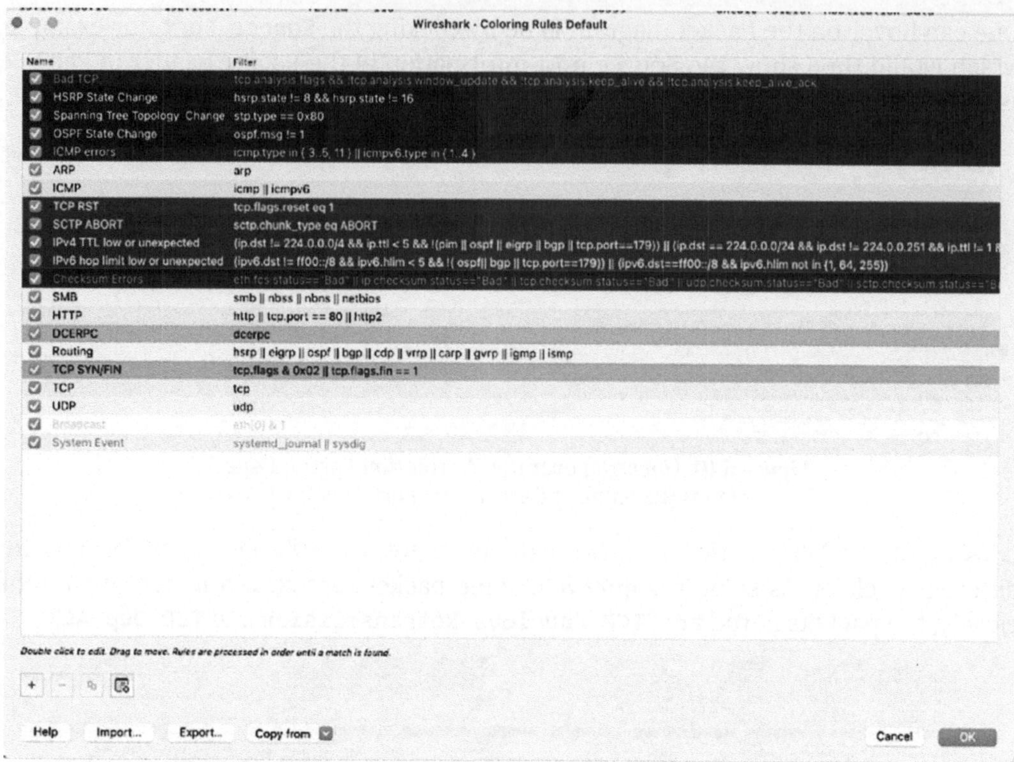

Figure 5.12: *One can also modify the Coloring Rules in Wireshark*

In order to change the color for the existing rule, click the specific rule name **"TCP RST"** and change the foreground or the background color as needed. The rules are processed from top to bottom until a match is found.

Let us create a new rule for source port **50539**.

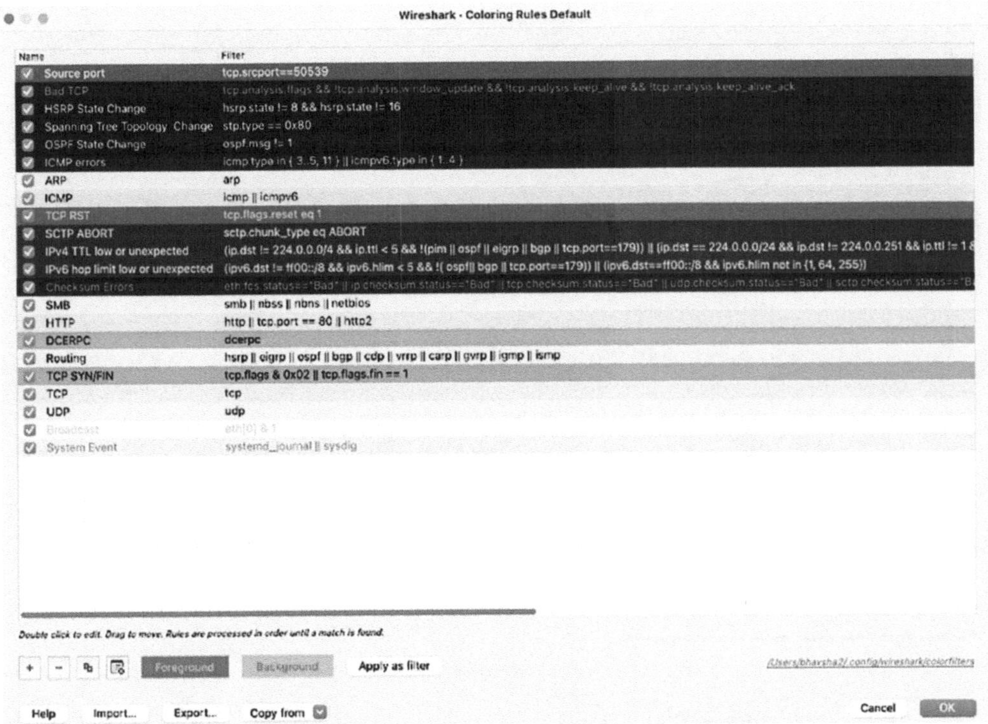

Figure 5.13: *Specific Attributes of OSI Layer can be modified by changing Foreground and Background Color*

The rule name is **`Source port`**, and the Filter is **`tcp.srcport==50539`**.

The Foreground color is set to **Purple,** and the Background color is set to **Green.**

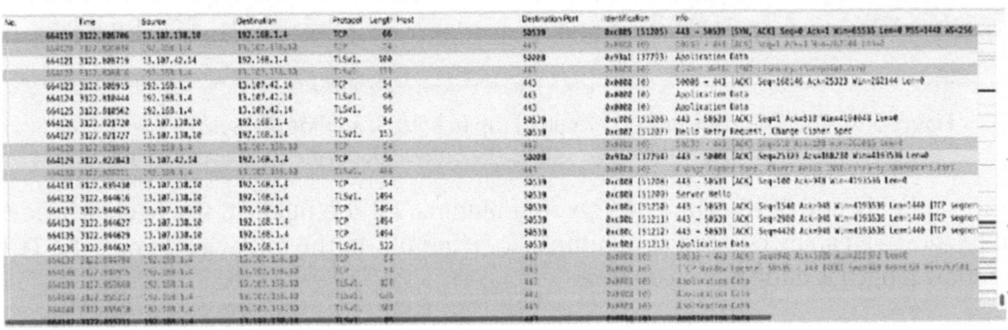

Figure 5.14: *Source Port Field was changed with the Foreground and Background Color changed*

As can be seen, the first rule that hits is the one that we created. Also, the TCP Spurious Retransmission is seen as green as it is for port **`50539`**.

If we change the order of the new rule, which is created at the bottom, then we see the same packet for source port **`50539`** is seen as red, as it processes the **`TCP spurious retransmission`** coloring rule and marks the packet in **red**.

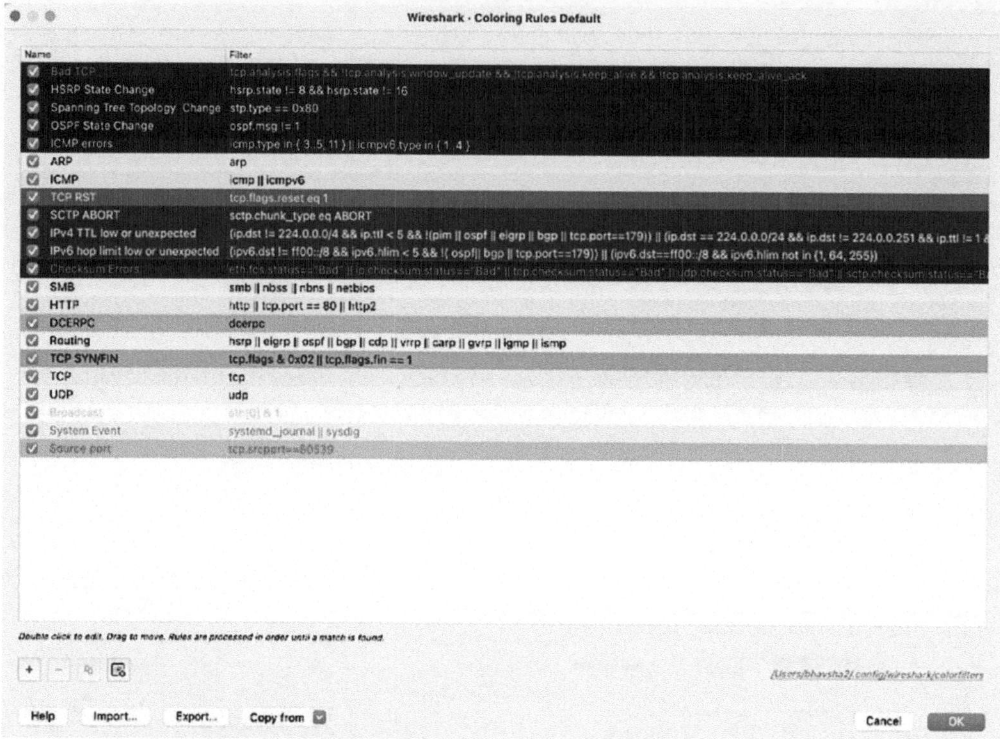

Figure 5.15: *Changing the Order of the Rule is also Possible*

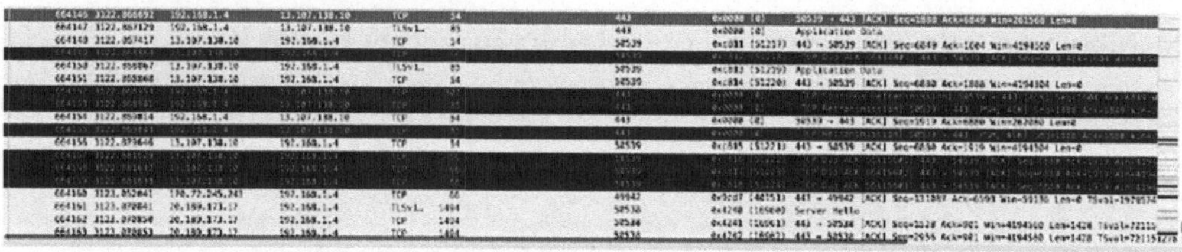

Figure 5.16: *The Coloring rule gets applied top to bottom so that the Source port which was Green earlier now shows red as the Source port rule is at the bottom*

Wireshark also gives the ability to create columns. All the fields in the packet header of IP and TCP can be created as columns. For example, in the following figure, the TCP window length is added as a column:

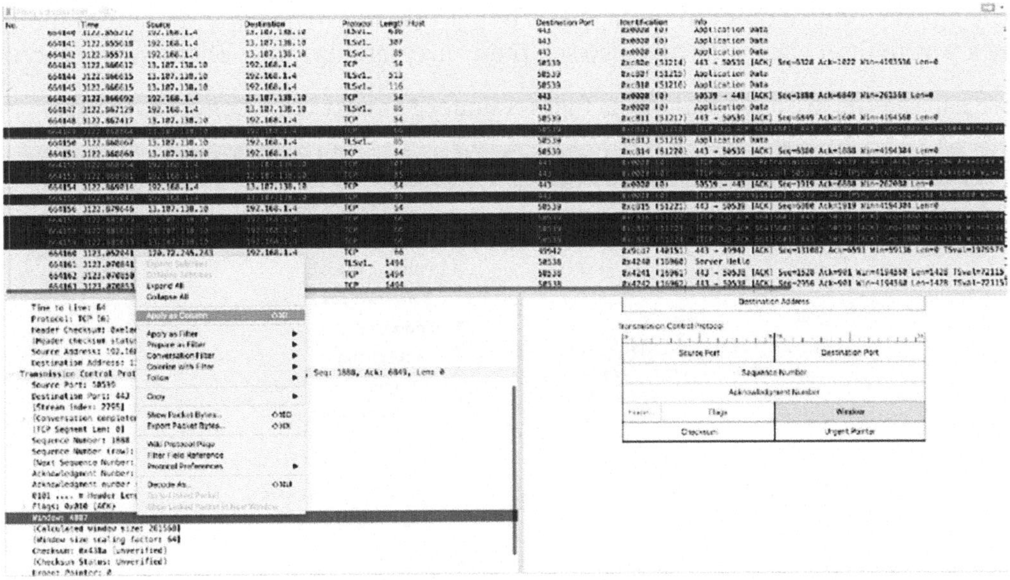

Figure 5.17: *Selecting the Appropriate TCP Field and applying as Column. Here the Window Length is selected as Column*

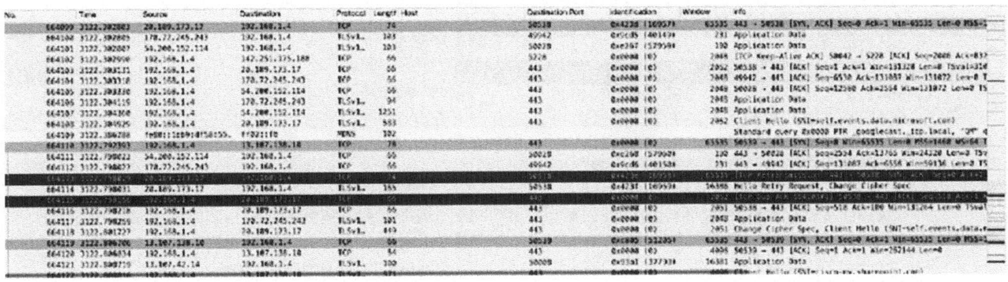

Figure 5.18: *Window Length now appears as a Column in Wireshark*

Similarly, if any column is not needed, it can also be removed. In the following example, the Identification column is being removed:

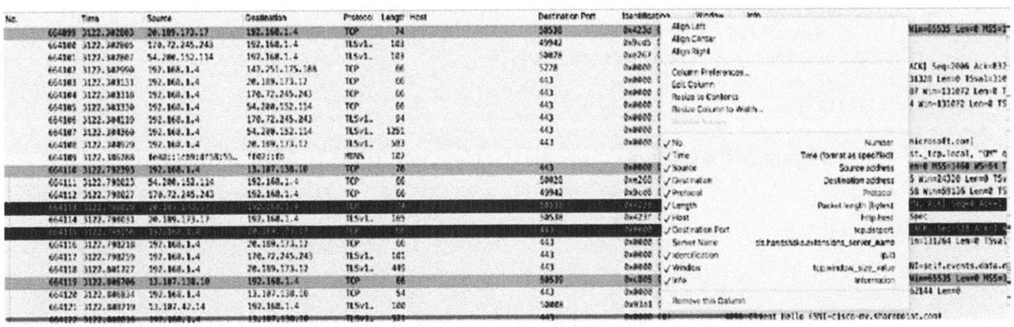

Figure 5.19: *Certain Columns can also be removed by performing a Right Click*

The amount of data that can be captured by Wireshark can be huge, and there should be a way to filter the traffic and also see the conversations that were being captured.

We can see these Conversations as follows under **Statistics** > **Conversations**.

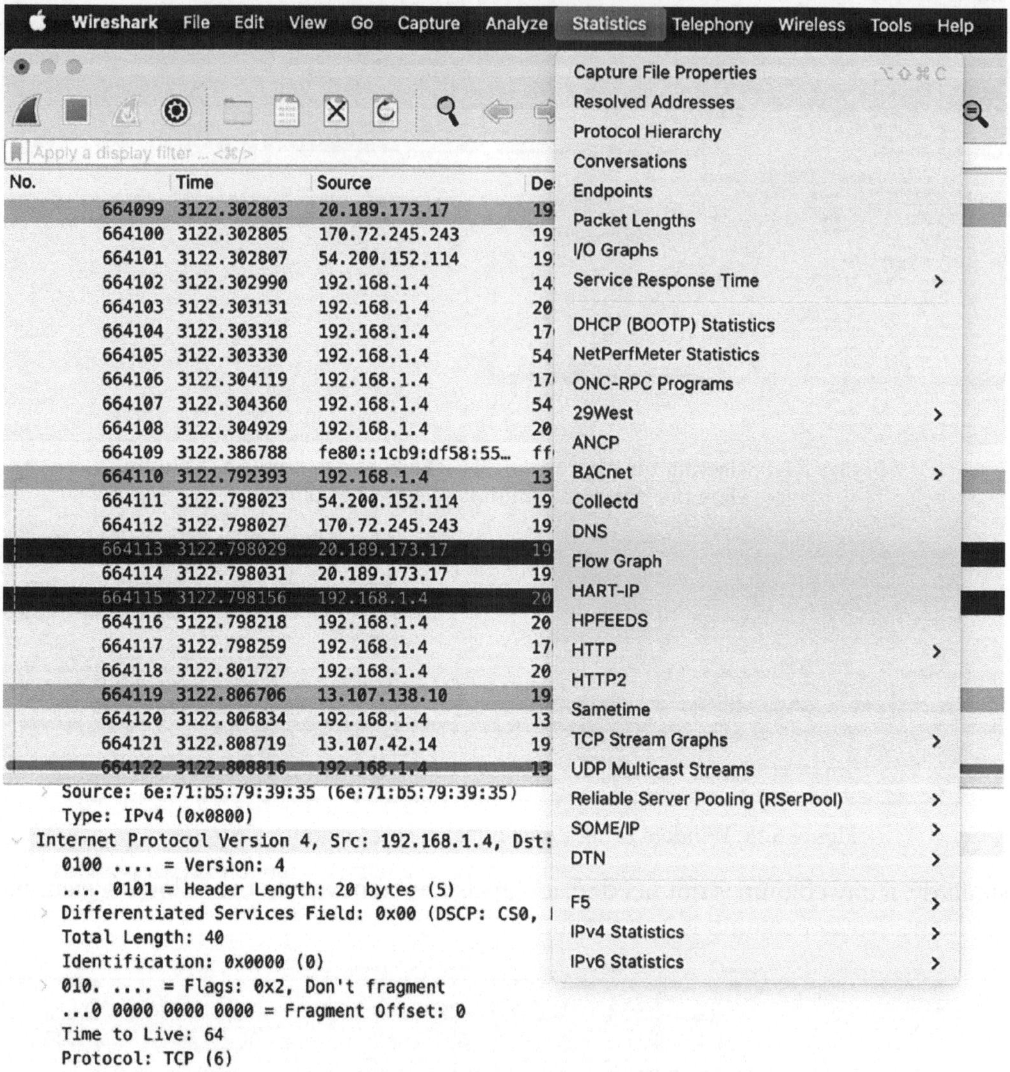

Figure 5.20: *Option to see all the Conversations in Wireshark*

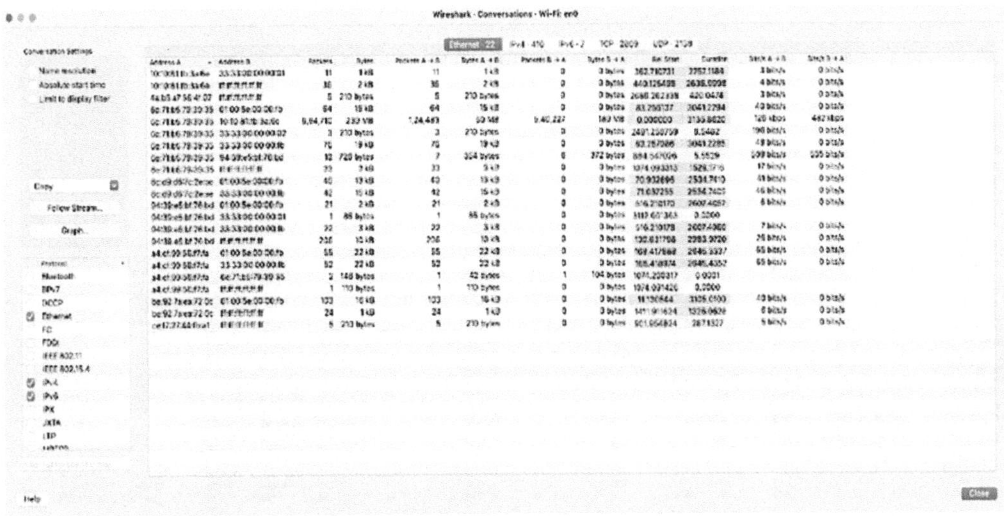

Figure 5.21: *Default Page of the Conversation Summary Pane*

The Conversation summary gives the statistics for all the packets that were being captured. As can be seen, it gives details on Ethernet frames, IPv4/IPv6 addresses, and also transport layer protocols such as TCP and UDP.

Looking at the IPv4 details, it captures all the IP addresses as part of the Conversation. As can be seen, it shows different IP pairs and also the amount of bytes/packets that were being transferred.

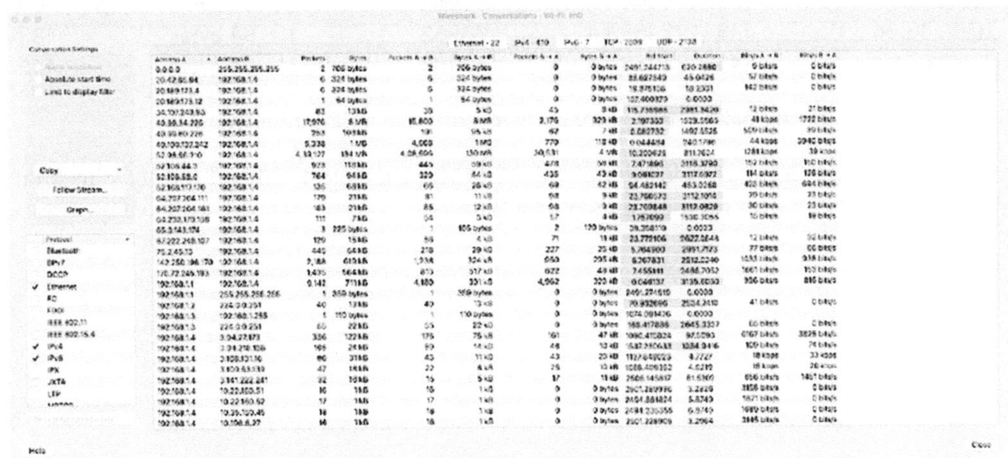

Figure 5.22: *IPV4 Tab in the Conversation Summary Pane*

The Conversation Summary pane also has a **`TCP tab`**, which shows the information at the **`TCP layer`**, such as the port on which the communication is happening.

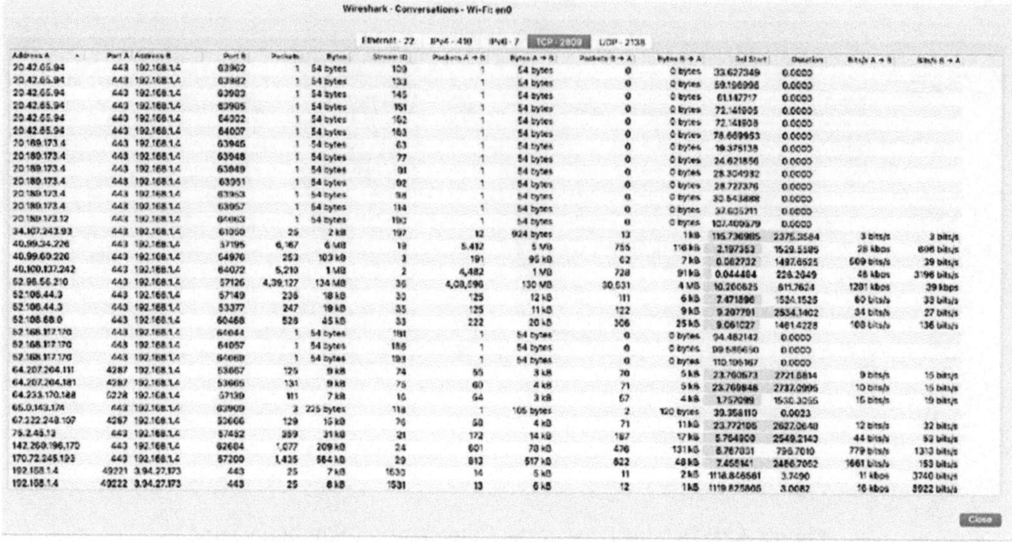

Figure 5.23: *TCP Tab in the Conversation Summary Pane*

One of the interesting fields in the TCP pane of Conversation Summary is Stream ID. Wireshark allocates a unique stream ID starting from 0 to each unique conversation. The way it assigns the stream ID is for every unique source IP, destination IP, source port, destination port, and protocol, such as TCP or UDP.

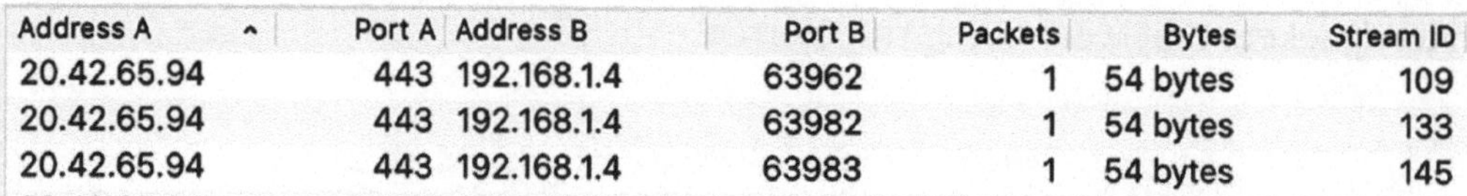

Address A	Port A	Address B	Port B	Packets	Bytes	Stream ID
20.42.65.94	443	192.168.1.4	63962	1	54 bytes	109
20.42.65.94	443	192.168.1.4	63982	1	54 bytes	133
20.42.65.94	443	192.168.1.4	63983	1	54 bytes	145

Figure 5.24: *Unique Stream Id for different TCP Connections*

If we look at the Wireshark UI, we can see that the Custom fields added by Wireshark are marked as **"[]"** and termed as **`Stream Index`**.

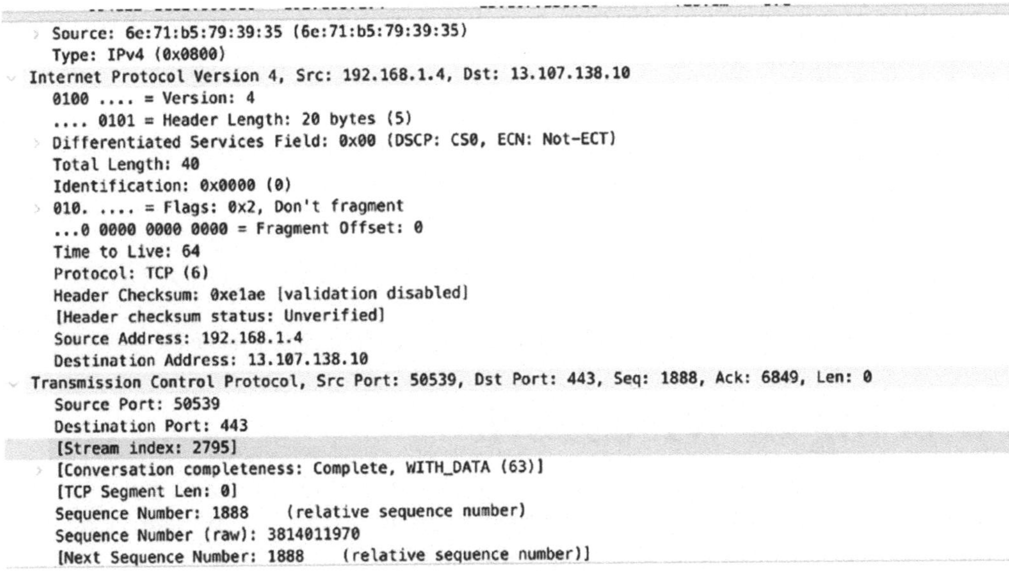

Figure 5.25: *Custom Fields added by Wireshark*

One other option Wireshark provides is TCP protocol preferences as follows:

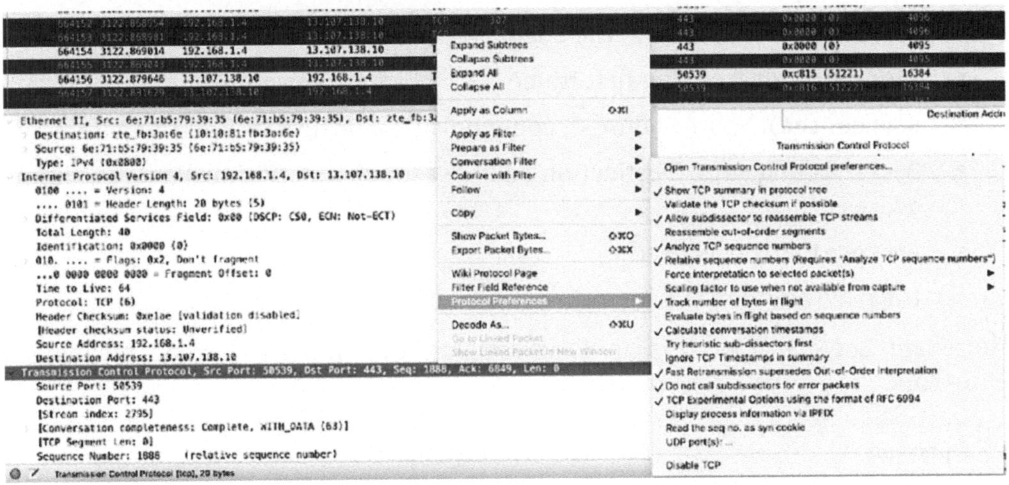

Figure 5.26: *Viewing the Protocol Preferences Options of TCP Layer*

One of the important fields that one would use in troubleshooting is "**Relative Sequence number**". As the name suggests, it is a relative that is calculated by Wireshark. As we learnt in previous chapters, TCP conversation is tracked by the **Sequence** and **Acknowledgement** numbers. With the relative sequence number, Wireshark assigns the first connection as sequence number **0**, and then everything starts getting incremented by 1. The relative sequence number can be seen as follows.

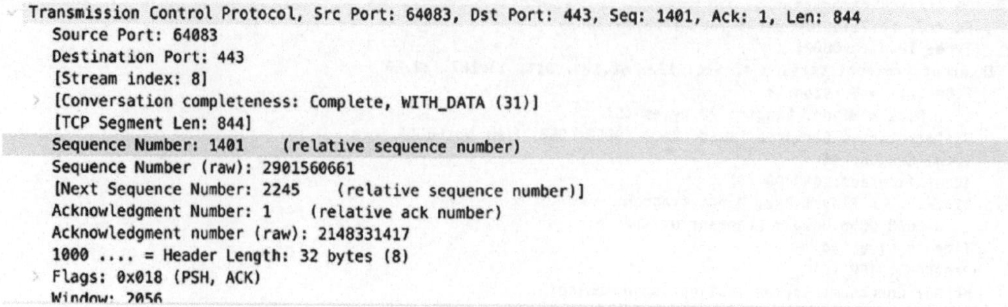

Figure 5.27: *It shows TCP Relative Sequence Number is enabled*

Filtering in Wireshark

We saw how Wireshark captures the data on the Network Interface. For any large amount of data, there should be some filters to analyze the data. Wireshark also has certain filters to be applied to look at specific data.

Let us try to understand these filters, which are mentioned as packet filters.

By default, Wireshark has default columns as follows:

- `No.`: Frame Number from the beginning of packet capture
- `Time`: Seconds from the first frame
- `Source(src)`: Source address, commonly IPv4 or IPv6 or Ethernet address
- `Destination(dst)`: Destination address, commonly IPv4 or IPv6 or Ethernet address
- `Protocol`: Protocol used
- `Length`: Length of the frame in bytes

There are Logical Operators in Programming that have the same meaning in Wireshark.

Operator	Description
and or &&	Logical AND
or or ||	Logical OR
xor or ^^	Logical XOR
not or !	Not(Negation)

Table 5.1: *Logical Operators and its Description*

Let us try to understand how to use these operators.

- `and or && ----- ip.src==192.168.1.4 and tcp.flags.fin==1`
- `or or || -------- ip.src==192.168.1.4 or ip.src==192.168.1.1`
- `Xor or ^^ ---- ip.src==192.168.1.4 xor ip.src==192.168.1.1`
- `Not or ! ------- not(ip.src==192.168.1.4)`

We would be applying these logical filters in the following text in Wireshark.

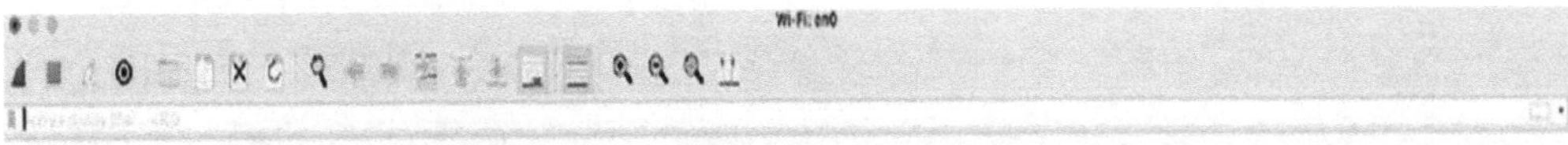

Figure 5.28: *Text Field in Wireshark where Filters would be entered*

As seen in the following figures, we have applied the filter for **`ip.src==192.168.1.4`**, where all the packets are displayed with source as **`192.168.1.4`**. The filter, which is applied in the form of **`ip.src==192.168.1.4`**, is called a filter expression.

ip.src==192.168.1.4

No.	Time	Source	Destination	Protocol
1	0.000000	192.168.1.4	52.108.147.15	TCP
2	0.004981	192.168.1.4	13.107.138.10	TCP
4	0.018318	192.168.1.4	13.107.138.10	TCP
5	0.020204	192.168.1.4	13.107.138.10	TCP
6	0.020228	192.168.1.4	13.107.138.10	TLSv1…
10	0.033694	192.168.1.4	13.107.138.10	TCP
11	0.033754	192.168.1.4	13.107.138.10	TCP
12	0.035302	192.168.1.4	13.107.138.10	TLSv1…
47	0.044938	192.168.1.4	40.100.137.242	TCP
80	0.046410	192.168.1.4	40.100.137.242	TCP
100	0.048320	192.168.1.4	40.100.137.242	TCP
115	0.050055	192.168.1.4	40.100.137.242	TCP
137	0.051643	192.168.1.4	13.107.138.10	TCP
138	0.051668	192.168.1.4	40.100.137.242	TCP
139	0.051757	192.168.1.4	13.107.138.10	TCP
160	0.053901	192.168.1.4	40.100.137.242	TCP
161	0.054059	192.168.1.4	13.107.138.10	TLSv1…
162	0.054312	192.168.1.4	13.107.138.10	TLSv1…
163	0.054678	192.168.1.4	13.107.138.10	TCP
164	0.054680	192.168.1.4	13.107.138.10	TCP
165	0.054689	192.168.1.4	13.107.138.10	TLSv1…
182	0.055155	192.168.1.4	40.100.137.242	TCP
184	0.055457	192.168.1.4	40.100.137.242	TCP
190	0.055714	192.168.1.4	40.100.137.242	TCP

Figure 5.29: *Filter to show All Packets whose Source IP is equal to 192.168.1.4*

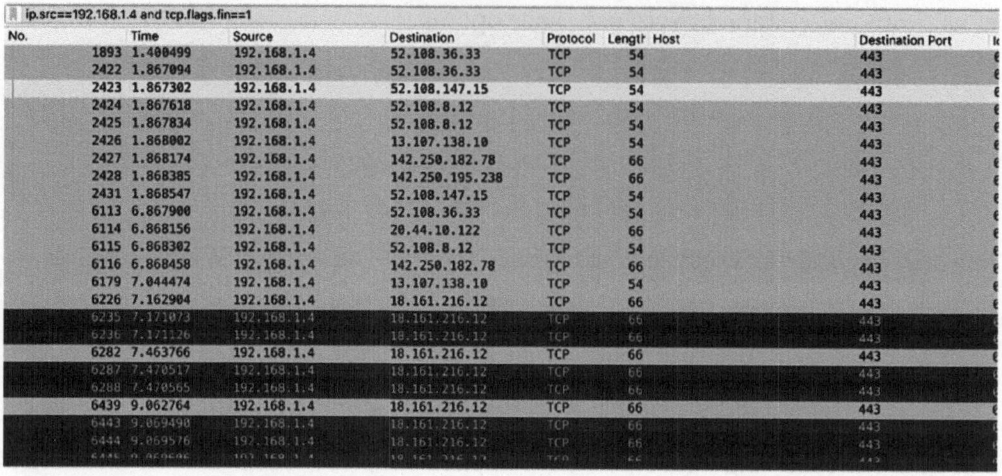

Figure 5.30: *Filter to show All Packets with Source IP equal to 192.168.1.4 and TCP Fin Flags*

If the Display filter expressions are not known, one can always look for specific data in Packet details and click **`Apply as filter`**, then click **`Selected`**.

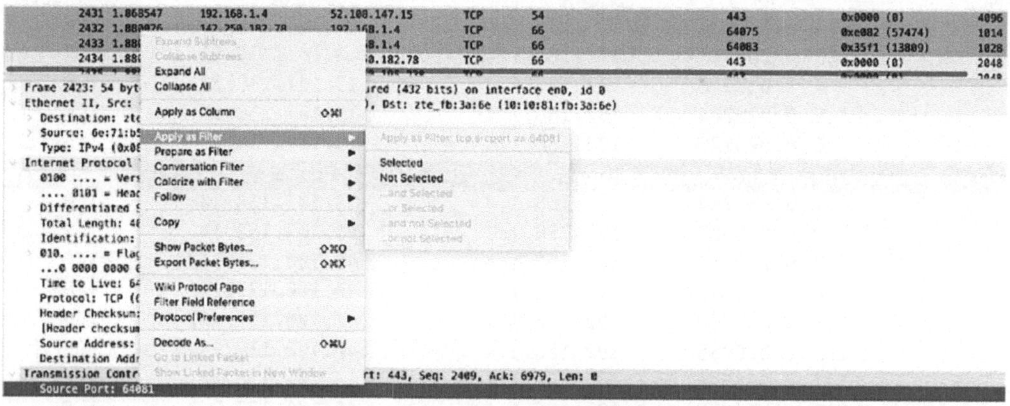

Figure 5.31: *Applying a Filter using the Options in the IP Header or TCP Header*

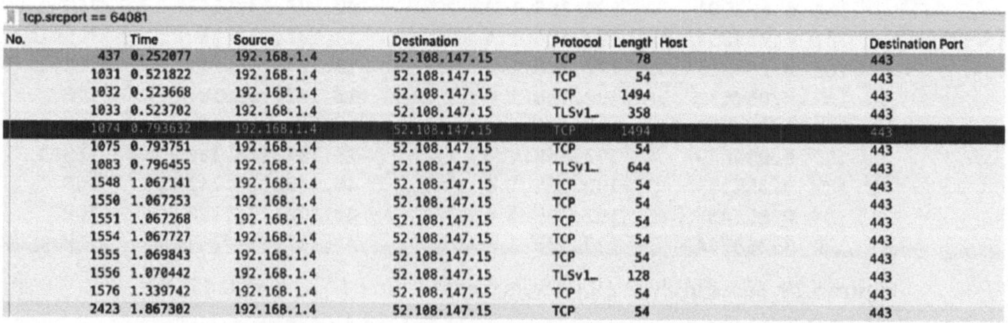

Figure 5.32: *Filter of tcp.srcport was created using Apply as Filter Option*

We can also look for the default filter expressions under **`Analyze`** > **`Display Filters`**.

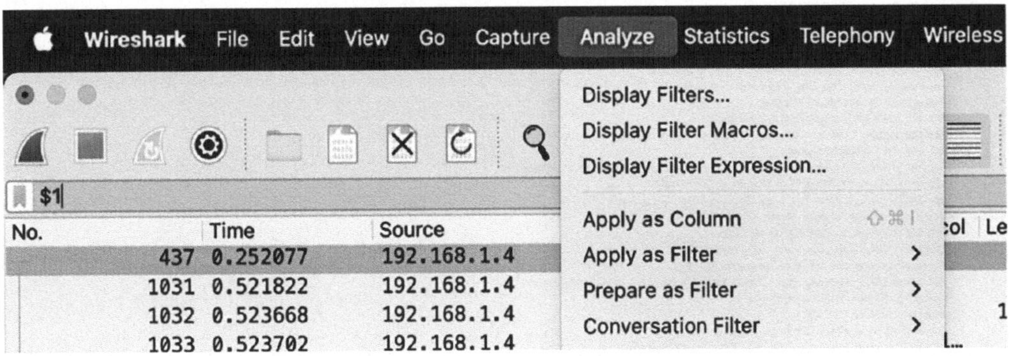

Figure 5.33: *Option for selecting Default Filter Expressions*

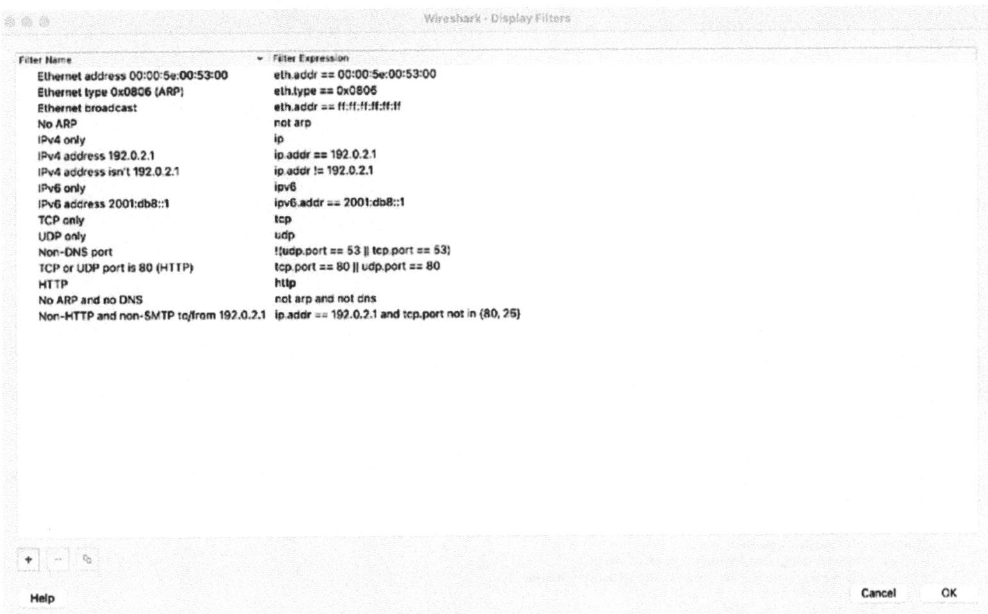

Figure 5.34: *Default Filter Expressions*

There is another option: **`Display Filter Expression`**.

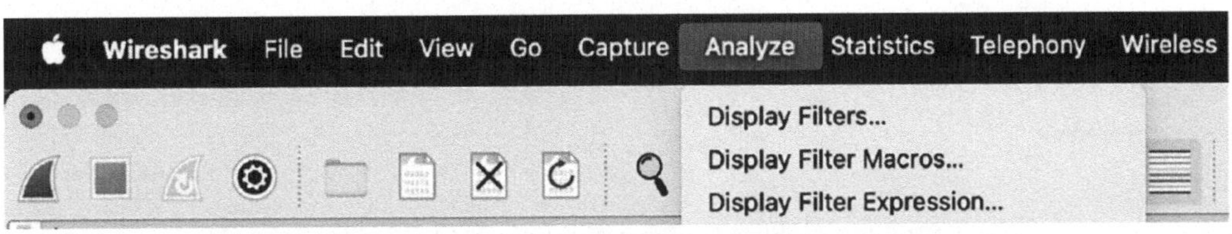

Figure 5.35: *Option to Select Display Filter Expression*

Here, one can see the filter expressions for all protocols. Let us look for TCP and IP.

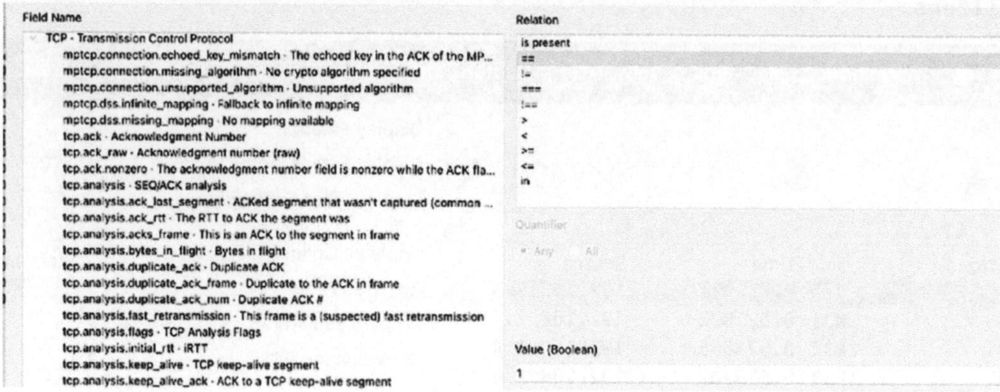

Figure 5.36: *Wireshark Pane shows all the Filter Names for Different Fields*

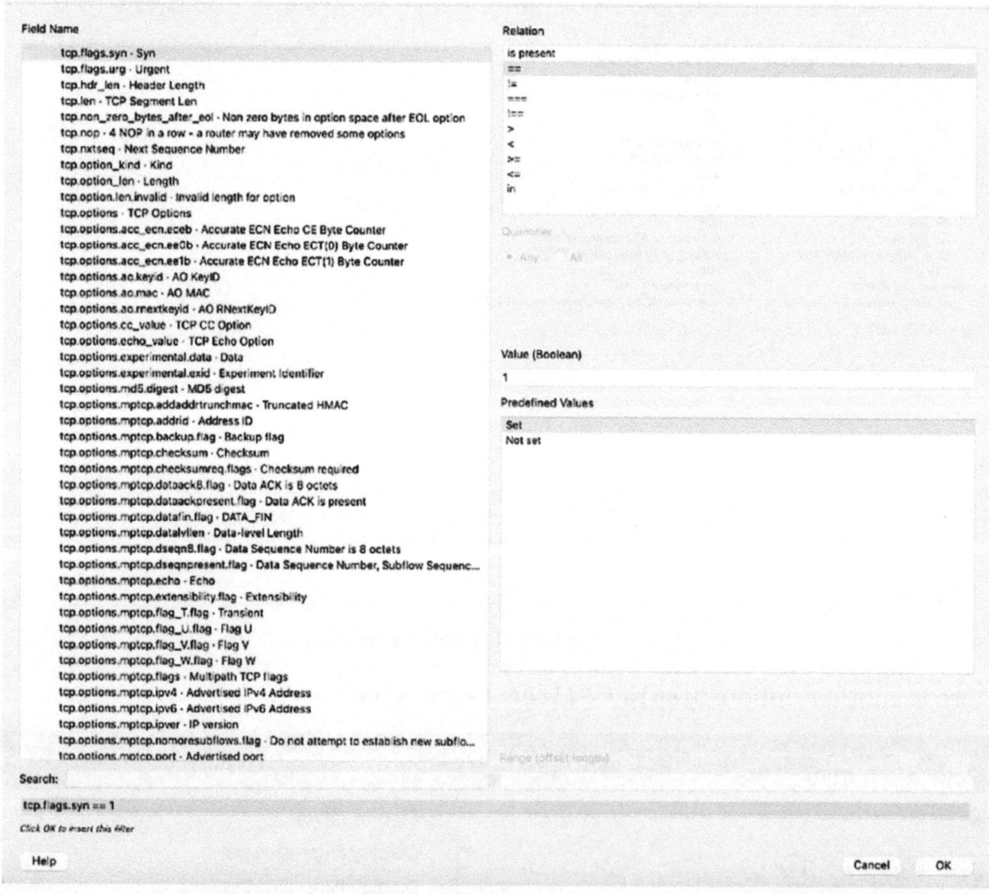

Figure 5.37: *Filter looking for Packets where TCP SYN Flag is enabled*

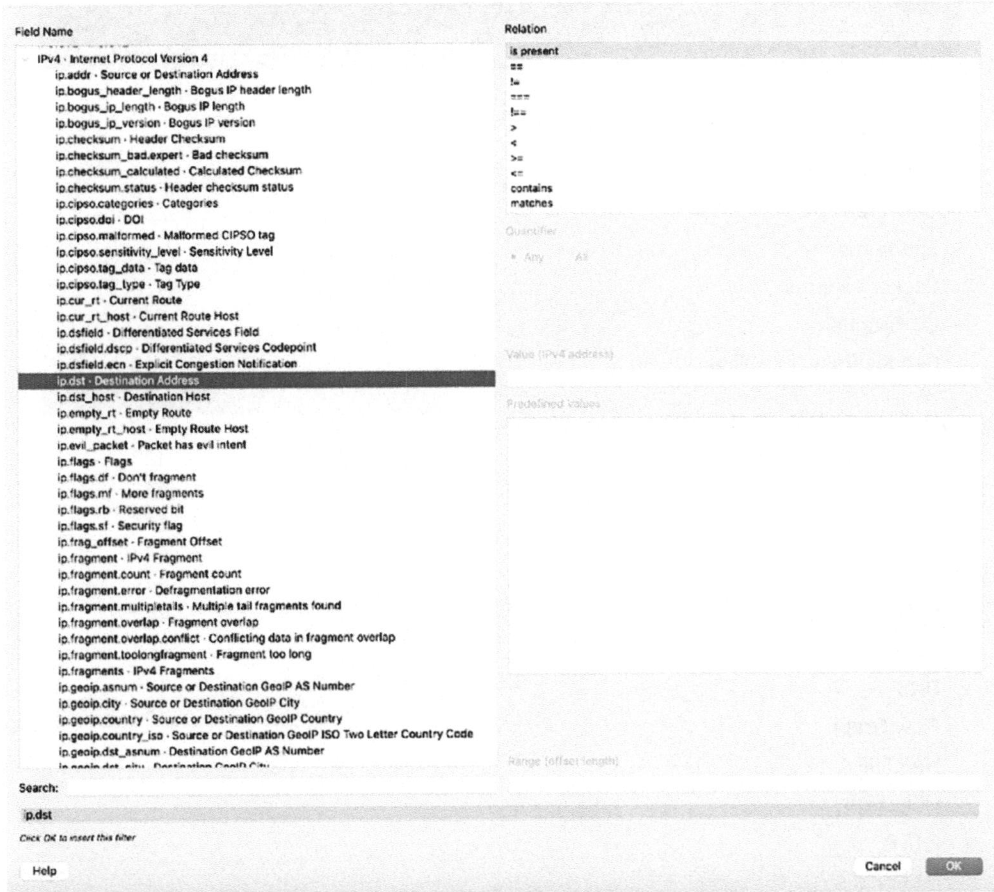

Figure 5.38: *Using Filter to check for all Destination Addresses filed in Wireshark Trace*

Along with the expression, we can also use the logical operator that we have learnt earlier.

Along with the Conversation Summary, we can also look for all IPv4 addresses under **`Statistics`** > **`IPv4 address`** > **`All Addresses`**.

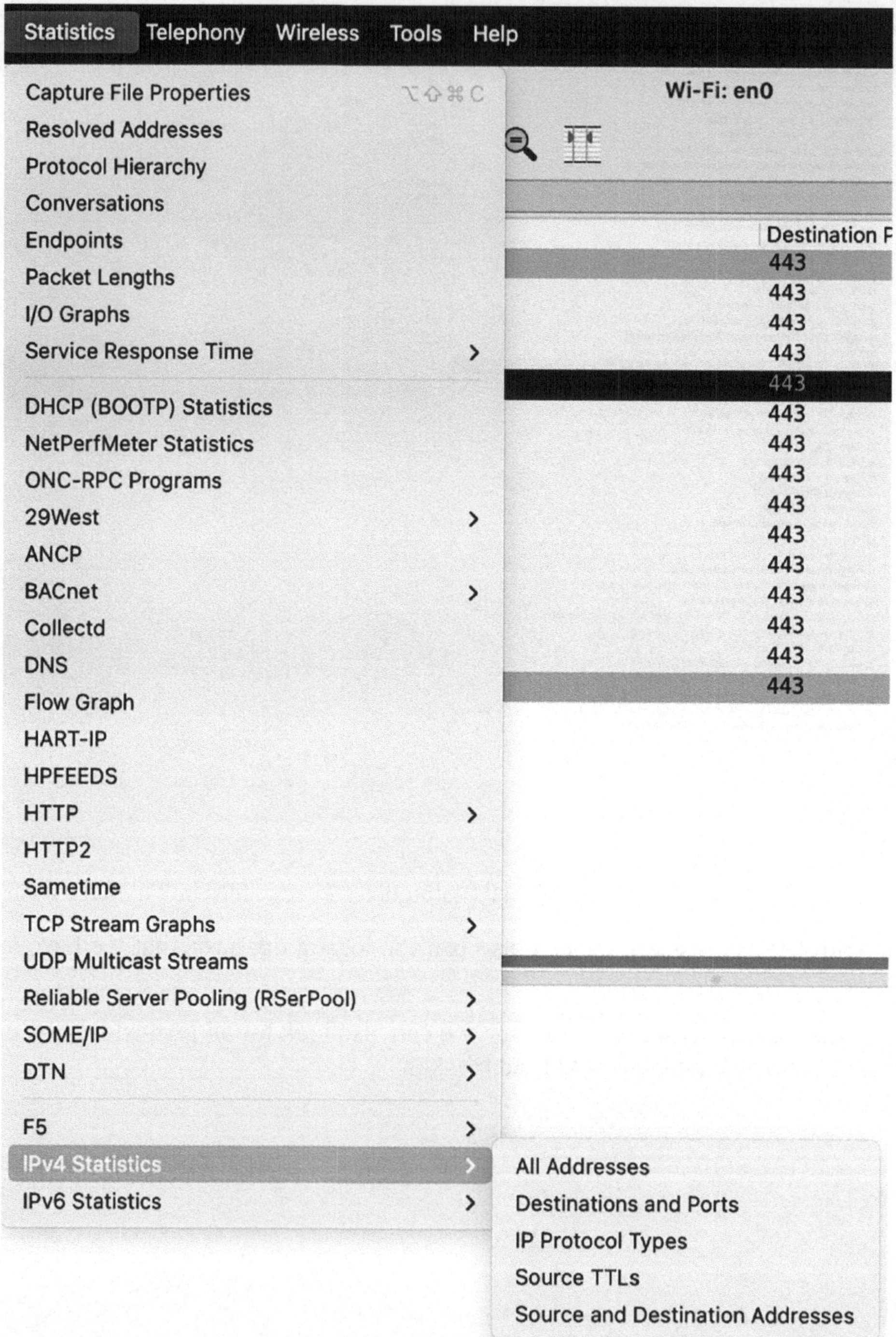

Figure 5.39: *Option to get a Quick Overview of All Addresses in the Wireshark Trace*

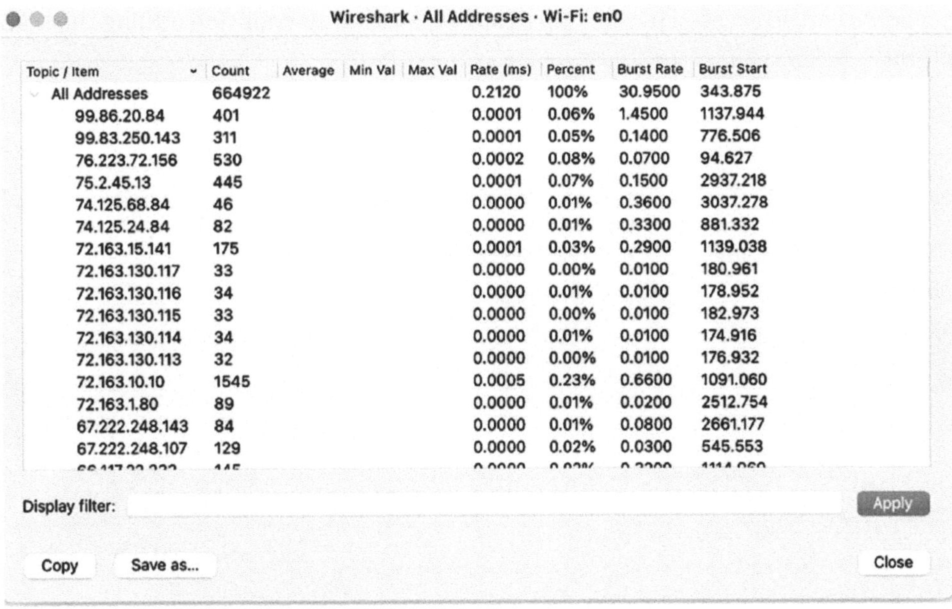

Topic / Item	Count	Average	Min Val	Max Val	Rate (ms)	Percent	Burst Rate	Burst Start
All Addresses	664922				0.2120	100%	30.9500	343.875
99.86.20.84	401				0.0001	0.06%	1.4500	1137.944
99.83.250.143	311				0.0001	0.05%	0.1400	776.506
76.223.72.156	530				0.0002	0.08%	0.0700	94.627
75.2.45.13	445				0.0001	0.07%	0.1500	2937.218
74.125.68.84	46				0.0000	0.01%	0.3600	3037.278
74.125.24.84	82				0.0000	0.01%	0.3300	881.332
72.163.15.141	175				0.0001	0.03%	0.2900	1139.038
72.163.130.117	33				0.0000	0.00%	0.0100	180.961
72.163.130.116	34				0.0000	0.01%	0.0100	178.952
72.163.130.115	33				0.0000	0.00%	0.0100	182.973
72.163.130.114	34				0.0000	0.01%	0.0100	174.916
72.163.130.113	32				0.0000	0.00%	0.0100	176.932
72.163.10.10	1545				0.0005	0.23%	0.6600	1091.060
72.163.1.80	89				0.0000	0.01%	0.0200	2512.754
67.222.248.143	84				0.0000	0.01%	0.0800	2661.177
67.222.248.107	129				0.0000	0.02%	0.0300	545.553

Figure 5.40: *View of All Addresses in the Wireshark Trace*

As seen, it only shows the IP address details and not any protocols such as TCP or UDP.

Wireshark also gives an option to define macros. Macros are similar to the logic we write in programming languages to accept inputs. In Wireshark, these macros help in replacing complex filters with shortcuts.

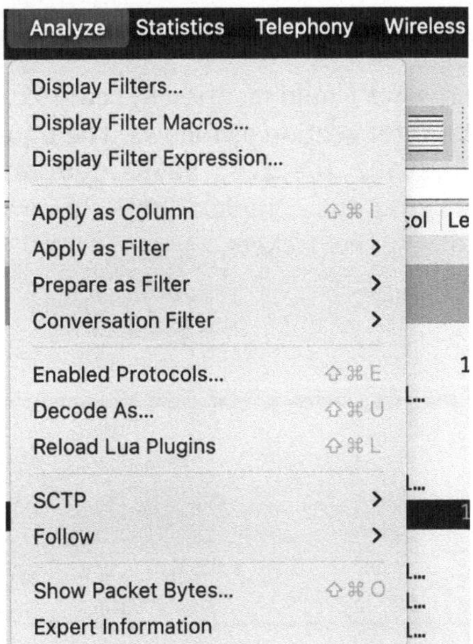

Figure 5.41: *Option to select Display Filter Macros*

The macros can be created by clicking **`Display Filter Macros`** and adding the macros required.

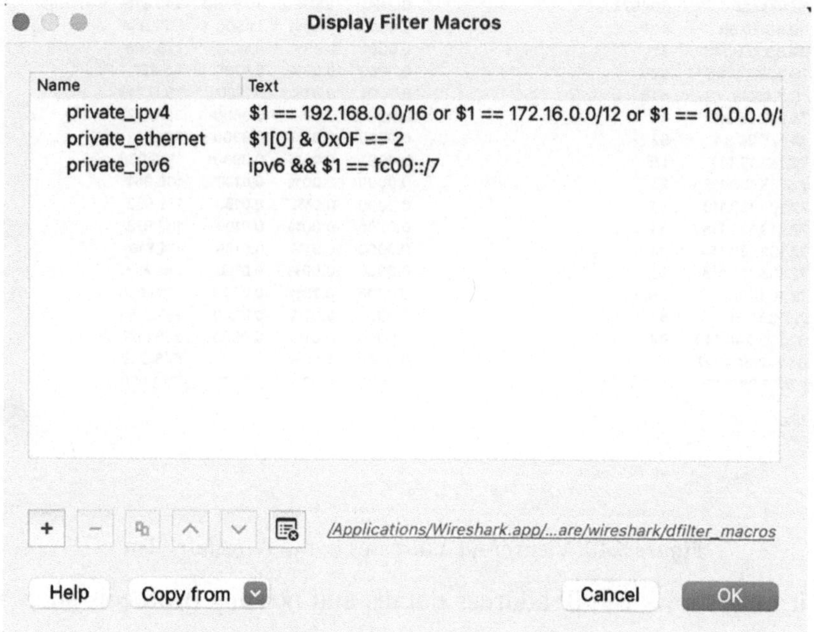

Figure 5.42: *Defining the Macro Function*

A macro named **`tcp`** is being created with the expression (**`ip.src == $1`** and **`ip.dst == $2`** and **`tcp.srcport == $3`** and **`tcp.dstport == $4`**)

$1,$2 are the inputs that the variables **`ip.src`**, **`ip.dst`** would be accepting.

In order to call these macros, we would mention **`${tcp:192.168.1.4;52.108.147.15;64078;443)`** in the display filter section as follows. The inputs which are provided to macro tcp are mapped as **`$1=192.168.1.4, $2=52.108.147.15, $3=64078, $4=443`**. The macros help in substituting the complex filters that we would be putting in the Wireshark display filter to view the packets.

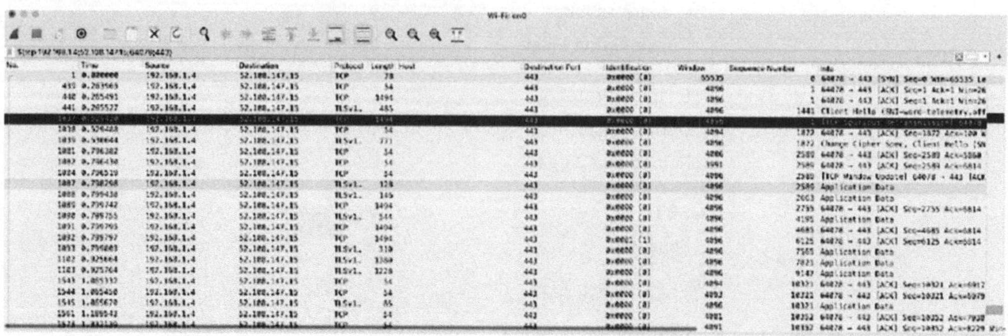

Figure 5.43: *Calling the Macros in the Filter Section in Wireshark*

The macros can also be defined in conjunction with the Logical operators such as **And** and **OR** as shown in the following figure:

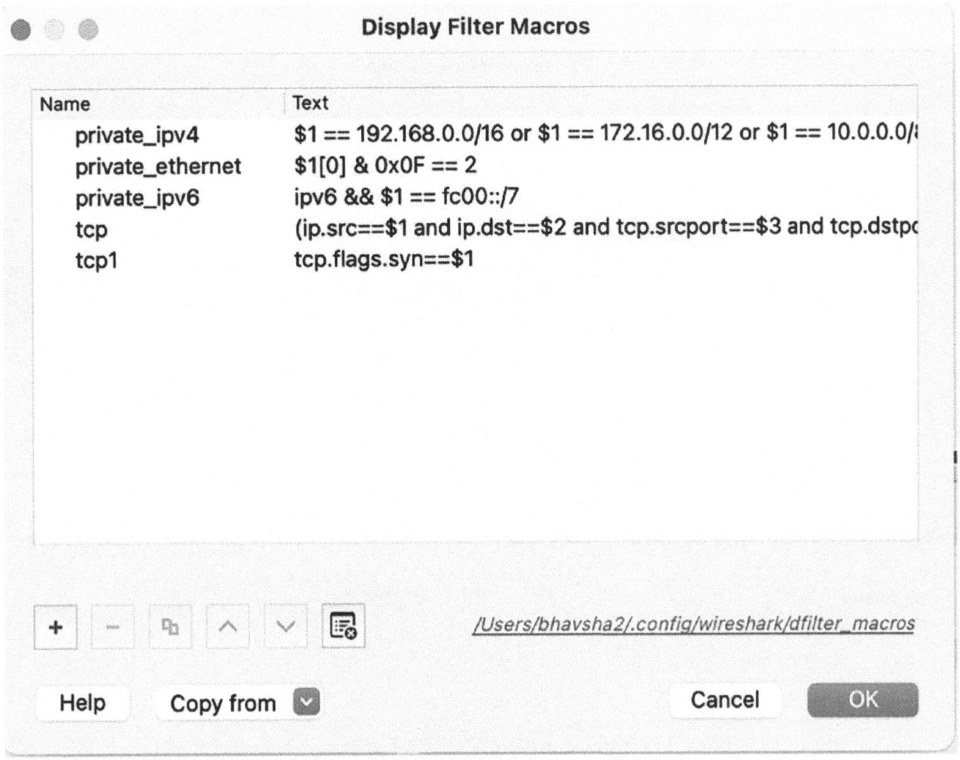

Figure 5.44: *Macros defined using Logical Operators*

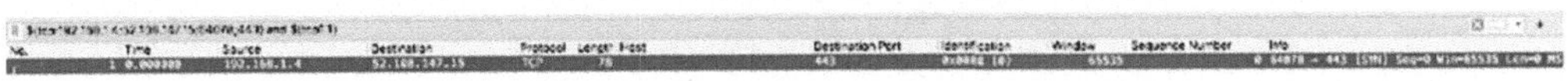

Figure 5.45: *Macros with Logical Operators*

Exporting Packets in Wireshark

We learnt how to select packets using specific filters for different packets in the OSI layer. The question comes if there is a possibility to export the packets and save locally. This is possible in Wireshark, where you can export the packets as shown in the following figure. Ideally, to export the packets, the first step would be to apply a filter to extract the specified packets from the large Wireshark file. In the following example, we have applied a filter for packets with source as **`192.168.1.4`** with **`ip.src==192.168.1.4`** as the filter. Under **`Wireshark`** > **`File`** > **`Export Specified packets`**.

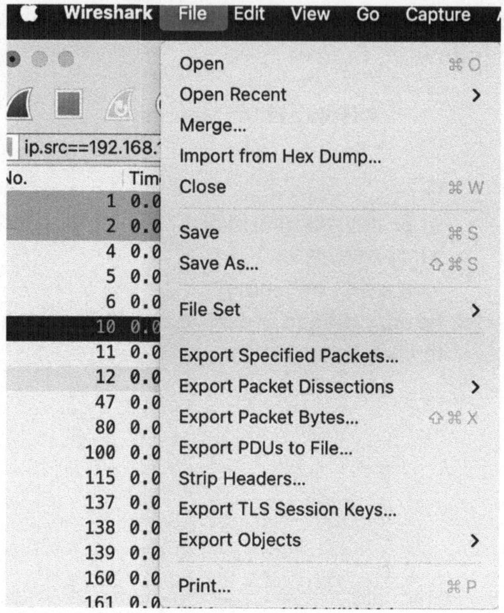

Figure 5.46: *Exporting Specific Packets from Wireshark Capture after applying the Filter*

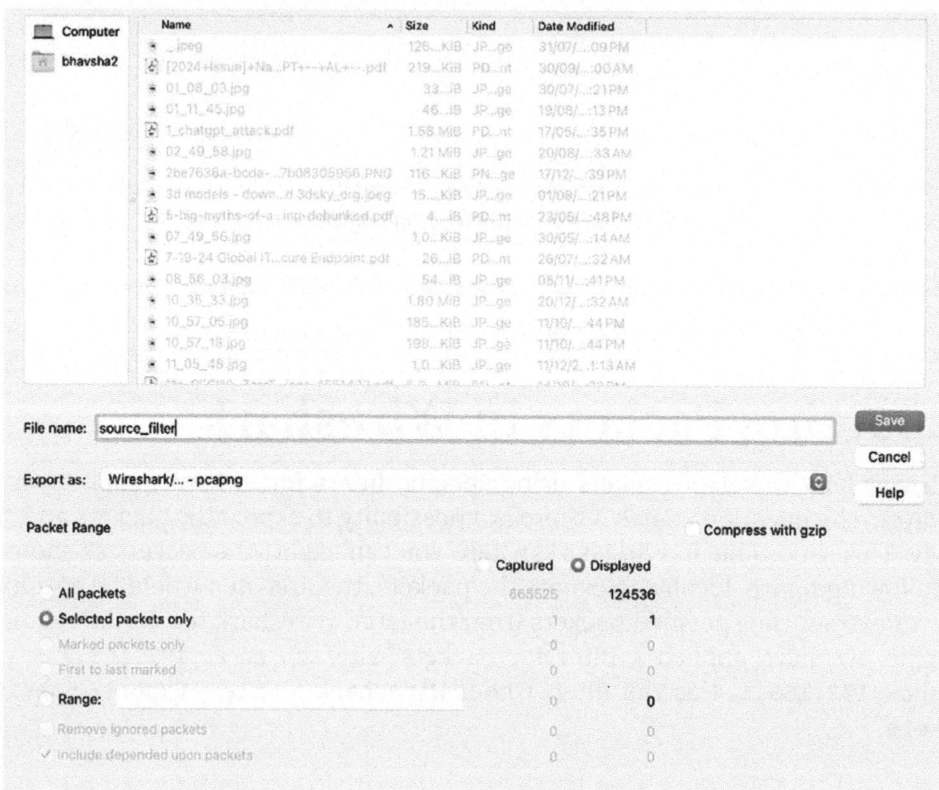

Figure 5.47: *Saving the Exported Packets in Wireshark*

While saving the file, as you can see, it shows All Packets and Selected packets as two options for saving the file. **All packets** displayed count as 124536 packets, while Selected packets only show 1 packet. By default, the selected packet only captures the **`client hello`** packet. So make sure the option All packets is selected while exporting the packets.

Wireshark also provides an option to export the packets in JSON format.

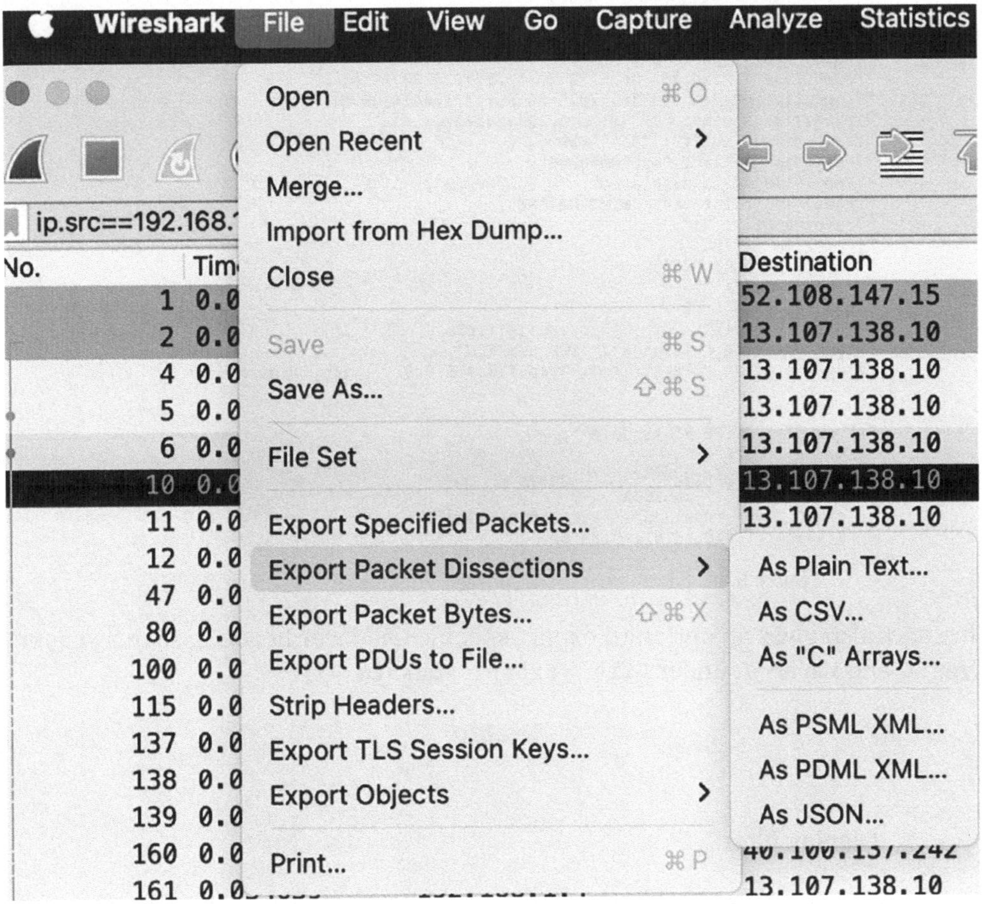

Figure 5.48: *Exporting the Packets captured in JSON*

```
[
  {
    "_index": "packets-2025-01-16",
    "_type": "doc",
    "_score": null,
    "_source": {
      "layers": {
        "frame": {
          "frame.section_number": "1",
          "frame.interface_id": "0",
          "frame.interface_id_tree": {
            "frame.interface_name": "en0",
            "frame.interface_description": "Wi-Fi"
          },
          "frame.encap_type": "1",
          "frame.time": "Jan 16, 2025 12:20:15.124424000 IST",
          "frame.time_utc": "Jan 16, 2025 06:50:15.124424000 UTC",
          "frame.time_epoch": "1737010215.124424000",
          "frame.offset_shift": "0.000000000",
          "frame.time_delta": "0.000000000",
          "frame.time_delta_displayed": "0.000000000",
          "frame.time_relative": "0.000000000",
          "frame.number": "1",
          "frame.len": "78",
          "frame.cap_len": "78",
          "frame.marked": "0",
          "frame.ignored": "0",
          "frame.protocols": "eth:ethertype:ip:tcp",
          "frame.coloring_rule.name": "TCP SYN/FIN",
          "frame.coloring_rule.string": "tcp.flags & 0x02 || tcp.flags.fin == 1"
        },
        "eth": {
          "eth.dst": "10:10:81:fb:3a:6e",
          "eth.dst_tree": {
            "eth.dst_resolved": "zte_fb:3a:6e",
            "eth.dst.oui": "1052801",
            "eth.dst.oui_resolved": "zte corporation",
            "eth.addr": "10:10:81:fb:3a:6e",
```


Figure 5.49: *File where the Exported Packets are saved in JSON*

Wireshark also gives an option to export specific OSI layer headers, such as **Layer 3**, **Layer 4**, and **Layer 7**, under **File** > **Export PDUs to File**.

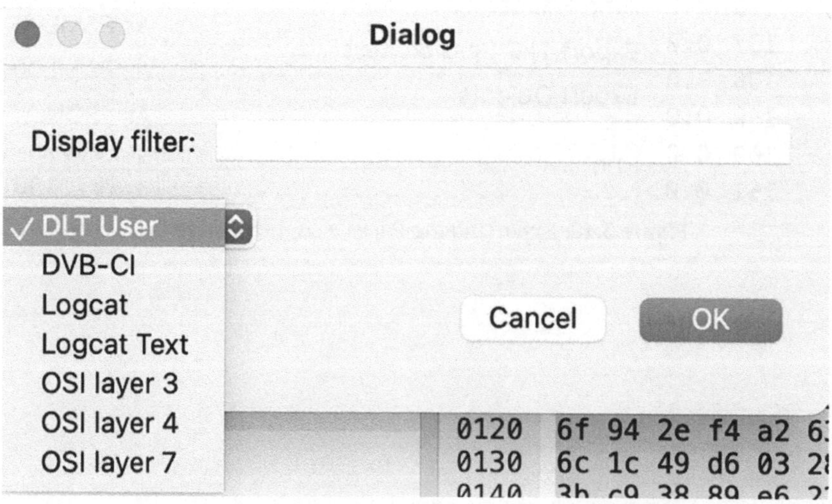

Figure 5.50: *Option to extract Specific OSI Layer Packets*

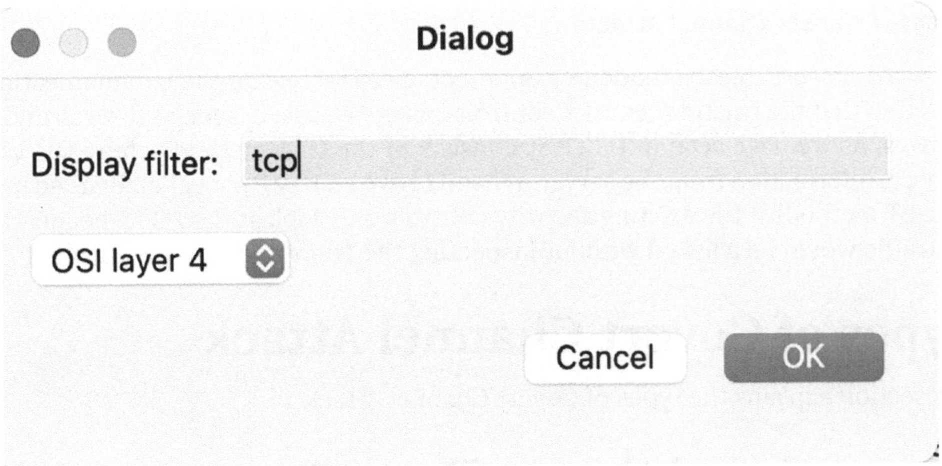

Figure 5.51: *TCP Filter along with the OSI Layer 4*

As seen in **pane 2**, it shows all the **Layer 4** details with no packet header details of **Layer 3**, which is the IP layer. This is helpful for looking for specific packet headers, such as **Layer 4**.

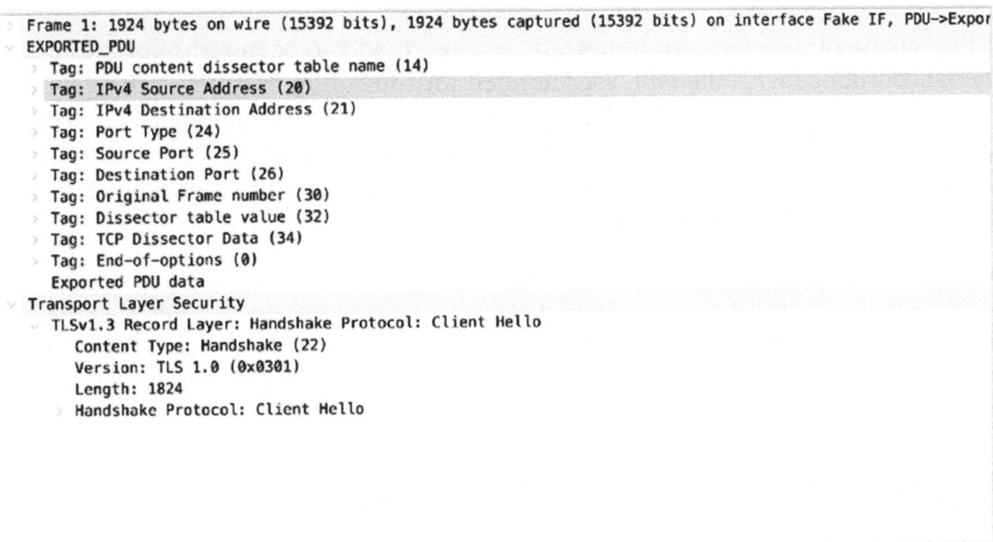

Figure 5.52: *Output Post the Filter is applied where Layer 4 Details of TCP are shown*

Covert Channel Attack

Let us apply the Wireshark skills that we learned and apply them to uncover the real-time attacks that can happen in the Enterprise Network. We would discuss **Covert Channel** attacks.

What is a Covert Channel Attack?

The word "covert" means hidden or undetectable. The reason the communication is hidden so that the existing security controls can be bypassed, such as firewall and IDS controls. As we have seen in HTTP, it consists of the GET method, where the client requests information from the server. What if I have an ICMP packet embedded inside the GET method? If the existing security controls only look at the HTTP header, then the traffic would be allowed without inspecting the content of the GET header.

Types of Covert Channel Attack

This section explains the types of Covert Channel Attack

Storage-based Covert Channels

This involves hiding data in some unexpected portion of the message. Ideally, the message is commonly encapsulated at each level of the OSI model. Logical pieces of information are added successively so that, following several protocols, we ensure end-to-end data integrity. These protocols include ICMP, DNS, TCP, or UDP.

In any protocol, headers are important as they hold the required information and are in accordance with the OSI layer defined for the communication to happen. Few parameters are optional, while others are mandatory for the sequencing and ordering of the packet. Thus, header fields are intended to facilitate the functioning of the protocol. It is expected that the headers not have any other information than what is defined as per RFC specifications.

For a better visualization of the power of covert channels, let us take some examples: Using the HTTP protocol, we could hide information inside cookies, user-agent, and some header fields. The TCP header also has some fields, such as destination port, source port, and TCP flags. Similarly, we can use ICMP echo request and reply packets.

Timing-based Covert Channels

With timing as a parameter, used in Morse code, we can use it in covert channels, too. There is no modification of the packets; information is instead hidden by manipulating delays, intervals of time between segments. For example, we could build a timing-based channel transmitting bits according to the interval of time between two packets.

Along with the information being concealed, there would be different encoding mechanisms that need to be decoded, which we would look at in the following captures.

Let us look at the Covert channel capture, which has been built as follows.

Analyzing Covert Channel Attack

Capture name: **`Channel.pcap`**

This capture has the Covert channel attack happening on the Network, and the idea is to find any anomaly in the conversation that can be traced. We would be analyzing any pattern in different headers and trying to find the data that is concealed.

As we learnt earlier, let us look at the Conversation statistics in Wireshark.

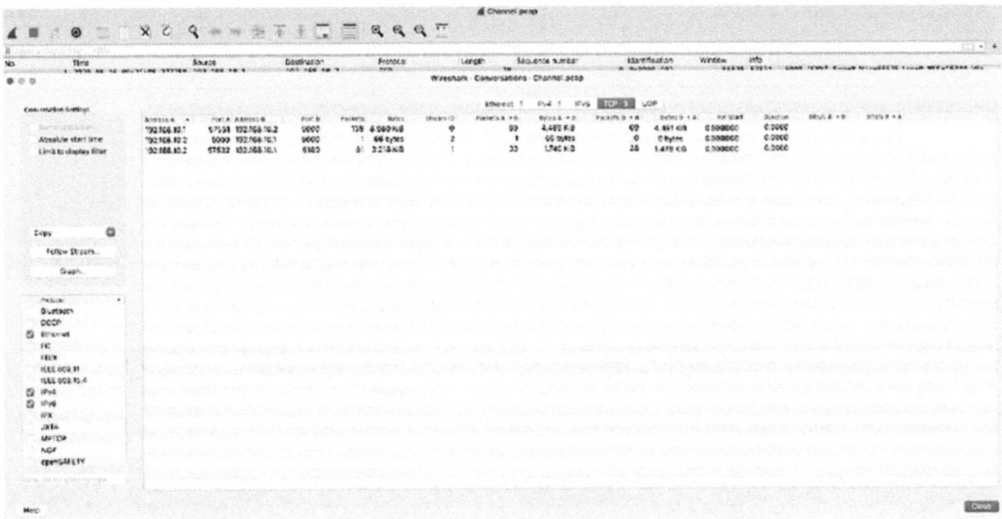

***Figure 5.53:** Looking at the Conversations Summary*

Here, we see there are 3 conversations as seen in *Figure* 5.53.

If we look at the ports for TCP communication, it is on destination port **`5000`** and destination address **`192.168.10.2`**.

As part of this capture, the Identification field has also been added as a column, as shown in *Figure* 5.54.

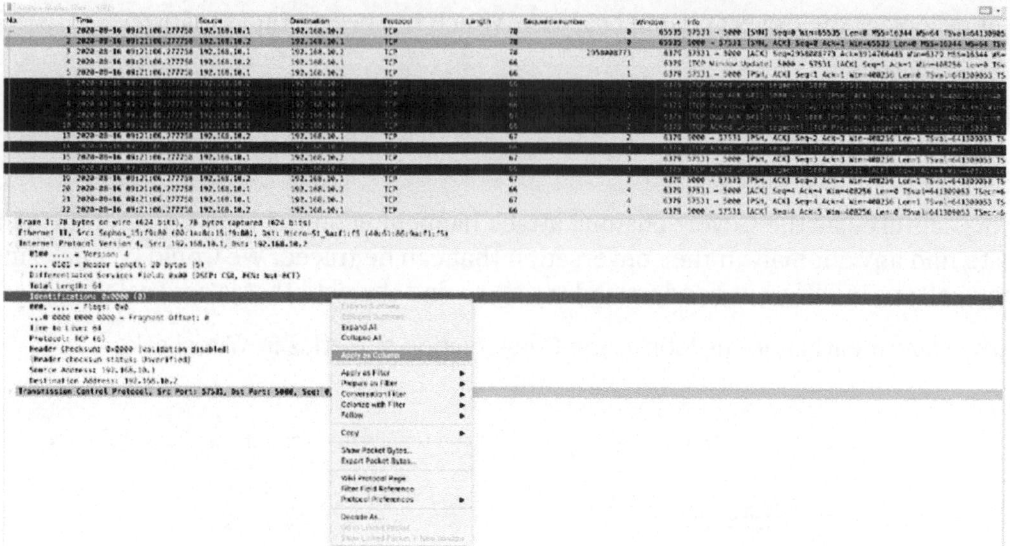

Figure 5.54: *Adding Identification Field in IP Header as part of Wireshark Column*

We can have different protocol fields as columns in Wireshark. Let us try to add Data to the TCP portion.

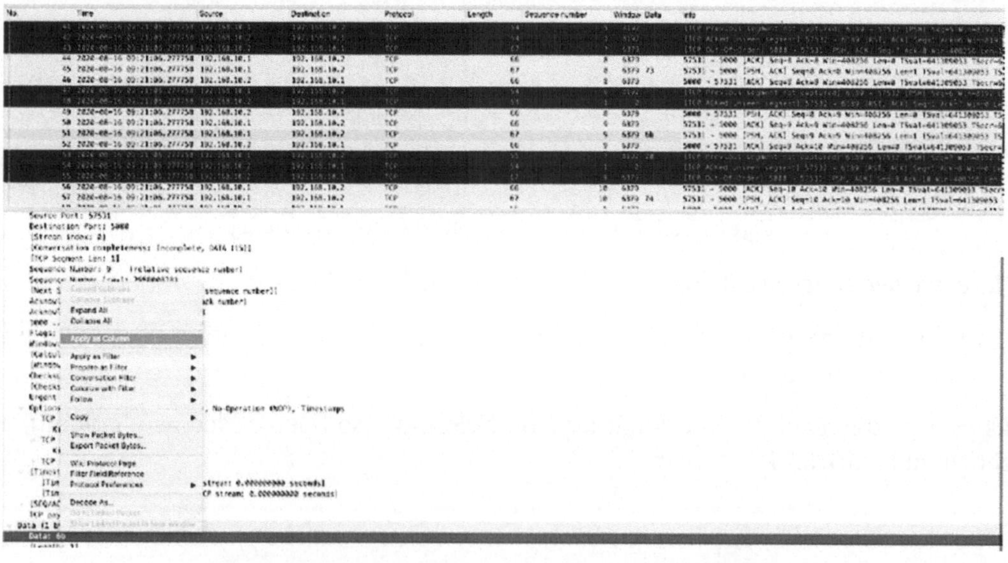

Figure 5.55: *Adding the TCP Data as Wireshark Column*

As you can see, the data field has different fields, such as **68**, **7a**, and so on, in packets. Let us try to understand what these bytes mean. Since these data are ASCII characters, let us try to look at the ASCII chart as shown in *Figure* 5.56.

dec	oct	hex	ch	dec	oct	hex	ch	dec	oct	hex	ch	dec	oct	hex	ch
0	0	00	**NUL** (null)	32	40	20	(space)	64	100	40	@	96	140	60	`
1	1	01	**SOH** (start of header)	33	41	21	!	65	101	41	A	97	141	61	a
2	2	02	**STX** (start of text)	34	42	22	"	66	102	42	B	98	142	62	b
3	3	03	**ETX** (end of text)	35	43	23	#	67	103	43	C	99	143	63	c
4	4	04	**EOT** (end of transmission)	36	44	24	$	68	104	44	D	100	144	64	d
5	5	05	**ENQ** (enquiry)	37	45	25	%	69	105	45	E	101	145	65	e
6	6	06	**ACK** (acknowledge)	38	46	26	&	70	106	46	F	102	146	66	f
7	7	07	**BEL** (bell)	39	47	27	'	71	107	47	G	103	147	67	g
8	10	08	**BS** (backspace)	40	50	28	(	72	110	48	H	104	150	68	h
9	11	09	**HT** (horizontal tab)	41	51	29	)	73	111	49	I	105	151	69	i
10	12	0a	**LF** (line feed - new line)	42	52	2a	*	74	112	4a	J	106	152	6a	j
11	13	0b	**VT** (vertical tab)	43	53	2b	+	75	113	4b	K	107	153	6b	k
12	14	0c	**FF** (form feed - new page)	44	54	2c	,	76	114	4c	L	108	154	6c	l
13	15	0d	**CR** (carriage return)	45	55	2d	-	77	115	4d	M	109	155	6d	m
14	16	0e	**SO** (shift out)	46	56	2e	.	78	116	4e	N	110	156	6e	n
15	17	0f	**SI** (shift in)	47	57	2f	/	79	117	4f	O	111	157	6f	o
16	20	10	**DLE** (data link escape)	48	60	30	0	80	120	50	P	112	160	70	p
17	21	11	**DC1** (device control 1)	49	61	31	1	81	121	51	Q	113	161	71	q
18	22	12	**DC2** (device control 2)	50	62	32	2	82	122	52	R	114	162	72	r
19	23	13	**DC3** (device control 3)	51	63	33	3	83	123	53	S	115	163	73	s
20	24	14	**DC4** (device control 4)	52	64	34	4	84	124	54	T	116	164	74	t
21	25	15	**NAK** (negative acknowledge)	53	65	35	5	85	125	55	U	117	165	75	u
22	26	16	**SYN** (synchronous idle)	54	66	36	6	86	126	56	V	118	166	76	v
23	27	17	**ETB** (end of transmission block)	55	67	37	7	87	127	57	W	119	167	77	w
24	30	18	**CAN** (cancel)	56	70	38	8	88	130	58	X	120	170	78	x
25	31	19	**EM** (end of medium)	57	71	39	9	89	131	59	Y	121	171	79	y
26	32	1a	**SUB** (substitute)	58	72	3a	:	90	132	5a	Z	122	172	7a	z
27	33	1b	**ESC** (escape)	59	73	3b	;	91	133	5b	[	123	173	7b	{
28	34	1c	**FS** (file separator)	60	74	3c	<	92	134	5c	\	124	174	7c	|
29	35	1d	**GS** (group separator)	61	75	3d	=	93	135	5d	]	125	175	7d	}
30	36	1e	**RS** (record separator)	62	76	3e	>	94	136	5e	^	126	176	7e	~
31	37	1f	**US** (unit separator)	63	77	3f	?	95	137	5f	_	127	177	7f	**DEL** (delete)

Figure 5.56: *Ascii Chart*

The first four data bytes correspond to **`68(h)`**, **`7a(z)`**, **`6d(m)`**, **`79(y)`**, which does not give any valid information. Let us keep on looking for other fields. Adding the **`Acknowledgement number`** and the **`Identification`** field as columns.

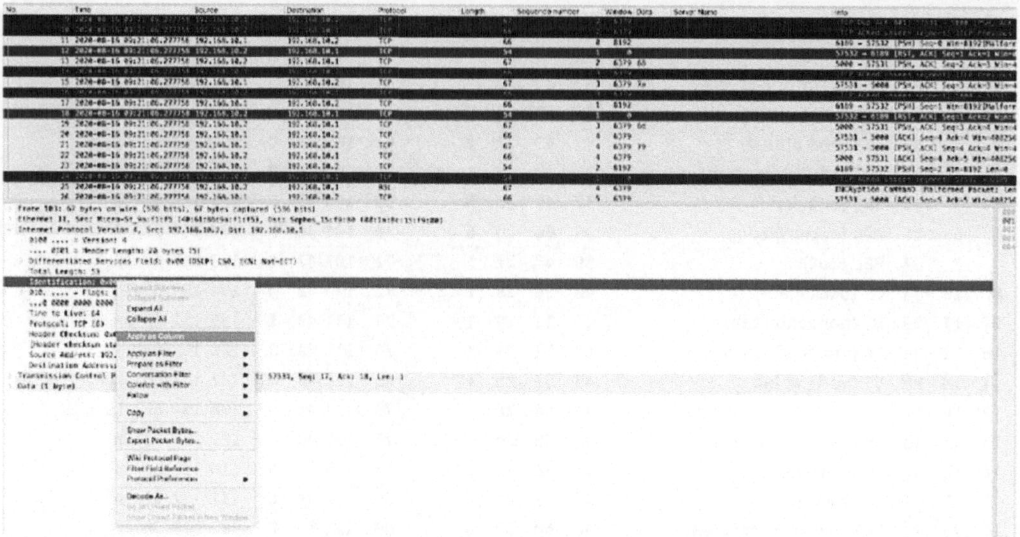

Figure 5.57: Adding Identification Field as Column

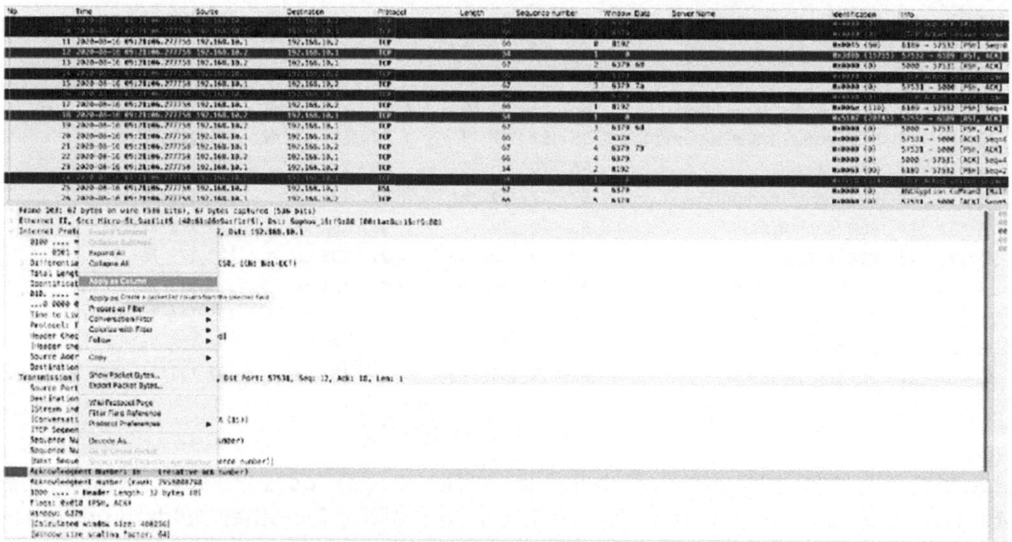

Figure 5.58: Adding Acknowledgement as Wireshark Column

As can be seen, the `Acknowledgement number` and `Identification` field are shown.

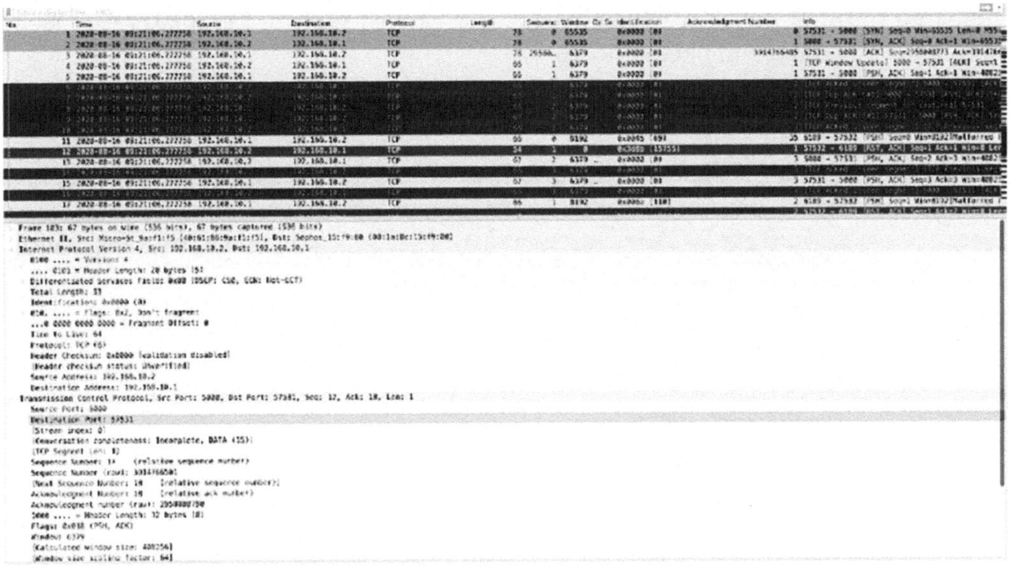

Figure 5.59: *Acknowledgement and Identification Field being added as Column*

If we carefully look at the **`Acknowledgement number`** of different packets, the relative **`ACK`** is enabled. Let us try to disable the **`Relative Acknowledgement number`** and look at the different values of the **`ACK`** number.

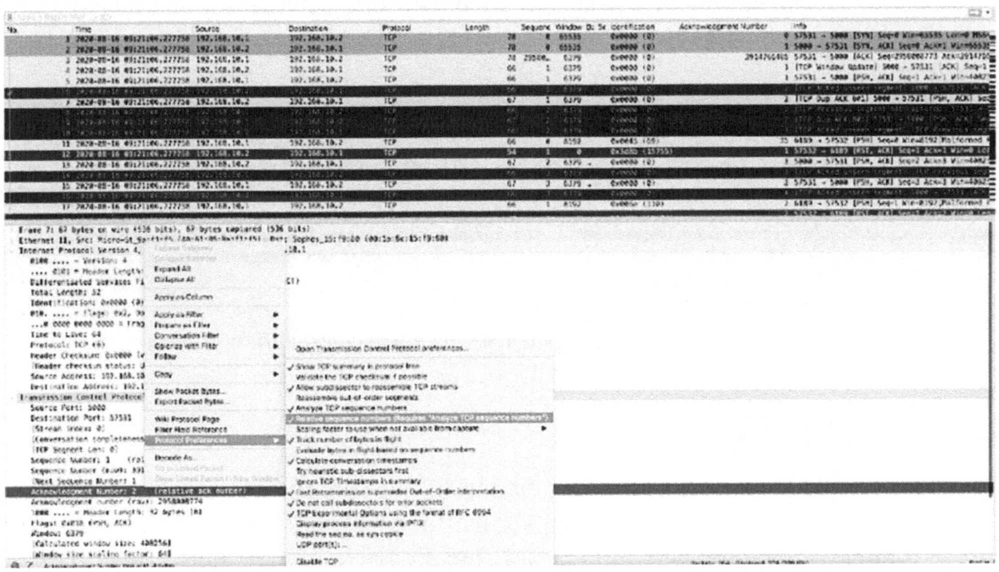

Figure 5.60: *Disabling Relative Acknowledgement Number*

If we analyze the packets after the relative TCP sequence numbers are disabled, we see that many packets have smaller acknowledgement values, such as **35**, **21**, as compared to other packets, which have larger values, such as **2958008777** in packet no **25** and **3914766489** in packet no **26**.

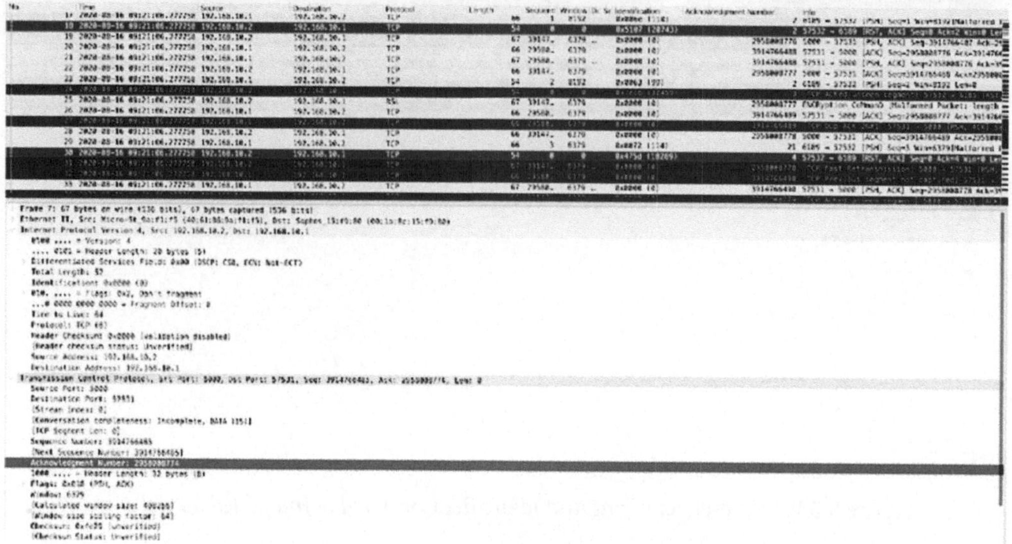

***Figure 5.61:** Viewing Acknowledgement Number of Different Packets*

Now let us look at the Identification field, and we can see that a few packets, such as packet no **17**, packet no **23**, packet no **29**, have values of **110**, **99**, **114** as compared to other values such as **15755** in packet no **12**, **20743** in packet no **18**, and **32459** in packet no **24**.

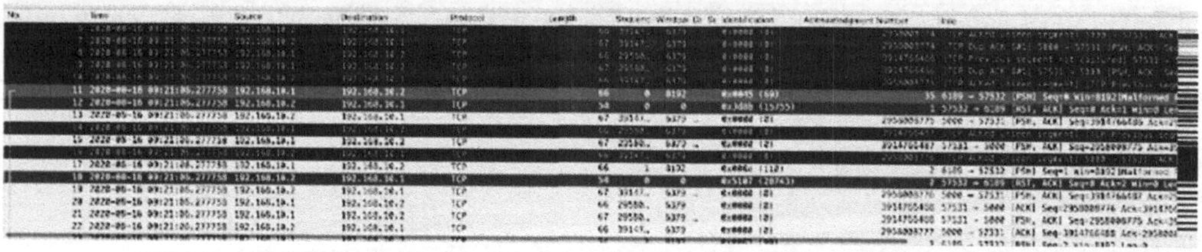

***Figure 5.62:** Different Values of Identification Fields for Different Packets*

Conclusion

We started with visualizing different panes in Wireshark and also how different packet headers and packet details are shown in Wireshark. We also looked at how different filters can be applied and extract specific packets. We learnt how to detect malicious intent in conversations between client and server by tracing the hidden content in Wireshark. We learnt how a Covert channel looks and how attackers can sneak a hidden conversation in a traditional protocol. The next chapter explains how to analyze Wireshark traffic.

CHAPTER 6

Tools to Analyze Wireshark Traffic

Introduction

We have learned how to analyze Wireshark traffic by looking at different fields, such as Conversations, and applying different filters. This process is manual, and it would be helpful to have some tools to analyze the Wireshark traffic and automate it. This chapter focuses on Pyshark to analyze the traffic.

Structure

In this chapter, we will discuss the following topics:

- Tool Installation
- Scripts to Analyze the Traffic

Tool Installation

Let us explore some tools to analyze Wireshark instead of manually visualizing packet captures.

There are a few tools, such as Scapy and Pyshark, that can help analyze these packet captures.

Let us explore how to use the Pyshark tool to analyze the capture by installing it on a Mac.

Steps to Install Pyshark

```
pip install pyshark
```

Collecting pyshark

```
Downloading pyshark-0.6-py3-none-any.whl (41 kB)

     ━━━━━━━━━━━━━━━━━━━━━━━━━━━━━━━━━━━━━━━━ 41.4/41.4 kB 598.2 kB/s eta 0:00:00
Requirement already satisfied: appdirs in /Users/bhavsha2/opt/anaconda3/lib/py-
thon3.9/site-packages (from pyshark) (1.4.4)
Requirement already satisfied: lxml in /Users/bhavsha2/opt/anaconda3/lib/py-
thon3.9/site-packages (from pyshark) (4.9.1)
Requirement already satisfied: packaging in /Users/bhavsha2/opt/anaconda3/lib/py-
thon3.9/site-packages (from pyshark) (21.3)
Collecting termcolor
  Downloading termcolor-2.4.0-py3-none-any.whl (7.7 kB)
Requirement already satisfied: pyparsing!=3.0.5,>=2.0.2 in /Users/bhavsha2/opt/an-
aconda3/lib/python3.9/site-packages (from packaging->pyshark) (3.0.9)
Installing collected packages: termcolor, pyshark
Successfully installed pyshark-0.6 termcolor-2.4.0

[notice] A new release of pip is available: 23.0 -> 24.0
[notice] To update, run: pip install --upgrade pip
```

Pyshark is an open source tool whose information is available on **https://github.com/KimiNewt/pyshark/**

We would be setting up Visual Studio, which is the IDE for writing code.

Downloading Visual Studio is straightforward, with the package for Mac available at https://visualstudio.microsoft.com/vs/mac/ and Windows at https://visualstudio.microsoft.com/downloads/

Figure 6.1: *Snippet of the Script to analyze the Covert Channel Capture We discussed in Chapter 5*

The first line imports all the packages from the Pyshark library. The second line loads the Capture file into a variable named **cap.** Now, we will look at the contents of the capture, which we have been viewing in Wireshark, by printing the contents of the variable **cap.**

The following is the output of the first packet of the capture. Each packet of the capture is viewed by iterating as an array object with an index **cap[0]** referring to the first packet.

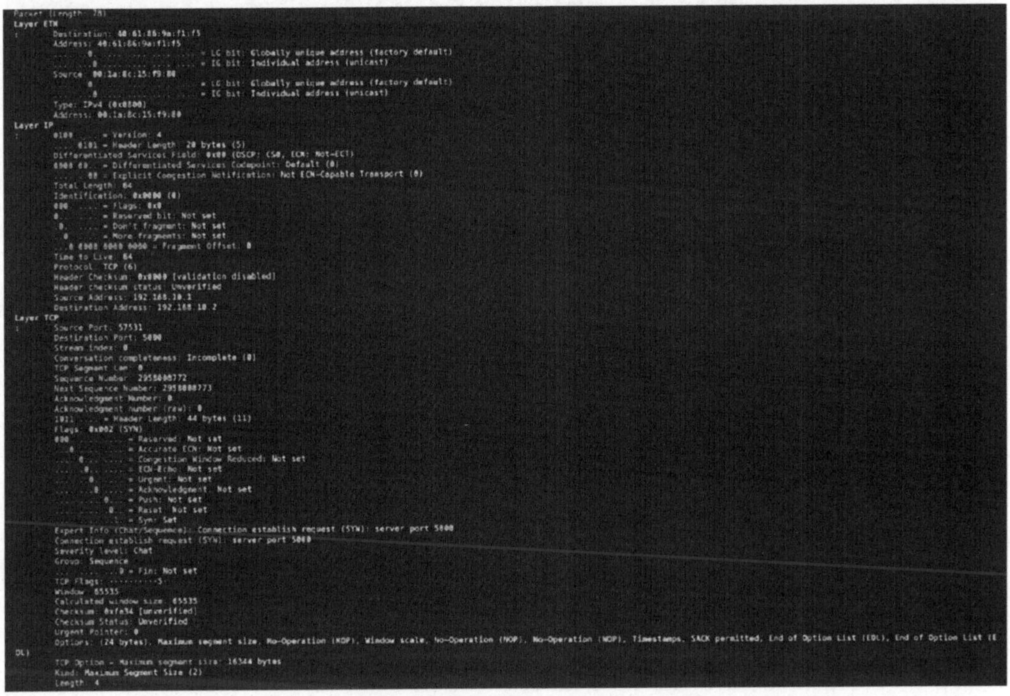

Figure 6.2: *Output of the First Packet as Part of the Script. Same Packet which was seen in Wireshark*

Below figure shows the information of the TCP header.

Figure 6.3: *Script Snippet which shows the TCP Header Information*

As seen in the output, each packet is divided into three layers: **Ethernet**, **IP**, and **TCP**.

Let us look at how the information can be accessed from each layer.

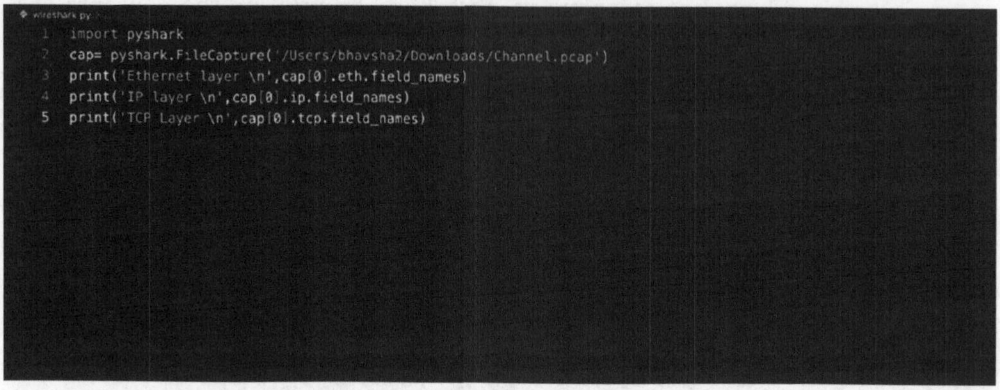

Figure 6.4: *Command to view the Ethernet, IP and TCP Layer Information of First Packet in the Capture*

Once the above script is executed we would get the below information from the Ethernet, IP and the TCP layer. As seen the information is outputted as a list in terms of keys. For example, the **`dst`** field is the MAC address in the Ethernet layer.

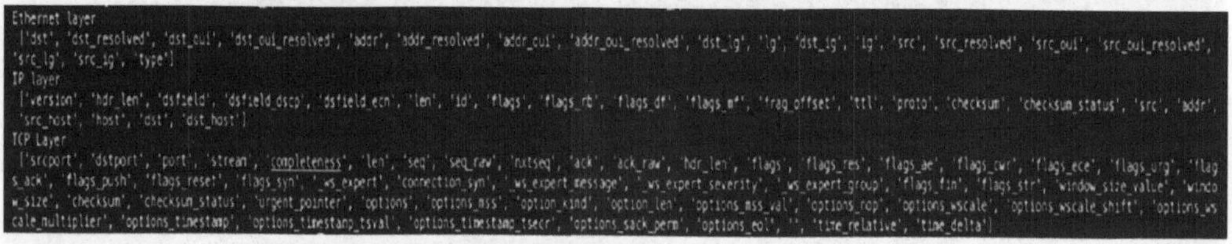

Figure 6.5: *Displays the Field Names and Not Values*

As can be seen, these are the individual fields in each layer, which we can view in Wireshark.

Let us look at how to parse through the field values of each layer.

Figure 6.6: *Extracting the Source and Destination mac Address of the First Packet*

The outputs for the preceding print statements are:

```
40:61:86:9a:f1:f5--- destination mac for 1st packet
00:1a:8c:15:f9:80--source mac for 1st packet
```

```
'IP layers as below'
print(cap[0].ip.src)
print(cap[0].ip.dst)

'TCP layers as below'
print(cap[0].tcp.srcport)
print(cap[0].tcp.dstport)
print(cap[0].tcp.seq)
print(cap[0].tcp.ack)
```

***Figure 6.7:** Extracting the IP Header and TCP Header Information*

The outputs for the preceding print statements are:

```
192.168.10.1
192.168.10.2
57531
5000
0
0
```

As we analyzed earlier, the **acknowledgement number** and the **Identification** field had smaller values compared to other packets. We will now examine the packet details using Pyshark.

```
Layer ETH
:       Destination: 40:61:86:9a:f1:f5
        Address: 40:61:86:9a:f1:f5
        .... ..0. .... .... .... .... = LG bit: Globally unique address (factory
        default)
        .... ...0 .... .... .... .... = IG bit: Individual address (unicast)
        Source: 00:1a:8c:15:f9:80
        .... ..0. .... .... .... .... = LG bit: Globally unique address (factory
        default)
        .... ...0 .... .... .... .... = IG bit: Individual address (unicast)
        Type: IPv4 (0x0800)
        Trailer: 01080a2639997d
        Expert Info (Note/Protocol): Didn't find padding of zeros, and an
        undecoded trailer exists. There may be padding of non-zeros.
        Didn't find padding of zeros, and an undecoded trailer exists. There may
        be padding of non-zeros.
        Severity level: Note
        Group: Protocol
        Frame check sequence: 0x2639997d [unverified]
        FCS Status: Unverified
        Address: 00:1a:8c:15:f9:80
Layer IP
:       0100 .... = Version: 4
        .... 0101 = Header Length: 20 bytes (5)
        Differentiated Services Field: 0x00 (DSCP: CS0, ECN: Not-ECT)
        0000 00.. = Differentiated Services Codepoint: Default (0)
```

```
        .... ..00 = Explicit Congestion Notification: Not ECN-Capable Transport
              (0)
        Total Length: 41
        Identification: 0x0045 (69)
        010. .... = Flags: 0x2, Don't fragment
        0... .... = Reserved bit: Not set
        .1.. .... = Don't fragment: Set
        ..0. .... = More fragments: Not set
        ...0 0000 0000 0000 = Fragment Offset: 0
        Time to Live: 64
        Protocol: TCP (6)
        Header Checksum: 0x7c87 [validation disabled]
        Header checksum status: Unverified
        Source Address: 192.168.10.1
        Destination Address: 192.168.10.2
Layer TCP
:       Source Port: 6189
        Destination Port: 57532
        Stream index: 1
        Conversation completeness: Incomplete (0)
        Short segment. Segment/fragment does not contain a full TCP header (might
        be NMAP or someone else deliberately sending unusual packets)
        Expert Info (Warning/Malformed): Short segment. Segment/fragment does not
        contain a full TCP header (might be NMAP or someone else deliberately
        sending unusual packets)
        Short segment. Segment/fragment does not contain a full TCP header (might
        be NMAP or someone else deliberately sending unusual packets)
        Severity level: Warning
        Group: Malformed
        Sequence Number: 0    (relative sequence number)
        Sequence Number (raw): 0
        Acknowledgment Number: 35
        The acknowledgment number field is nonzero while the ACK flag is not set
        Acknowledgment number (raw): 35
        1000 .... = Header Length: 32 bytes (8)
        Flags: 0x008 (PSH)
        000. .... .... = Reserved: Not set
        ...0 .... .... = Accurate ECN: Not set
        .... 0... .... = Congestion Window Reduced: Not set
        .... .0.. .... = ECN-Echo: Not set
        .... ..0. .... = Urgent: Not set
        .... ...0 .... = Acknowledgment: Not set
        .... .... 1... = Push: Set
        .... .... .0.. = Reset: Not set
        .... .... ..0. = Syn: Not set
        .... .... ...0 = Fin: Not set
        TCP Flags: ········P···
```

```
            Window: 8192
            Calculated window size: 8192
            Window size scaling factor: -1 (unknown)
            Checksum: 0x44de [unverified]
            Checksum Status: Unverified
            Urgent Pointer: 0
            Options: (12 bytes), No-Operation (NOP)
            TCP Option - No-Operation (NOP)
            Kind: No-Operation (1)
            Time since the first frame in this TCP stream: 0.000000000 seconds
            Time since the previous frame in this TCP stream: 0.000000000 seconds
            Timestamps
            Expert Info (Note/Protocol): The acknowledgment number field is nonzero
            while the ACK flag is not set
            Severity level: Note
            Group: Protocol
```

As can be seen for packet **11**, the **Identification** field and **acknowledgement number** look interesting when compared to the same fields in other packets.

If there are two fields, and since the packet capture has some message concealed, there might be an encryption mechanism in place to hide the data. One of the common encryption algorithms used is the XOR cipher, along with other algorithms such as RSA. Let us try performing XOR between the Identification ^ Ack number.

```
xor = int(cap[10].ip.id,16)
xor1= int(cap[10].tcp.ack)
result = xor ^ xor1
print('first charachter is',chr(result))
```

Figure 6.8: *The XOR Cipher applied on Packet 10*

The output of the preceding print statement is **first character is f**

Let us look at the contents of other packets where the acknowledgement number and the Identification field are unique.

The other packet is packet number **16**, as follows.

```
Layer ETH
:       Destination: 40:61:86:9a:f1:f5
        Address: 40:61:86:9a:f1:f5
        .... ..0. .... .... .... .... = LG bit: Globally unique address (factory
        default)
        .... ...0 .... .... .... .... = IG bit: Individual address (unicast)
        Source: 00:1a:8c:15:f9:80
        .... ..0. .... .... .... .... = LG bit: Globally unique address (factory
        default)
```

```
        .... ...0 .... .... .... .... = IG bit: Individual address (unicast)
        Type: IPv4 (0x0800)
        Trailer: 01080a2639997d
        Expert Info (Note/Protocol): Didn't find padding of zeros, and an
        undecoded trailer exists. There may be padding of non-zeros.
        Didn't find padding of zeros, and an undecoded trailer exists. There may
        be padding of non-zeros.
        Severity level: Note
        Group: Protocol
        Frame check sequence: 0x2639997d [unverified]
        FCS Status: Unverified
        Address: 00:1a:8c:15:f9:80
Layer IP
:       0100 .... = Version: 4
        .... 0101 = Header Length: 20 bytes (5)
        Differentiated Services Field: 0x00 (DSCP: CS0, ECN: Not-ECT)
        0000 00.. = Differentiated Services Codepoint: Default (0)
        .... ..00 = Explicit Congestion Notification: Not ECN-Capable Transport (0)
        Total Length: 41
        Identification: 0x006e (110)
        010. .... = Flags: 0x2, Don't fragment
        0... .... = Reserved bit: Not set
        .1.. .... = Don't fragment: Set
        ..0. .... = More fragments: Not set
        ...0 0000 0000 0000 = Fragment Offset: 0
        Time to Live: 64
        Protocol: TCP (6)
        Header Checksum: 0x0000 [validation disabled]
        Header checksum status: Unverified
        Source Address: 192.168.10.1
        Destination Address: 192.168.10.2
Layer TCP
:       Source Port: 6189
        Destination Port: 57532
        Stream index: 1
        Conversation completeness: Incomplete (36)
        Short segment. Segment/fragment does not contain a full TCP header (might
        be NMAP or someone else deliberately sending unusual packets)
        Expert Info (Warning/Malformed): Short segment. Segment/fragment does not
        contain a full TCP header (might be NMAP or someone else deliberately
        sending unusual packets)
        Short segment. Segment/fragment does not contain a full TCP header (might
        be NMAP or someone else deliberately sending unusual packets)
        Severity level: Warning
        Group: Malformed
        Sequence Number: 1    (relative sequence number)
        Sequence Number (raw): 1
```

```
Acknowledgment Number: 2
The acknowledgment number field is nonzero while the ACK flag is not set
Acknowledgment number (raw): 2
1000 .... = Header Length: 32 bytes (8)
Flags: 0x008 (PSH)
000. .... .... = Reserved: Not set
...0 .... .... = Accurate ECN: Not set
.... 0... .... = Congestion Window Reduced: Not set
.... .0.. .... = ECN-Echo: Not set
.... ..0. .... = Urgent: Not set
.... ...0 .... = Acknowledgment: Not set
.... .... 1... = Push: Set
.... .... .0.. = Reset: Not set
.... .... ..0. = Syn: Not set
.... .... ...0 = Fin: Not set
TCP Flags: ········P···
Window: 8192
Calculated window size: 8192
Window size scaling factor: -1 (unknown)
Checksum: 0x30e7 [unverified]
Checksum Status: Unverified
Urgent Pointer: 0
Options: (12 bytes), No-Operation (NOP)
TCP Option - No-Operation (NOP)
Kind: No-Operation (1)
Time since first frame in this TCP stream: 0.000000000 seconds
Time since previous frame in this TCP stream: 0.000000000 seconds
Timestamps
Expert Info (Note/Protocol): The acknowledgment number field is nonzero
while the ACK flag is not set
Severity level: Note
Group: Protocol
```

Figure 6.9: *XOR Cipher applied on Packet 16*

The output of the preceding print statement is **`second character is 1`**. Thus, if we look at the first two characters, they are **fl**.

Let us try to look at other packets and find the hidden message.

```
result = chr((int(cap[10].ip.id,16)) ^ (int(cap[10].tcp.ack))) + chr((int(-
cap[16].ip.id,16)) ^ (int(cap[16].tcp.ack))) + chr((int(cap[22].ip.id,16))
^ (int(cap[22].tcp.ack))) + chr((int(cap[28].ip.id,16)) ^ (int(cap[28].tcp.
ack))) + chr((int(cap[34].ip.id,16)) ^ (int(cap[34].tcp.ack))) + chr((int(-
cap[40].ip.id,16)) ^ (int(cap[40].tcp.ack))) + chr((int(cap[46].ip.id,16))
```

```
^ (int(cap[46].tcp.ack))) + chr((int(cap[52].ip.id,16)) ^ (int(cap[52].tcp.
ack))) + chr((int(cap[58].ip.id,16)) ^ (int(cap[58].tcp.ack))) + chr((int(-
cap[64].ip.id,16)) ^ (int(cap[64].tcp.ack))) + chr((int(cap[70].ip.id,16)) ^

(int(cap[70].tcp.ack))) + chr((int(cap[76].ip.id,16)) ^ (int(cap[76].tcp.
ack))) + chr((int(cap[82].ip.id,16)) ^ (int(cap[82].tcp.ack))) + chr((int(-
cap[88].ip.id,16)) ^ (int(cap[88].tcp.ack))) + chr((int(cap[94].ip.id,16)) ^
(int(cap[94].tcp.ack))) + chr((int(cap[100].ip.id,16)) ^ (int(cap[100].tcp.
ack))) + chr((int(cap[106].ip.id,16)) ^ (int(cap[106].tcp.ack))) + chr((int(-
cap[112].ip.id,16)) ^ (int(cap[112].tcp.ack))) + chr((int(cap[118].ip.id,16))
^ (int(cap[118].tcp.ack))) + chr((int(cap[124].ip.id,16)) ^ (int(cap[124].
tcp.ack))) + chr((int(cap[130].ip.id,16)) ^ (int(cap[130].tcp.ack))) +
chr((int(cap[136].ip.id,16)) ^ (int(cap[136].tcp.ack))) + chr((int(cap[142].
ip.id,16)) ^ (int(cap[142].tcp.ack))) + chr((int(cap[148].ip.id,16)) ^ (in-
t(cap[148].tcp.ack))) + chr((int(cap[154].ip.id,16)) ^ (int(cap[154].tcp.
ack))) + chr((int(cap[160].ip.id,16)) ^ (int(cap[160].tcp.ack))) + chr((int(-
cap[166].ip.id,16)) ^ (int(cap[166].tcp.ack))) + chr((int(cap[172].ip.id,16))
^ (int(cap[172].tcp.ack))) + chr((int(cap[178].ip.id,16)) ^ (int(cap[178].
tcp.ack))) + chr((int(cap[184].ip.id,16)) ^ (int(cap[184].tcp.ack))) +
chr((int(cap[190].ip.id,16)) ^ (int(cap[190].tcp.ack))) + chr((int(cap[196].
ip.id,16)) ^ (int(cap[196].tcp.ack)))
print(result)      The message is flag{C0VeRt_istN3t_Sn_Secure_70}
```

We learnt to analyze the Covert channel captures using the Pyshark tool and to analyze anomalies in different fields of IP packets. The example shown here was built to show how a Covert channel attack is being seen in Enterprise Network. In an Ideal Covert channel attack there would be more complex algorithms and more fields to look for to decode the Information which is being transferred.

Conclusion

This chapter covered Covert channel attacks and how to interpret them in Wireshark. As a security analyst, one needs Wireshark skills to analyze these attacks and prevent them from causing network outages. In the next chapter, we will discuss Malware Analysis on Wireshark.

Chapter 7
Malware Analysis on Wireshark

Introduction

This chapter provides an insight into using Wireshark in analyzing malware over the network. We will discuss the different stages of attack and will analyze actual Malware on Wireshark. As part of this chapter, the author has also created a malware that would help in understanding the techniques of identifying the malware on Wireshark. For analyzing the actual malware on Wireshark, we need to have collectors that have collected the traces from the infected machine.

Structure

In this chapter, we will cover the following topics:

- Introducing Malware
- Tracing Malware in Wireshark
- Attack Kill Chain Model
- Analyzing Breach Incident Reported
- Drawing Correlations Using Wireshark Trace

Introducing Malware

Since we have now understood how to use Wireshark, we will try to apply the knowledge in analyzing different malware that results in the machines getting infected.

What is Malware?

As the name suggests, it is a software that damages the system by running an injected process that communicates to the attacker's hosted server over the Internet. This might result in several PII information getting leaked and causing the systems to crash. The malware would be delivered in the form of spyware or ransomware. The transport layer for this malware could be over the network via email, or it can be through free software downloads.

Let us look at a recently launched malware called **`"Xloader"`**. The malware uses multiple file types, such as PDF, XLSX, and RTF, for initial infection and execution. It is also designed to drop three modules in memory and execute the final payload using the Process Hollowing technique. Xloader is a class of Formbook malware that extracts data from the HTML page.

Following is how the malware was downloaded on the endpoint machine:

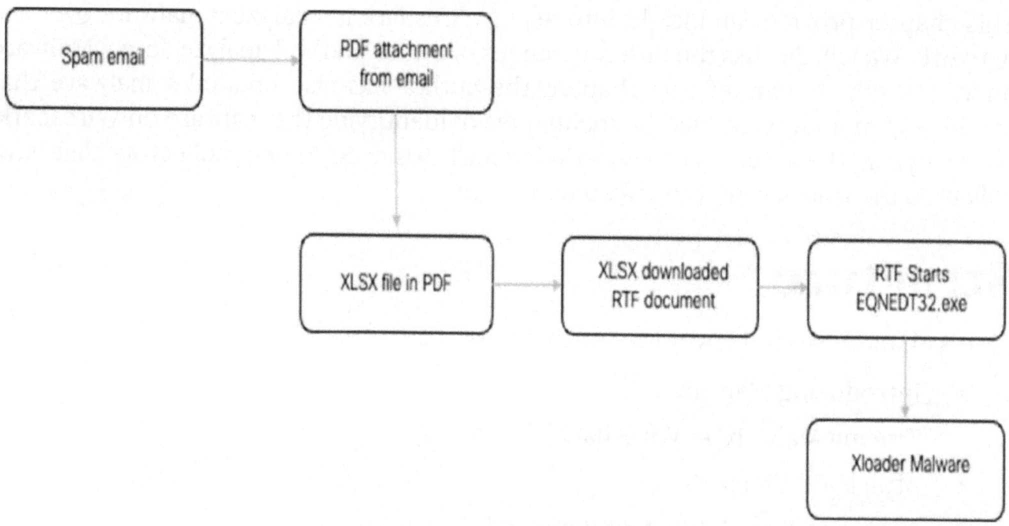

***Figure 7.1**: Steps for Loading Malware*

Snapshot of the email that was received:

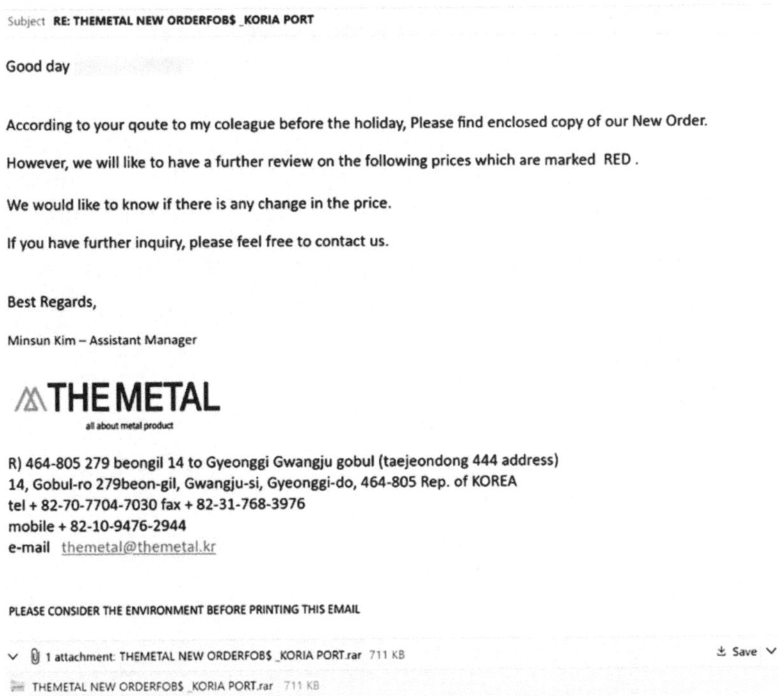

Subject RE: THEMETAL NEW ORDERFOB$ _KORIA PORT

Good day

According to your qoute to my coleague before the holiday, Please find enclosed copy of our New Order.

However, we will like to have a further review on the following prices which are marked RED .

We would like to know if there is any change in the price.

If you have further inquiry, please feel free to contact us.

Best Regards,

Minsun Kim – Assistant Manager

THE METAL
all about metal product

R) 464-805 279 beongil 14 to Gyeonggi Gwangju gobul (taejeondong 444 address)
14, Gobul-ro 279beon-gil, Gwangju-si, Gyeonggi-do, 464-805 Rep. of KOREA
tel + 82-70-7704-7030 fax + 82-31-768-3976
mobile + 82-10-9476-2944
e-mail themetal@themetal.kr

PLEASE CONSIDER THE ENVIRONMENT BEFORE PRINTING THIS EMAIL

1 attachment: THEMETAL NEW ORDERFOB$ _KORIA PORT.rar 711 KB Save

THEMETAL NEW ORDERFOB$ _KORIA PORT.rar 711 KB

Figure 7.2: *Snapshot of the email which was used for loading the Malware*

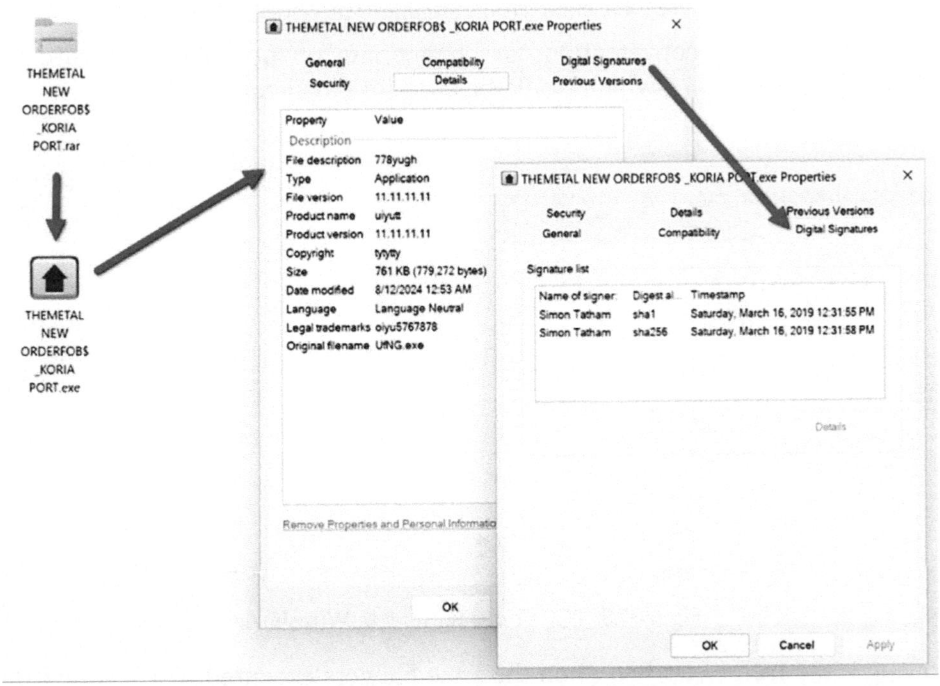

Figure 7.3: *The exe which was downloaded from the email*

Tracing Malware in Wireshark

Let us try to look at the malware traces in Wireshark. The captures were taken when the machine was infected with this malware, that is, post the email was opened on the endpoint machine and the executable was being run. We will try to identify what the malware does when it is accidentally installed on the endpoint machine.

Let us first look at the conversation summary for different hosts, seen as follows:

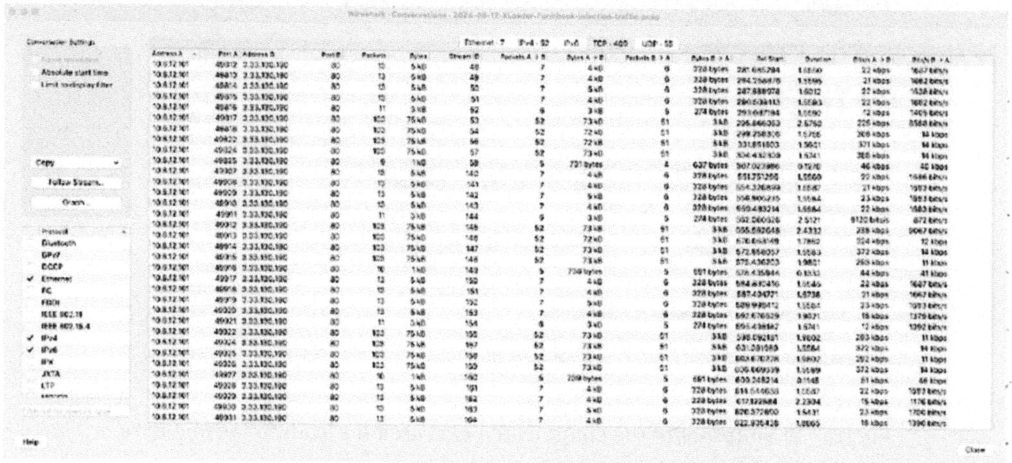

Figure 7.4: *Conversation Summary in Wireshark*

As seen, most of the conversations are happening on port **80**. There are a few conversations on port **443**, which would be used for email conversations.

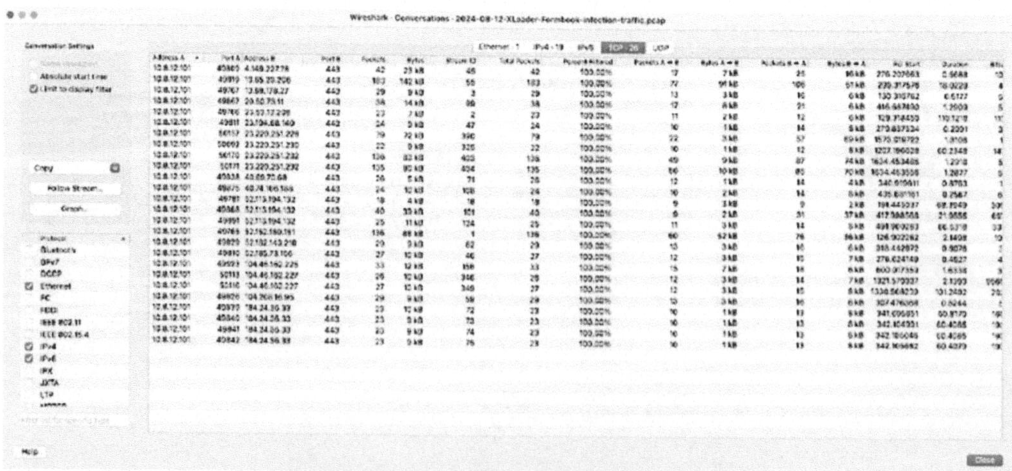

Figure 7.5: TCP Conversations in Wireshark

Following is the traffic capture when the **.exe** file gets executed. This traffic capture was taken from an endpoint when the Malicious exe was getting executed. Ideally in a larger Enterprise Network there would be continuous Capture points on different Endpoints.

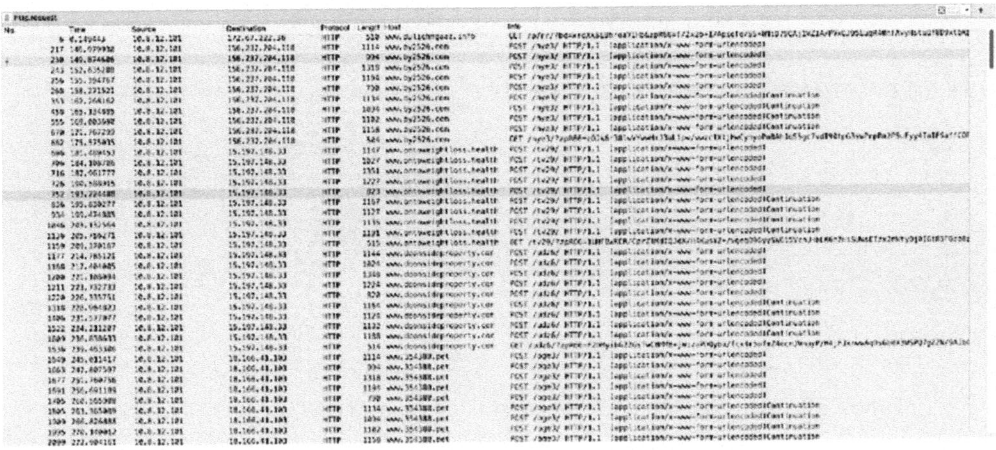

Figure 7.6: *Filter to look at Different HTTP Requests*

Following is the capture once the machine has been infected, and it makes a set of **POST** requests to the server **by2526.com**:

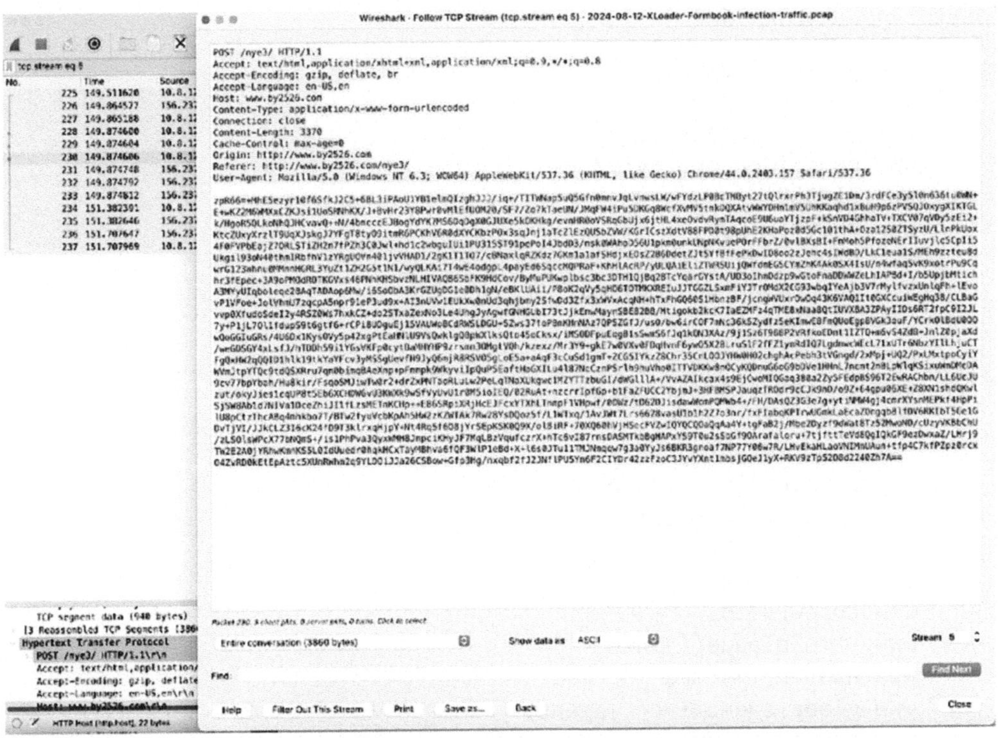

Figure 7.7: *Tracing the HTTP POST Request*

There are also some **GET** requests along with the **POST** requests, as follows:

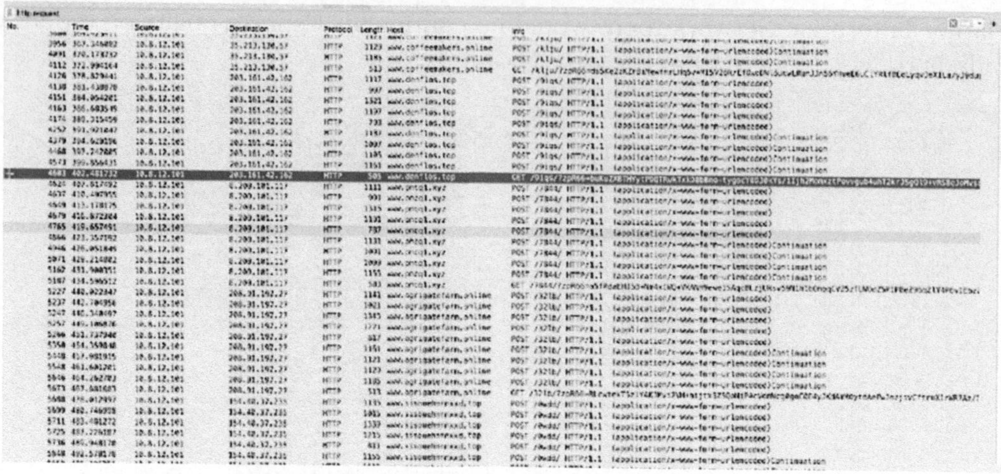

***Figure 7.8**: Analyzing the HTTP Request which shows GET and POST Headers*

This brings us to determine the Indicators of Compromise. The domains that were communicated while the machine was infected. Indicators of Compromise are the assets which were communicated when the device was compromised or when the exe was Installed on the machine which resulted in Command and Control Communication from the Infected machine.

```
www.dulichngaaz[.]info
www.by2526[.]com
www.ontoweightloss[.]health
www.doonsideproperty[.]com
www.354388[.]pet
www.qkotc[.]xyz
www.dressroza[.]com
www.coffeemakers[.]online
www.denflos[.]top
www.pmcq1[.]xyz
www.agrigatefarm[.]online
www.askvanta[.]com
www.wowsomefan[.]store
www.physicallyfit[.]org
www.agiantsbar[.]com
www.ueimg[.]xyz
www.sisouehnmnxxd[.]top
www.screw[.]lol
www.steelplaque[.]info
www.huanle[.]store
www.globalexecutive[.]agency
www.connectionbyebd[.]com
www.cradunk[.]com
```

Another form of malware is Gootloader Malware, which is a multi-functional malware that is known to target Windows systems. It can download additional malicious payloads, which can allow attackers to carry out a range of harmful activities. The flow of the attack is as follows:

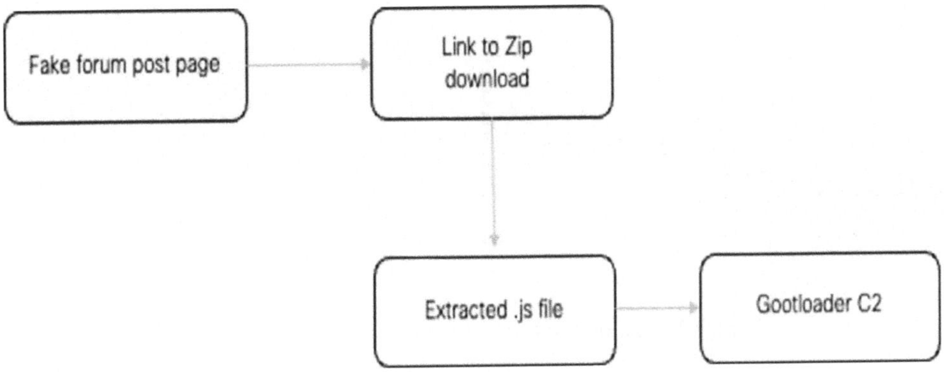

Figure 7.9: *Flow of the GootLoader Malware*

Let us look at the Wireshark traces when the endpoint machine visits the fake form site and tries to download the zip file on the post.

As compared to previous malware capture, here we can see most of the transactions are happening on HTTPS, while a few transactions are on port **80**.

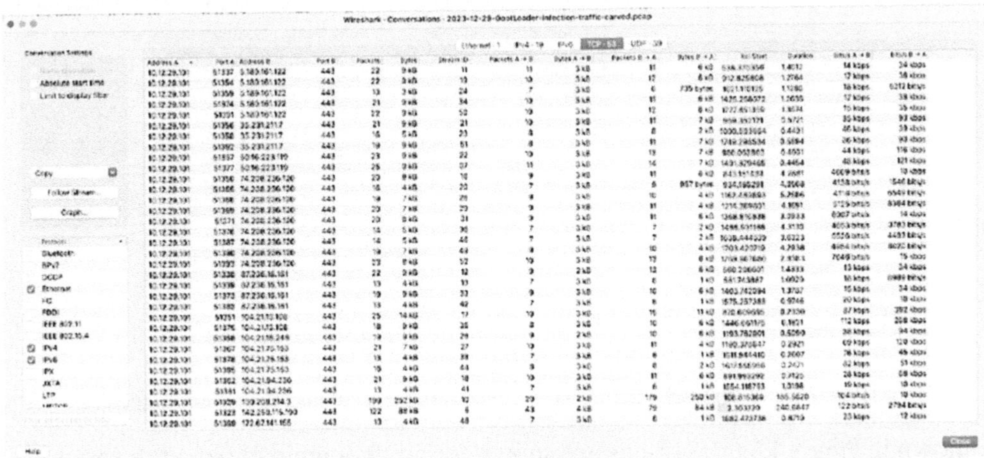

Figure 7.10: *Conversation Summary for Wireshark when Gootloader Malware gets Installed*

As shown in *Figure* 7.10, the Conversation Summary shows Communication happening on Port **443**.

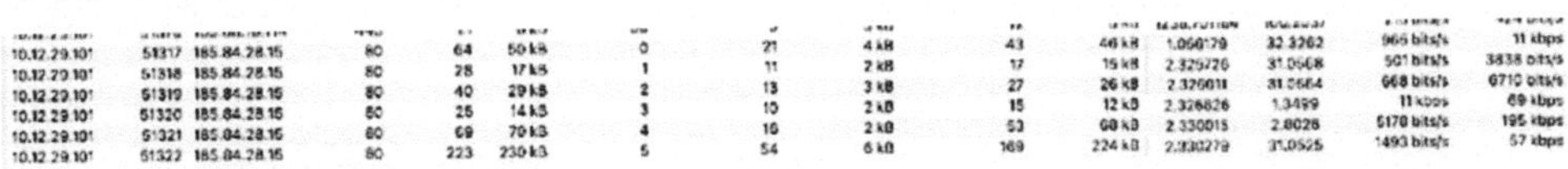

10.12.29.101	51317	185.84.28.15	80	64	50 kB	0	21	4 kB	43	46 kB	1.060179	32.3262	966 bits/s	11 kbps
10.12.29.101	51318	185.84.28.15	80	28	17 kB	1	11	2 kB	17	15 kB	2.329726	31.0568	501 bits/s	3838 bits/s
10.12.29.101	51319	185.84.28.15	80	40	29 kB	2	13	3 kB	27	26 kB	2.326011	31.0664	668 bits/s	6710 bits/s
10.12.29.101	51320	185.84.28.15	80	25	14 kB	3	10	2 kB	15	12 kB	2.326826	1.3499	11 kbps	69 kbps
10.12.29.101	51321	185.84.28.15	80	69	70 kB	4	16	2 kB	53	68 kB	2.330015	2.8026	5170 bits/s	195 kbps
10.12.29.101	51322	185.84.28.15	80	223	230 kB	5	54	6 kB	169	224 kB	2.330279	31.0525	1493 bits/s	57 kbps

Figure 7.11: *Conversation Summary for Wireshark showing HTTP Packets*

As shown in *Figure* 7.11, the Conversation Summary shows Communication happening on Port **80**.

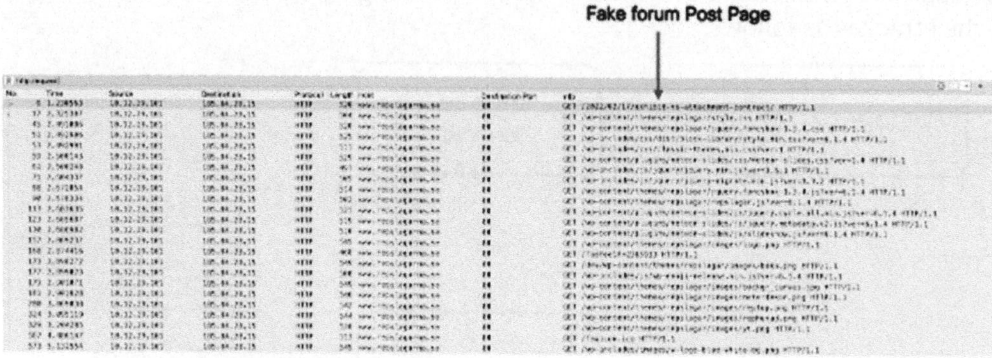

Figure 7.12: *Analyzing the Wireshark Traces on port 80*

As shown in *Figure* 7.12, all the **HTTP** requests are being displayed. Since the Gootloader malware step consists of Downloading the zip file let's try to find the Wireshark trace where the ZIP file gets downloaded.

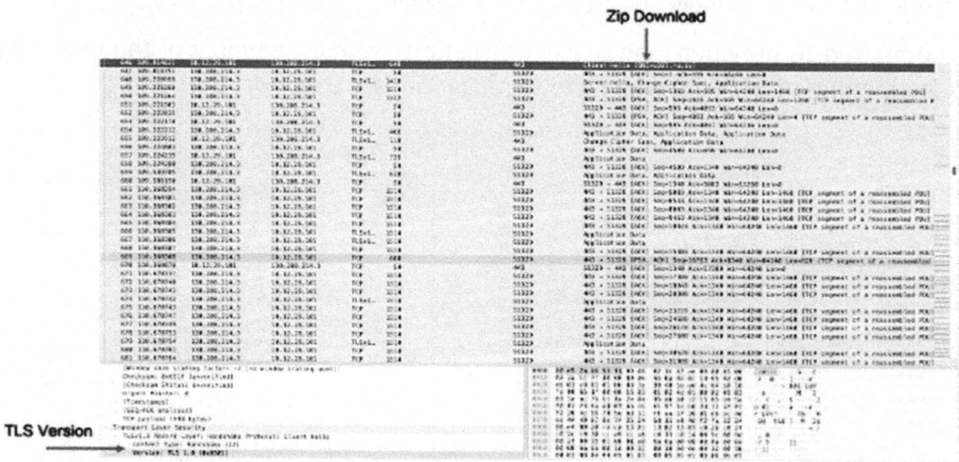

Figure 7.13: *Wireshark Packet which shows the ZIP File getting downloaded*

As shown in *Figure* 7.13, the traces are shown for a ZIP download from the server.

Figure 7.14: A Web Page from *repslagarna.se*

This is how the website looks, and if you notice, Chrome detects it as a Deceptive site, which means it is **High risk**. The reason for this is that it is using TLS 1.0. In the above capture, we downloaded the **`Exhibit versus Attachment Contract`** Zip file.

The Indicators of Compromise found are as follows, which were communicated once the endpoint was affected:

```
https://tattoo-mall[.]ru
https://parubok-lesia[.]com
https://latesthentai[.]com
https://gambrick[.]com
https://instawp[.]com
https://diskodrugarputovanja[.]rs
```

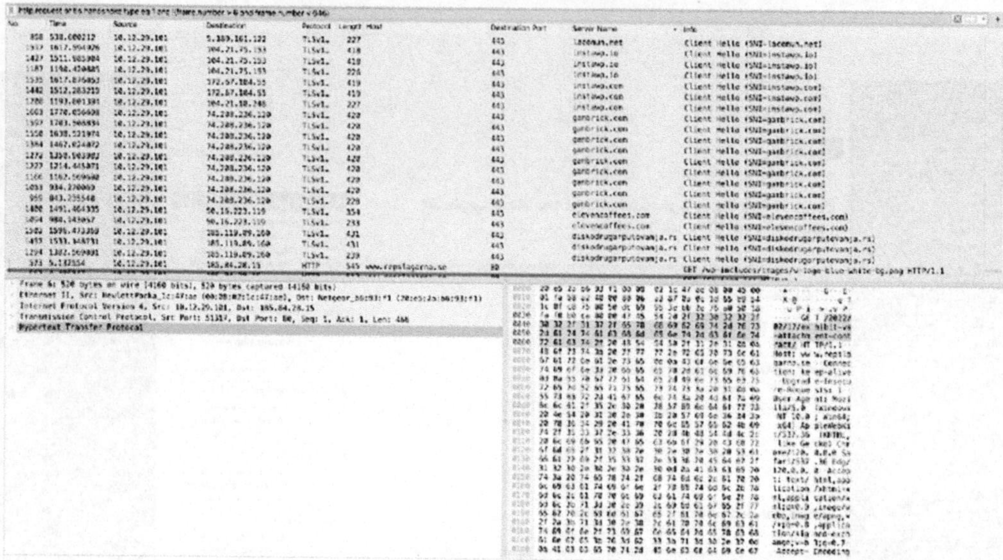

Figure 7.15: *Wireshark Trace showing Different Indicators of Compromise*

The filter **`tls.handshake.type==1`** means we are requesting Client Hello and **`tls.handshake.type==2`** means we are filtering for **`Server Hello`**.

By looking at the captures, we analyzed the traffic while the endpoint machine was infected with malware. The traffic originated in unknown domains from where the malicious scripts were downloaded.

Attack Kill Chain Model

Now we will deep dive into an attack kill chain model, which is referenced in lockheedmartin.com.

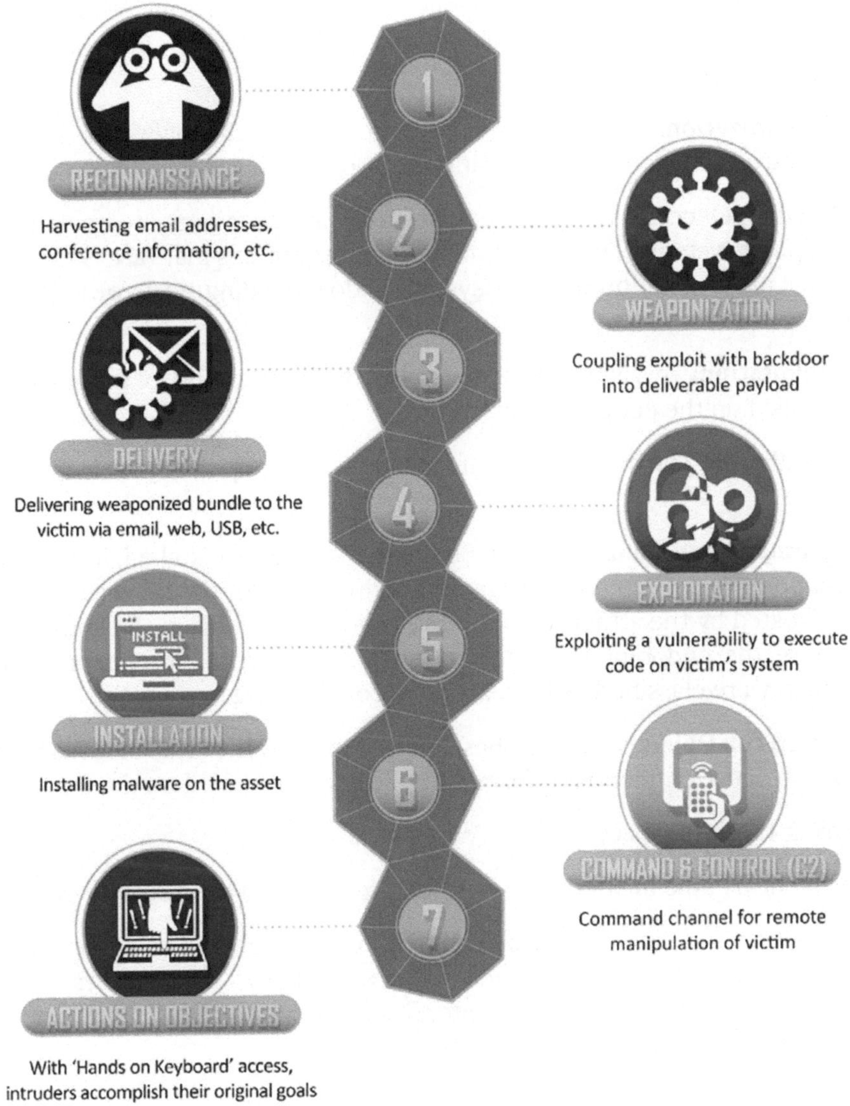

***Figure* 7.16:** *Attack Kill Chain Model*

This explains the stage of the attack before the target is identified and compromised. The term attack kill chain has been coined from a military term, which involves research on the target before it starts attacking it.

The sequence of steps has been explained as follows:

1. **Reconnaissance:** This phase includes gaining more information about the network. This can be carried out either actively or passively. For example, `nmap` scan for the network. One of the drawbacks of Active reconnaissance is that

the attacker can be identified, while passive reconnaissance results in looking at the social media profiles of the system administrator, but the information might not be more relevant.

2. **Weaponization:** This phase is ammunition, where the malware is created. The malware can be created with different tools, such as Metasploit.
3. **Delivery:** Once the malware is created, the attacker wants to implant it on the endpoint systems. The most common delivery of this malware is via email. The other most common delivery system is downloading posts or software from free websites.
4. **Exploitation**: This is the phase to exploit the vulnerability of the software to be installed on the endpoint system.
5. **Installation:** The malware gets installed on the endpoint system as part of this phase
6. **Command and Control(C2)**: Once the malware gets installed, it influences the endpoint system to make outbound connections to the servers, which would be hosted by the attacker on the Internet. We saw this in the above captures, where the endpoint system makes a connection to unregistered domains, which were classified as **Indicators of Compromise.**
7. **Actions on Objectives:** This phase includes where the attacker asks for ransom or extracts Confidential Information, which can be sold on the Dark Web.

Let us look at these stages of attack in Wireshark.

Following is the sample Incident that has been reported to the Security Analyst:

In Ideal Situation the Enterprise would report of a breach and as a Security Analyst you need to understand how the breach occurred and how the attackers were able to Intrude in the Network and perform Lateral movement (Discovering other assets in the Enterprise Network)

Analyzing Breach Incident Reported

Incident Summary

Figure 7.17: *Security Breach Analysis*

A security breach was reported in a financial organization named "Zenith". Some confidential files were leaked online. It is suspected that the laptop of their CFO, John Doe, was compromised.

Zenith's CISO has contacted us to identify the source of the breach and how the data breach happened.

In order to identify the cause of the data breach Security Analyst asked for specific information, as follows:

- Approximate timestamp of the Issue
- IP address of the possible infected machine (**`192.168.10.10`**)
- If the customer has network collectors in place that provide captures from the network
- Email address of the person whose laptop was possibly compromised (jdoe@zenith.com)

The goal of the Security Analyst is to look for Indicators of Compromise by answering the following questions when the Malware was installed:

- What are the hidden file types?
- What is the encoding format of the hidden code?
- What is the decoded content exactly?

The Security Analyst was able to get a Wireshark trace of the CISO's infected machine from different network collectors in the Infrastructure.

Drawing Correlations using Wireshark Trace

We have looked at the Conversations Summary, and we will deep dive into **`Protocol Hierarchy`** in Wireshark.

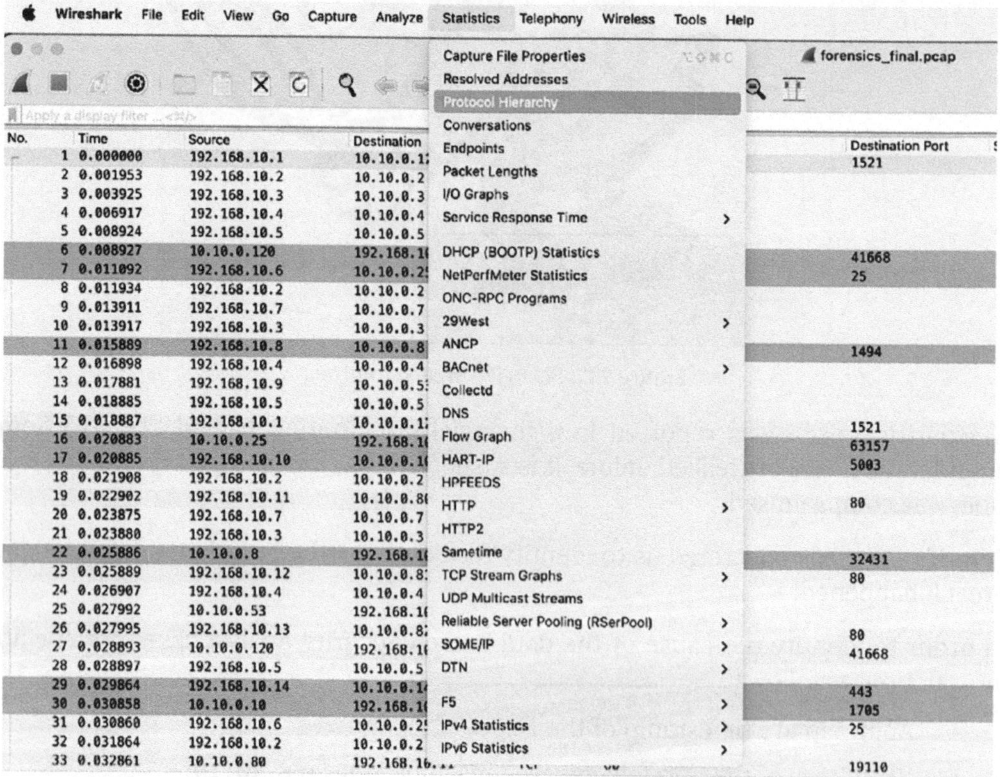

Figure 7.18: *Similar to Conversation Summary in Wireshark we have Protocol Hierarchy*

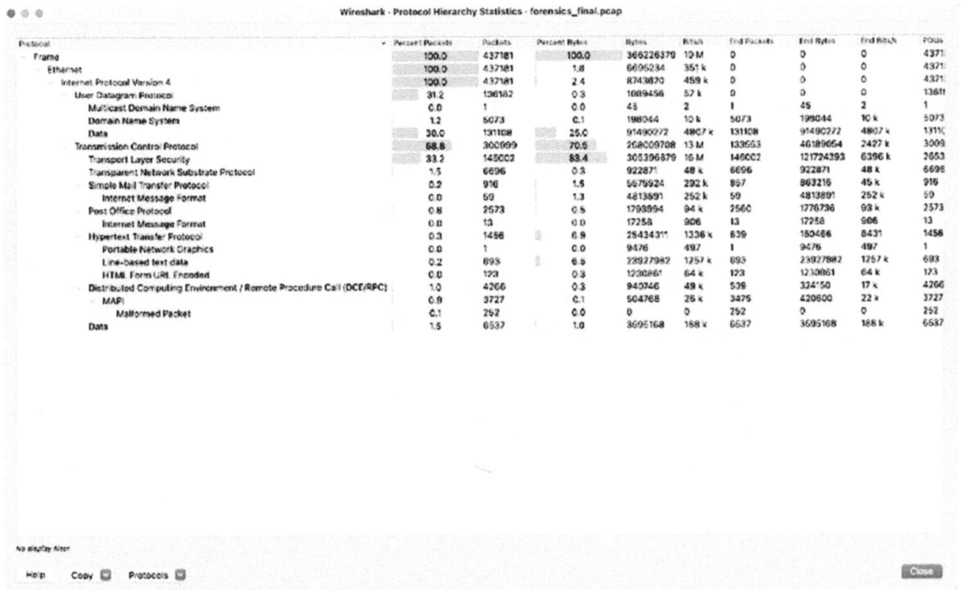

Figure 7.19: *Snapshot of Different Packets as per the Protocol*

The **`Protocol Hierarchy`** shows the traffic across different protocols. As seen, it shows all traffic is **`IPV4`** and the **`Layer 4 transport layer`** traffic is on both TCP and UDP. It also shows some traffic on **`SMTP`**, which means some email traffic would have been seen on the infected machine.

Since we know the IP address of the infected machine, we would filter with the IP address **`192.168.10.10`**. As we are looking at the Installation stage of the attack, we would see if some data is getting exfiltrated.

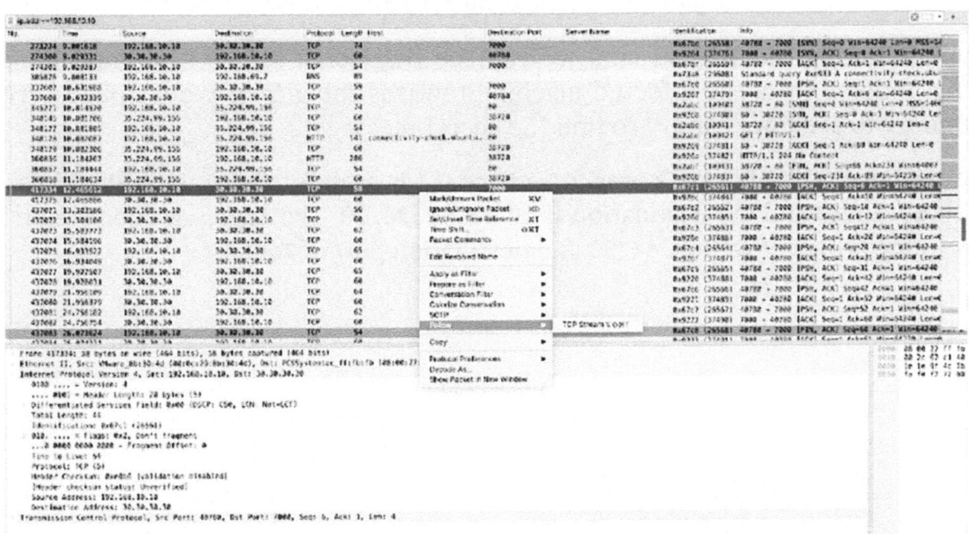

Figure 7.20: *Filtering the Traffic on the Basis of Infected Machine IP Address*

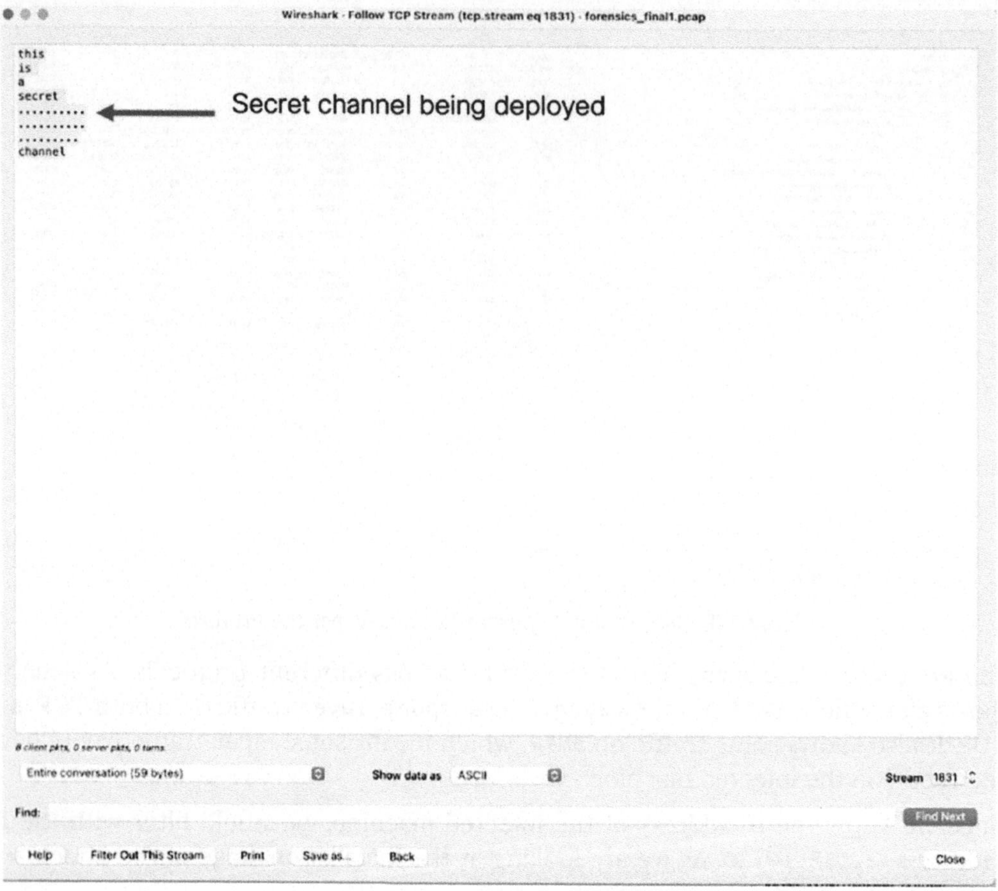

***Figure 7.21:** Output of the Follow TCP Stream*

While following the TCP stream, we can see that some secret communication is being initiated from the infected machine towards the attacker-controlled server. Let us try to see if we can try to find the secret message.

The message of **`"this is a secret channel"`** is seen for the source IP address of **`192.168.10.10`** and the destination IP of **`30.30.30.30`**. The **`layer 4`** information for this traffic is on source port **`40780`** and destination port of **`7000`**.

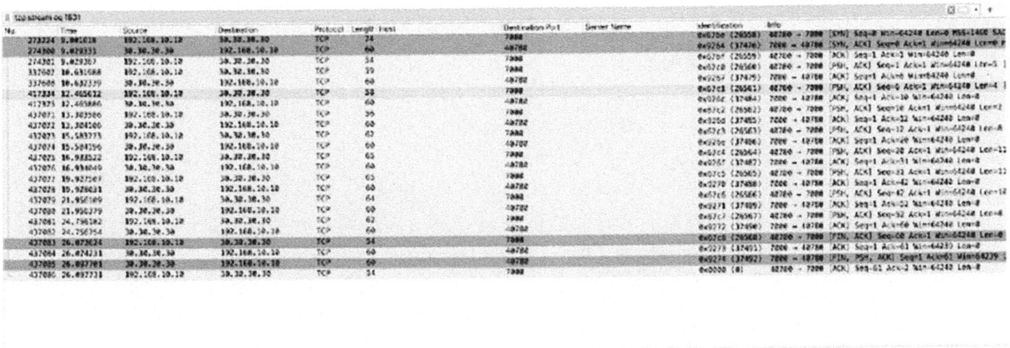

Figure 7.22: *Snapshot of the TCP Stream on which the Secret Communication was done*

Let us try to see if any other communication is being seen on the same source and destination, but on different ports. As we can see, the communication is happening on port **8000**.

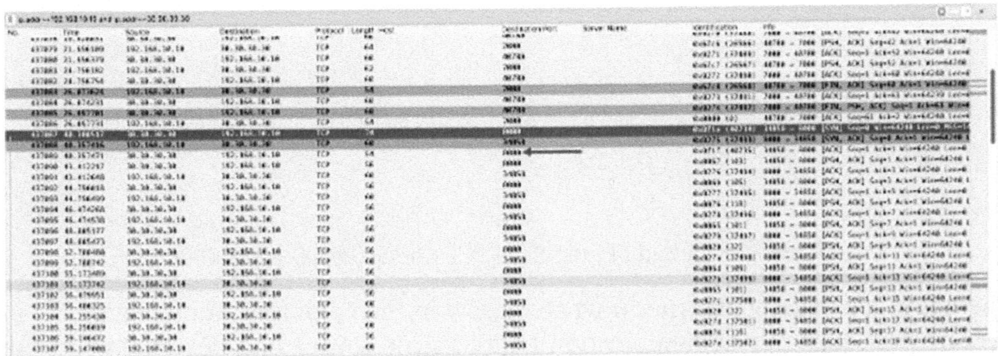

Figure 7.23: *Looking for Communication on Other TCP Ports*

If we try to follow the TCP stream for the conversation between **192.168.10.10** and the destination IP of **30.30.30.30** on port **8000**, we see the message as **"......."**

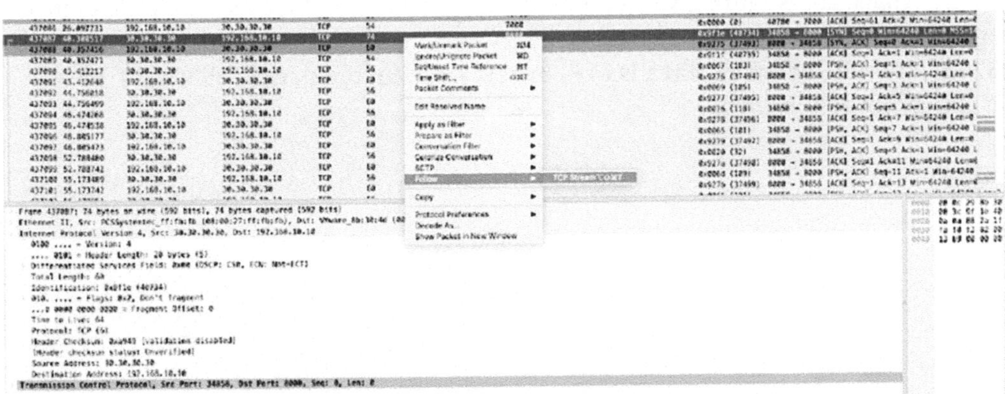

Figure 7.24: *Following TCP Stream on TCP port 8000*

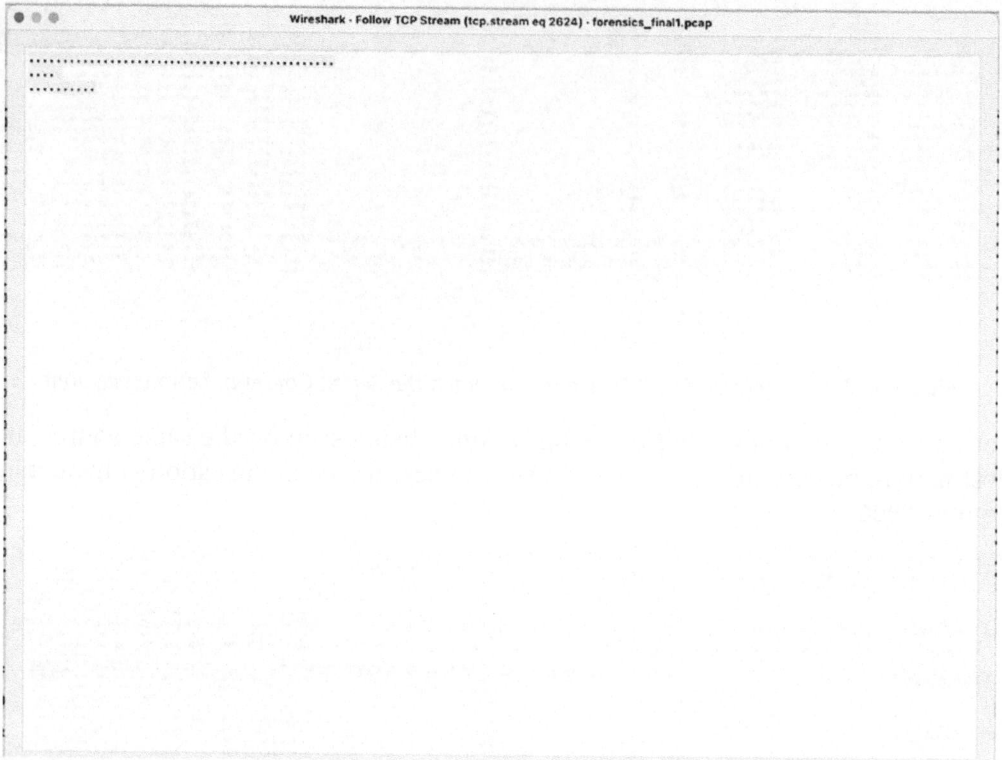

***Figure** 7.25: Output of the Follow TCP Stream on TCP port 8000*

The above message holds true to what we saw in the communication channel being **secret.** Why does this communication for the same source and destination on port **8000** show "....." while the communication on port **7000** shows the message **"this is a secret channel"**. Can you think why this could be?

Let us try to understand in which field of the transport layer the message **"this is a secret channel"** is seen. If we remember the **Transport layer**, there is Data in TCP segments on which the application tries to share the data. Looking at the packet no **337607**, the **TCP segment data** is of **5 bytes**. As seen, the data in Hex is **74 68 69 73 0a** and in ASCII it is **This**.

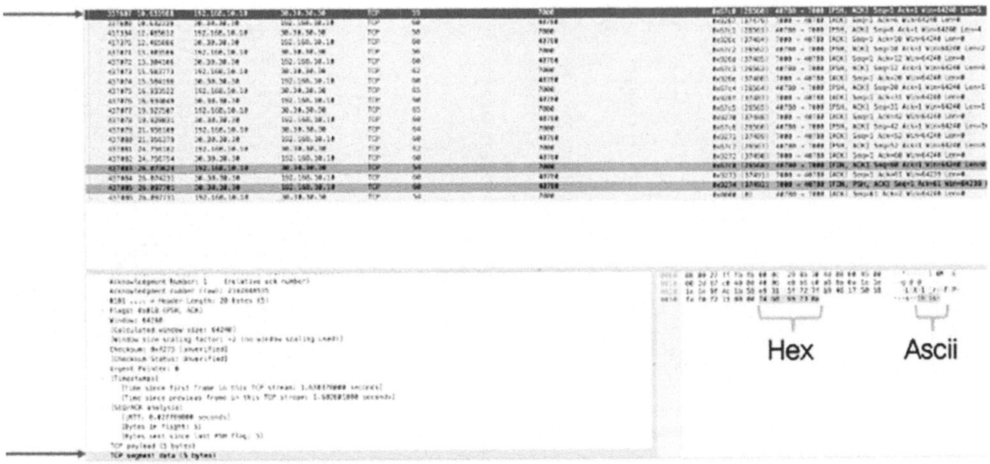

***Figure 7.26:** Wireshark Trace showing Details of Packet No. 337607*

As seen in packet **`417334`**, the next **`data segment`** is of **`4 bytes`** with data as **`is`** and **2 whitespaces.**

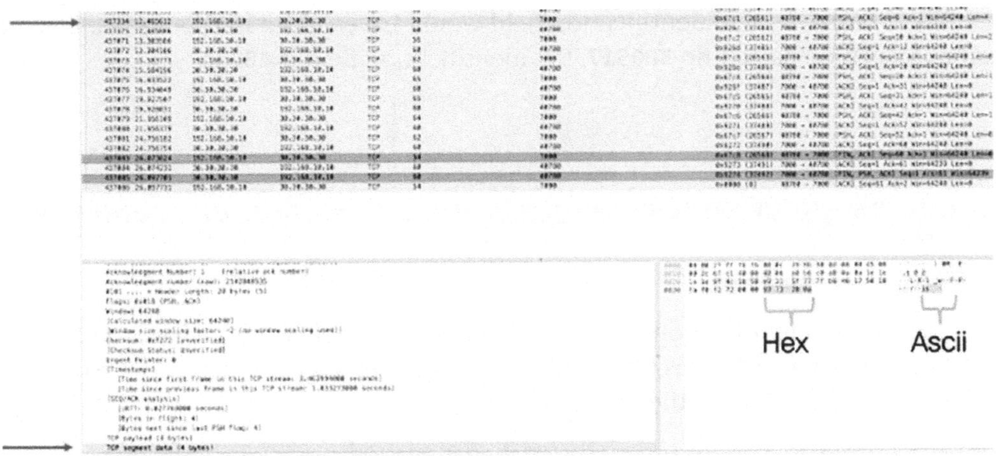

***Figure 7.27:** Wireshark Trace showing Details of Packet No. 417334*

This answers us why the stream for the traffic between **`192.168.10.10`** and **`30.30.30.30`** on port **`8000`** shows .... because the data in the TCP segment is empty. Does that mean there is no data because we have found that the conversation is through some secret channel? Let us try to look for other headers from where we can get some information. What can be other headers? Let us look at the IP header. The IP header has the Identification field along with the source and destination IP addresses. Hence, **`Identification`** field as a column has been added.

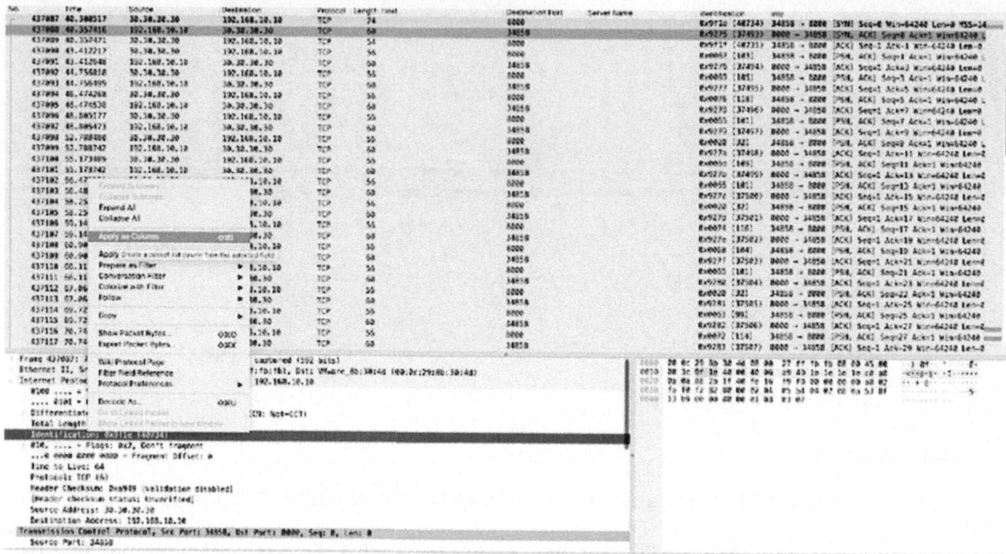

Figure 7.28: *Applying Identification Field as Column*

In an ideal scenario, the Identification field would have values in thousands. Like, for example, seen on packet no **300517**, the identification field is **40734**.

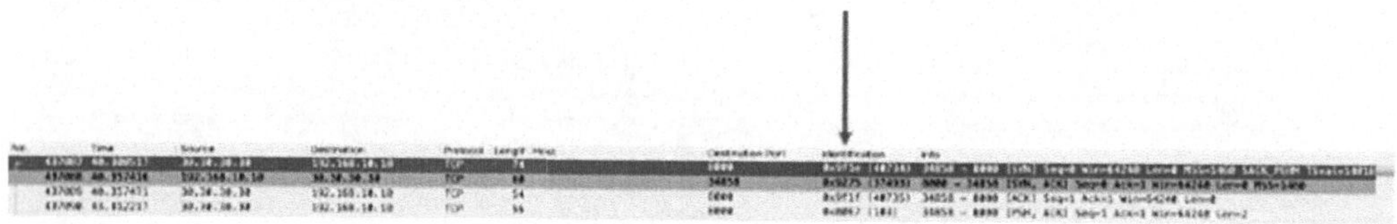

Figure 7.29: *Identification Fields for Different Packets*

If we look at the Identification fields of other packets, such as for packet no **437090**, it is **103,** for packet **437092**, it is **105,** and for packet no **437094**, it is **118.** If we look at the ASCII table, then **103** gives the character **'g'**.

Let us try to create a script to extract all the characters.

We would be using Scapy to extract these characters. The following is the script:

```
from scapy.all import *
from scapy.utils import *
p=rdpcap("forensics_final1.pcap")
for packets in p:
        If packets.haslayer(TCP):
                If packets[TCP].dport==8000:
                        file.write(packets[IP].id)
```

After extracting these bytes, we get the message **"give me the credentials in file"**. The first conversation on port **7000** gave the hint in the form of a secret channel. The second conversation on port **8000** gave the message **"give me the credentials**

in file". There is a file that the attacker would have downloaded from its server. This means that the conversation between **192.168.10.10** and the server **30.30.30.30** would be on a different port.

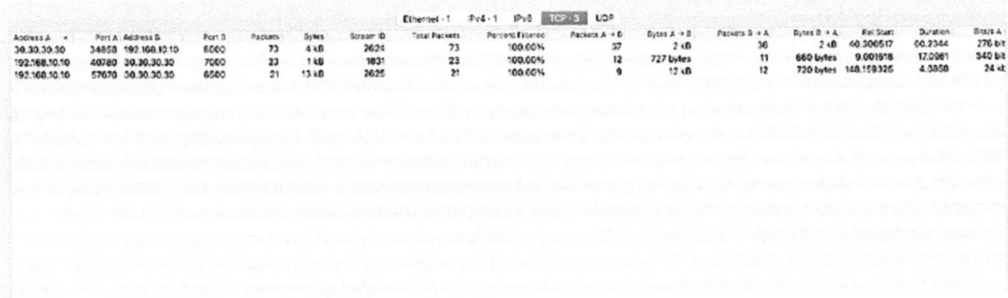

Figure 7.30: *Conversation Summary in Wireshark*

As we can see, there is another conversation on port **8500**.

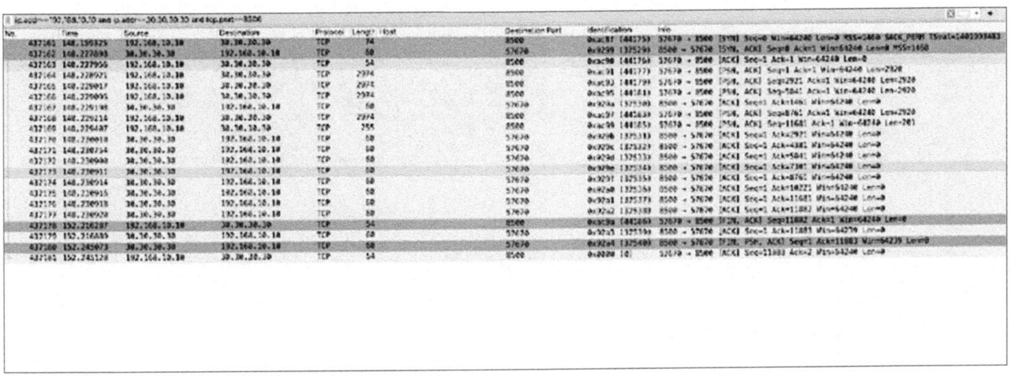

Figure 7.31: *Wireshark Trace showing Conversation on port 8500*

If we have followed the **TCP** stream on this conversation, we see as follows:

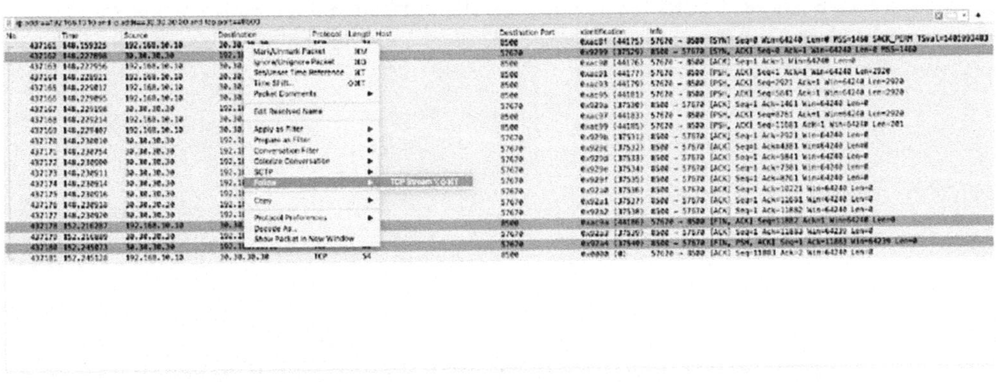

Figure 7.32: *Follow TCP Stream for Conversation on port 8500*

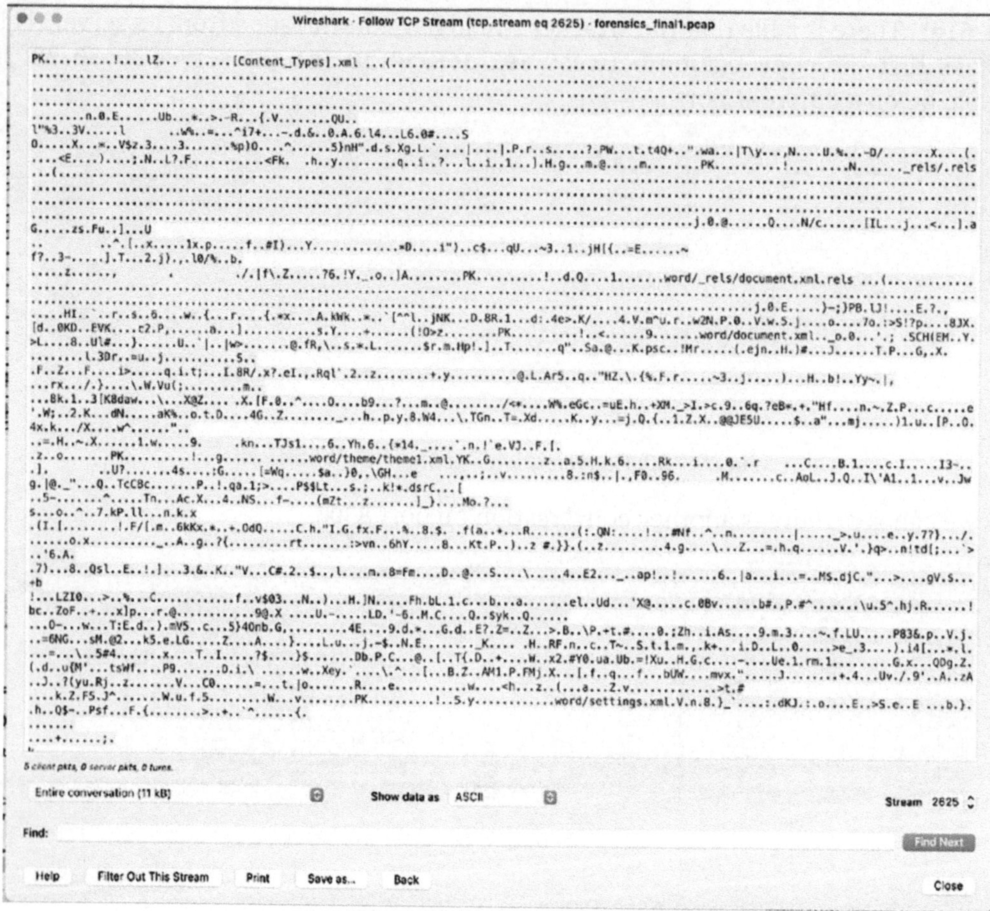

Figure 7.33: *Output of the Follow TCP Stream*

As can be seen, it looks to be some file where the signature shows in the form of **XML** and also starts with **PK**. Let us try to change the format from ASCII to raw bytes.

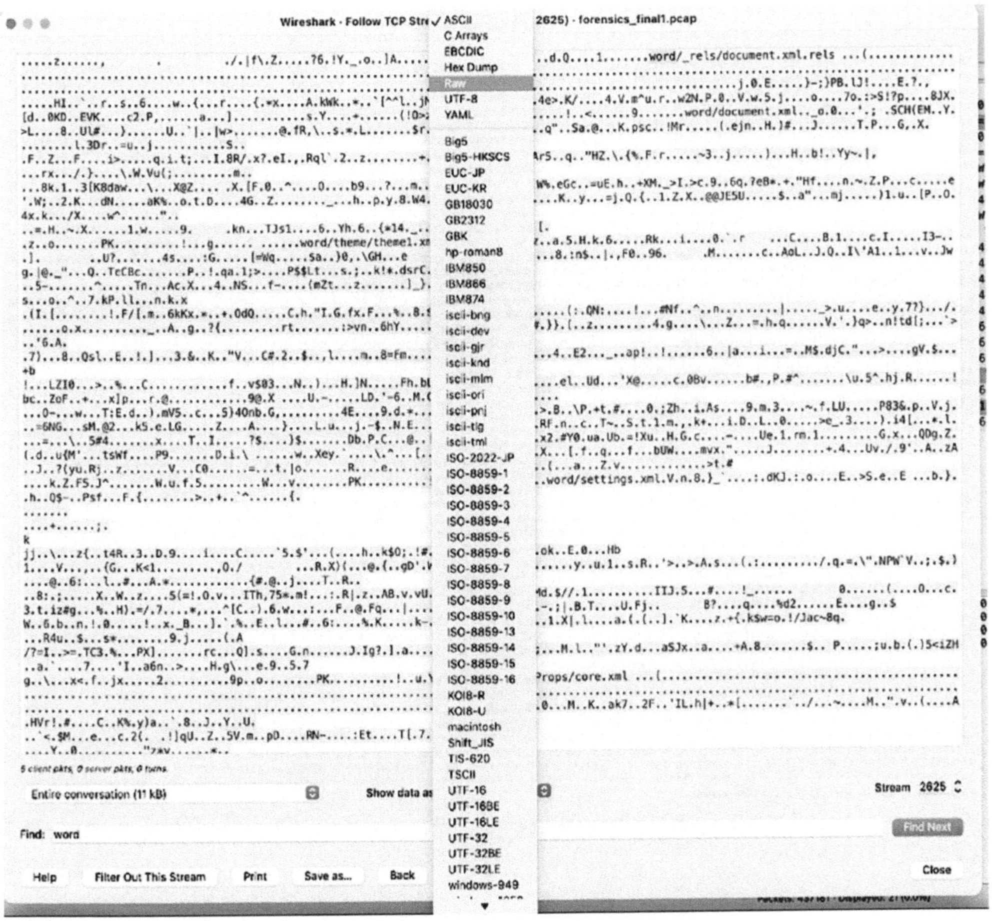

Figure 7.34: *Changing the Structure from ASCII to Raw*

The raw bytes are seen as follows:

Figure 7.35: *Viewing the Raw Bytes on Wireshark*

The starting bytes are **504b**. Looking at the https://www.garykessler.net/library/file_sigs.html we can see that a file signature of **504b** indicates a text file.

Let us try to extract this file of raw bytes by clicking **"Save as"**:

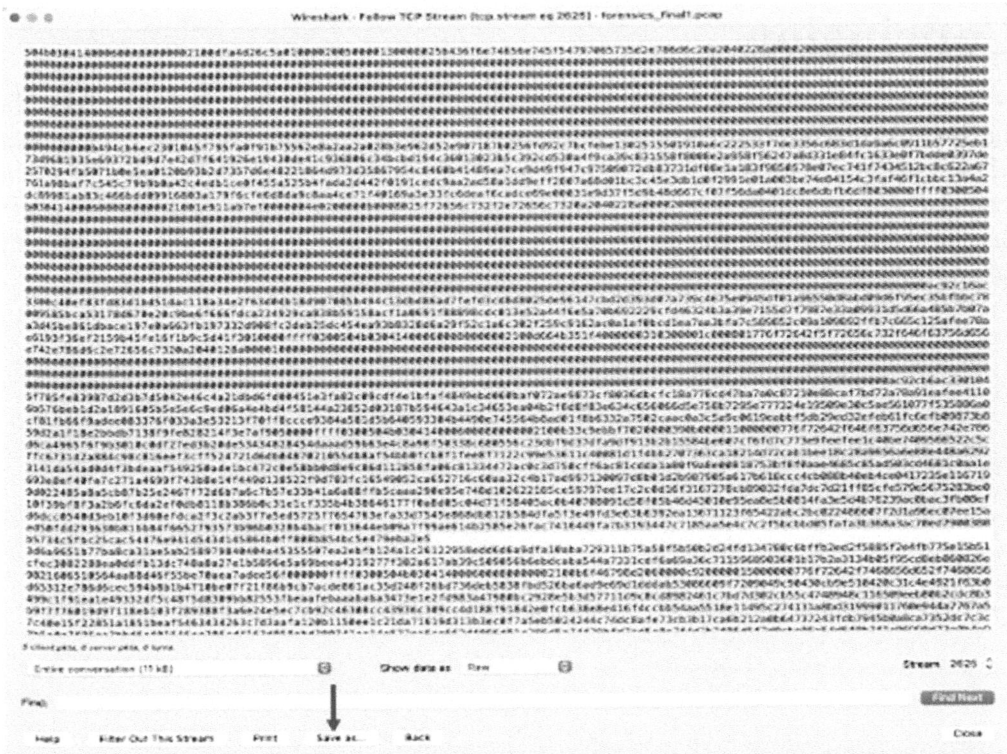

Figure 7.36: *Saving the File from Wireshark*

Once we save this file and open it, the contents of the file are as follows:

Figure 7.37: *Contents of the File extracted from the Wireshark*

The content of the file shows **`"Hidden info"`**. This is a sample file which was created to showcase the different stages of attack. Ideally the next stage would be to diagnose this file as it would have different Macros and understand the different Malicious elements included as part of the File.

Conclusion

Wireshark lays the foundation for analyzing malware over the network when the machine gets infected. Thus, it is important to understand that Wireshark traces help when it is taken that the machine is infected. The capture points can be directly on the machine, or they can be taken from different collectors in the network. We also learnt that **Indicators of Compromise** can be derived from the Wireshark traces, which were taken while the malware was implanted on the machine.

Index

P

S

T

V

W

Z